A DICTIONARY OF BUDDHISM

A DICTIONARY
OF BUDDHISM

Introduction by T. O. Ling

CHARLES SCRIBNER'S SONS, NEW YORK

Abbreviations

acc. to	according to
attr.	attribute(d)
anc.	ancient
b.	born
BC	Before Christian Era
Buddh., Bhm.	Buddhist(s), Buddhism
C.	Central
c.	*circa*, about
CE	Christian Era
cent.	century
ch.	chapter(s)
Chi.	Chinese
Chr.	Christian
cmp.	compare
comy.	commentary
d.	died
doc.	doctrine, doctrinal
E.	East, Eastern
Eng.	English
esp.	especially
estab.	establish(ed)
gen.	general(ly)
hist.	history, historical
import.	important, importance
incl.	include(d), including
indic.	indicate(s), indicating
intro.	introduce(d), introduction
lit.	literally, literature
Mhy.	Mahayana

Abbreviations

mod.	modern
partic.	particular(ly)
prob.	probable, probably
poss.	possible, possibly
ref.	refers, reference
relig.	religion, religious
repr.	represent(ed), or reprint, acc. to context
Skt.	Sanskrit
syn.	synonym(ous)
Thv.	Theravādin(s)
trad.	tradition(ally)
trans.	translation
vv.	verses
→	cross reference
→→	cross reference to subjects named

Bibliographical Notes

A.N., AN	*Anguttara-Nikaya*
A.N.E.T.	*Ancient Near Eastern Texts Relating to the Old Testament,* ed. J. B. Pritchard, Princeton University Press, 2nd edn., 1955.
B.S.O.A.S.	*Bulletin of the School of Oriental and African Studies,* London
C.H.I.	*Cambridge History of Iran*
D.I.	*Der Islam*
D.N., DN	*Digha-Nikaya*
D.P.P.N.	*Dictionary of Pali Proper Names*
D.T.Z.	*The Dawn and Twilight of Zoroastrianism,* by R. C. Zaehner, London, 1961
E.R.E.	*Encyclopaedia of Religion and Ethics,* ed. J. Hastings, 12 vols. and Index vol., Edinburgh, 1908–26
H.B.	*Hinduism and Buddhism,* 3 vols., by Sir C. Eliot (1921, repr. 1954)
J.B.R.A.S.	*Journal of the Bombay Branch of the Royal Asiatic Society*
J.R.A.S.	*Journal of the Royal Asiatic Society of Great Britain*
K.N.	*Khuddaka-Nikaya*
Massignon, Hallaj	L. Massignon, *La passion . . . d'al-Hallaj,* 2 vols. (Paris, 1922)
M.N.	*Maijjhima-Nikaya*
R.A.C.	*Reallexikon für Antike und Christentum,* hrg. T. Klauser, Stuttgart (from 1950)
R.Ae.R-G	*Reallexikon der ägyptischen Religionsgeschichte,* by H. Bonnet, Berlin, 1952

Bibliographical Notes

R.G.G.	*Die Religion in Geschichte und Gegenwart*, 3. Aufl., hrg. K. Galling, Bände I–VI, 1957–62, Tübingen
S.B.E.	*Sacred Books of the East*
S.N.	*Samyutta-Nikaya*
S.O.	*Sources orientales.* A series comprising volumes, variously entitled and by various contributors from 1959, Paris

Introduction

It is hoped that the publication here in separate form of what was originally part of a larger volume will be of service to two additional classes of readers: first, those who require a comprehensive but brief introduction to Buddhist history and culture; second, those whose primary concern is with the study of Southeast Asia.

It will be seen from the style and arrangement of the entries that the primary intention is to provide a work of reference for scholars. These entries have been extracted from the earlier work, *A Dictionary of Comparative Religion* (1970), edited by the late Professor S. G. F. Brandon, to whom the present writer takes this opportunity of paying personal tribute, as one who was outstandingly humane and unfailingly kind, generous in his encouragement of younger scholars, and of deservedly high international reputation for his own meticulously careful and often pioneering scholarship.

The decision to publish these entries on Buddhism as a separate book was prompted by the realization that there is in the West a keen and growing interest in Buddhism, especially among young people. This interest leads the novice into a new cultural world, and into frequent encounters with what are at first strange and occasionally difficult terms. In Western literature on the subject these are sometimes translated into the reader's language; sometimes, when they are virtually untranslatable, they are not. Either way, many of these terms have technical connotations which, as in any other serious intellectual discipline, need to be mastered. Moreover, the literature of Buddhism, in Pāli, Sanskrit, Tibetan, Chinese, and other languages of Asia, is vast; the student of the subject needs to be able to refresh his memory

Introduction

concerning this or that piece of text, its date and contents, and so on. These are the occasions when a book of reference of the present sort saves time and also makes available material that might otherwise require resort to specialist libraries.

In addition to this primary purpose, however, the present volume can be used to provide sustained introductory reading on Buddhism. The following method is suggested. The entry "Buddhism: general survey" should be consulted first. After this the cross references contained in it should be followed up, that is, entries on other pages, indicated by the symbol →. For instance, the reader would, after reading the general survey, turn to the entry headed "Buddha, Gotama." In reading this he would encounter other cross references. Then he could go on to the next entry mentioned in the general survey, "Sākyas," again following up cross references found there. By the time he had reached the latter part of the general survey article it would probably be unnecessary to consult all the cross references, as some of them would already have been consulted in another connection.

Similarly, the reader who is engaged in Southeast Asian studies should consult first of all the entries on Burma, Cambodia and Laos, Indonesia, and Thailand. Then following up the cross references he would consult the entries on "Theravada," "Literature, Buddhist," "Sangha," and so on. Other important entries in connection with the Buddhist culture of Southeast Asia are: Almsgiving; Devotions; Discipline; Fasting; Festivals; Four Holy Truths; Holy Days; Jataka; Kamma; Monasteries; Ordination; Pali; Pagoda; and Self-Immolation. The advantage of such use of the dictionary is that it can be easily adapted to whatever degree of knowledge the reader may already possess. Pali and Sanskrit words are shown with diacritical marks when they appear as head words to entries; thereafter they are often printed in a more popular form, e.g., Vinaya-Piṭaka and Vinaya-Pitaka.

T. O. LING

A DICTIONARY OF BUDDHISM

A

Abhidhamma (Pali); (Skt.) **Abhidharma** Thematic arrangement and logical development of Buddha's teaching.
Whereas the doc. of Buddha contained in → *Sutta-Pitaka* is
discursive (in form of parables, anecdotes, metaphors,
etc.), and refers to persons and places, the A. is entirely abstract, precise and impersonal. The beginning of schemati-
zation of ideas is found in → *Anguttara-Nikaya*, part of
Sutta-Pitaka, and prob. repr. an early form of A. Such lists
of topics for mnemonic or catechetical purposes known as
mātikā were used by monks in earliest period; from these
developed the A. The A. is concerned mainly with analysis
of psychical or mental phenomena and their interrelation-
ships. The many poss. different states of consciousness are
described and their mental and moral constituent elements
enumerated, being classified acc. to their capacity to produce wholesome or unwholesome → karma. These elements or → *dhammas* are regarded as always being in state
of interdependence with other *dhammas* within vast rela-
tional net. The study of A. requires considerable applica-
tion, powers of memory, and perseverance, and is trad. the
occupation of monks. It is intensively studied at certain
monasteries. A. is spec. assoc. with the → Theravada.
Burma has long reputation for A. studies. Strong interest in
A. has developed in Ceylon also in mod. times, partly stimulated by European converts (→ *Abhidhamma-Pitaka*).
Nyanaponika, *Abhidhamma Studies* (1949); H. V. Guen-
ther, *Philosophy and Psychology in the Abhidharma* (1957);
Lama Anagarika Govinda, *The Psychological Attitude of
Early Buddhist Philosophy* (1961); W. F. Jayasuriya, *The Psy-
chology and Philosophy of Buddhism* (1963).

Abhidharma-Kośa

Abhidharma-Kośa An import. Buddh. treatise of → *Sarvāstivādin* sch.; attr. to → Vasubandhu. A.K. consists of two parts: *A.K.-Kārikā*, a collection of 600 verses, and *A.K.-Bhāsya*, a prose commentary on these verses. The whole forms a compendium of the → *Abhidharma* of the Sarvāstivāda, and is arranged under nine heads: elements (*dhātu*); faculties (*indriya*); world (*loka*, i.e., forms of existence and varieties of living beings); action (*karma*); proclivities or inclinations (*anusaya*); stages in removal of defilement (*pudgala-marga*); types of knowledge (*jñāna*); types of meditation (*samādhi*); lastly, an exam. of theories of the 'person' (*pudgala-viniścaya*). This last section is an independent treatise intended to refute in partic. idea of individual *ātman*, advocated by Brahman philosophers and by the Buddh. Vatsiputrīyas, a sect that affirmed reality of individual *pudgala*, or person (Pudgala-vādins). In monasteries in India, in time of → I-Tsing, the A.K. was used as intro. to study of Buddh. thought. While it is a compendium of Sarvastivādin Abh. doc. (as the → Abhidhammattha-Sangaha is of → Theravādin), A.K. offers also an interpretation recognised as moving in direction of the → Sautrantikas, and thus towards → Mahāyāna Buddhism. It was an import. instrument of propagation of Buddhism in China, and produced much commentarial literature. The text of A.K. is in Skt., the original of which was lost in India; it has been preserved in Chinese and Tibetan trans. From Chinese versions a French trans. was made by L. de la Vallée Poussin (6 vols., Paris, 1923–31). In 1934 and 1936 a Skt. version was discovered in Tibetan monasteries by Indian scholar Rahula Sanskrityayana. Text of *Karika* portion was pub. by V. V. Gokhale (*The Text of the Abhidharmakośakārikā of Vasubandhu, JBRAS*, vol. 22).

Abhidharma-Piṭaka (Sarvāstivādin) A-P. of the → Sarvastivadin school differs completely from *Abhidhamma-Piṭaka* of Thv. in names of books it contains, although some of subject-matter coincides. The seven books of this school's A-P. are: (1) *Sangiti-pariyaya-pada*; (2) *Dharma-skandha*; (3) *Dhatukaya-pada*; (4) *Prajnapti-pada*; (5) *Vijnana-pada*; (6) *Prakarana-pada*; (7) *Jnana-prasthana*. Of these the closest

Abhidharma-Piṭaka

in content to a Thv. Abh. text is (2), which has chapters co-inciding with 14 of the 18 chapters of the Thv. *Vibanga*. Whereas language of Thv. A-P. is Pali, that of the Sarvas-tivadins was Skt.; but now is preserved in Chinese and Ti-betan trans. only.

Abhidharma-Piṭaka (Theravādin) Third section of Buddh. Pali canonical scriptures, or → *Tipitaka*. Preserved by Thvs. of S. E. Asia, this is one of two extant collections of Abh. texts. The other is that of the → Sarvastivadins. Thv. A-P. consists of seven books: (1) *Dhammasangani* (enumeration of *dhammas*, or entities); (2) *Vibhanga* (the treatises); (3) *Dhātu-kathā* (discussion about *dhatus*, or elements); (4) *Puggala-paññatti* (categories of individuals); (5) *Kathā-Vat-thu* (areas of dispute, or points of controversy); (6) *Yamaka* (the pairs); and (7) *Patthāna* (causality). Of these (1) and (7) are together said to present quintessence of Abh. (1) follows the analytical method of reducing all phenomena to ultimate constituent entities or *dhamas;* while (7) is con-cerned with synthesis, or causal relationships which exist between dhammas in actual human existence, which are not necessarily the same as 'common-sense' relationships which appear on surface of life. (2) is a collection of 18 treatises, each of which deals with some fundamental cate-gory of B. analysis: the 5 → *khandhas*, the 12 → *ayatanas*, the 18 → *dhatus*, the → 4 holy truths, etc. (3) comprises hundreds of questions and answers rel. to the *khandhas, ayatanas* and *dhatus*. (4) is smallest of books of A-P. and differs from other works in dealing with a popular or 'com-mon-sense' concept, that of the 'individual,' a concept not regarded as valid or even helpful in B. thought gen. (→ An-atta); the main body of work consists of enumeration and brief definition of over 300 different human types. (5) deals with controversies that had arisen among Buddhists by about mid. of 3rd cent. BC, e.g., whether in any absolute sense a human individual (*pudgala*) could be said to exist, each question being followed by the unorthodox answer and its refutation; the book is trad. attr. to Thera Moggalip-putta-Tissa, who is said to have recited it at 3rd Buddh. Council held at Pataliputra in time of → Asoka. (6) is a

5

Abhidhammika

work on logic, in so far as it consists of Abh. propositions, each of which is examined in its reverse form. Since Thv. and Sarvastivadin A-Ps. differ in list of books which each contains, the compiling of the A-P. was, in each case, prob. carried out after separation of these 2 schools, *c.* 300 BC, since the Vinaya and Sutta Ps. of the 2 schools are the same. → *Abhidharma-Pitaka* (Sarvāstivādin).
Nyanatiloka Mahathera, *Guide through the Abhidhamma-Pitaka* (1957).

Abhidhammika Buddh. monk who is specialist in study of → *Abhidhamma.* This does not mean that he is unacquainted or unconcerned with the other two Pitakas of Buddh. canon, but that he has specially mastered the *Abh.* The Buddha is described in → *Atthasalini* as first A.; this is an anachronism since development of → *Abh. Pitaka* took place some time after Buddha's decease. In anc. Buddhism, A.s were among → Theravadins held in higher esteem than other monks. The Chinese Buddh. pilgrim → Fa Hsien mentions a → stupa built in honour of the *Abh.* at which A.s performed devotions on Buddh. holy days.

Abhidhammattha-Saṇgaha Compendium (*saṇgaha*) of meaning (*attha*) of → *Abhidhamma.* → Theravada B. work of 12th cent. by → Anuruddha. Has been and still is most widely used primer and handbook for Abh. study in Thv. countries. Since material is presented in extremely condensed form, it has produced crop of commentaries espec. in Burma and Ceylon. Was trans. into English by S. Z. Aung of Burma and ed. by Mrs. Rhys-Davids as *Compendium of Philosophy* (1910, 1956).

Abhiññā Supernatural knowledge or insight, accord. to Buddh. thought, possessed by Buddha and by those who have reached advanced stage of spiritual development. It is supernatural in so far as not characteristic of generality of men, but only of those who have transcended certain ordinary human limitations. Is mentioned in Buddh. scriptures as seventh in series of nine results of apprehension of → 4 holy truths; its position in series indic. its importance, the eighth and ninth being enlightenment and *nibbana* (D. III.XXIX). Is frequently attr. to Buddha in Pali scriptures; by

6

Ācārya

his A. or insight, Buddha has knowledge of realities not immediately apparent to ordinary men. He 'knows the universe, with its devas, with → Mara, with Brahma, the whole creation, with recluse and brahman, the world of men and devas, by his own *abhinna* he knows' (D.I.87 etc.).
T. O. Ling, *Buddhism and the Mythology of Evil* (1962), pp. 68, 96, etc.

Abode → Vihāra (*Pali*).

Abortion Act of A., i.e. terminating life of a foetus, is explicitly mentioned in Buddh. canonical scriptures, in the → *Vinaya-Pitaka*, as a grave offence. If A. is brought about by Buddh. monk, or if he is in any way a party to the procuring of an A., by offering advice as to the method, or supplying abortive medicine, penalty is expulsion from monkhood. This is in accord. with Buddh. view that destruction of life is a moral transgression.

Absolute, The In Pali Buddh., nearest approach to West. philosophical notion of the A. is that which is ref. to in canon as the unconditioned (*asankhata*). Certain other negative adjectives also are used in this connection: not-born (*ajātam*), not-become (*abhūtam*), and not-made (*akatam*). Thus the Buddha is repr. as saying, 'Monks there is that which is not-born, not-become, not-made and unconditioned. If this not-born, not-become, not-made and unconditioned were not, then there would be apparent no release from that which is born, become, made and conditioned.' (*Udāna*, VIII:3) Since it is to → *nibbāna* that adj. 'unconditioned' is applied elsewhere (AN I:152; SN IV:359 etc.), it may be assumed that it is *nibbāna* which is to be understood as the A. in Pali Buddh.

In Mhy. Buddh. it is the universal 'void' or → *śūñyatā*, which becomes the A., espec. as repr. in → Nagarjuna's doc. In the further development, or poss. synthesis, repr. by Asanga's → Yogācāra system of thought, it was the → *ālayavijñāna*, the abode of consciousness, which repr. the A. In all these cases, the A., however represented, was identified with goal of Buddh. relig. life.

Ācārya (Skt.); Acariya (Pali) in Buddhism. In Buddhism the teacher or instructor (*ācārya*) plays an indispensable role.

Access-Concentration

As it has existed historically, Buddhism has always involved social relationship, even when this is at minimum level of teacher and pupil: the 'solo' Buddh. is a rare exception. *Ācārya* is one of 2 main types of teacher; other is *upadhyaya* (Skt.), or *upajjhāya* (Pali). Orig. A. was teacher of → *dhamma* or doctrine, while *upajjhāya* was moral preceptor, whose function it was to encourage and correct learner-monk. A. was thus custodian of Buddh. viewpoint or trad. doc., and it was his responsibility to ensure its preservation and accurate transmission. In early period, the role of *upajjhāya* was regarded as more import.; this reflected primary importance within the Buddh. community of moral discipline. When transmission of essential Buddh. teaching became more difficult by reason of unsettled conditions of times, role of A. was regarded as having an importance equal to that of *upajjhāya*. When → Buddhaghosa's *Visuddhimagga* was composed, role of A. had become even more import. than that of *upajjhāya* (*Vis.* 81, etc.).

Relationship between A. as teacher and junior monk as pupil, or *antevāsika,* was similar to that expected between father and son, i.e., one of reciprocal confidence and respect.

Access-Concentration (*Upacāra Samādhi*) Term used in Buddhism for a stage of meditation in which concentration on a moral object has reached the degree that precedes entrance into state of absorption, or → *jhāna* (→ Samadhi).

Adi-Buddha Term used in → Mhy. Buddhism, espec. in Nepal and Tibet, for the 'primordial Buddha,' the Buddha without beginning. Necessity for such concept arises within context of developments in Mhy. Buddhism, where, as Snellgrove comments, the term A.-B. 'serves to distinguish the basic idea of buddha-hood from secondary buddha-forms.' Since term is found in Java as well as Nepal and Tibet, it is considered that it may have originated in the Mhy. of Bengal and thence have spread to both these regions. It was in connection with esoteric, Tantric Buddhism → Vajrayāna, that concept was first developed; although embryo of concept can be found in earlier Buddh. thought. When notion of a plurality of Buddhas had developed in Tantric Buddhism, where there is belief in 5 Buddhas, thought of as different coexistent forms of one principle rather than (as in earlier Buddh. thought) forming an hist. succession, this led in turn to re-emphasis on one original Buddha who is central principle of Buddha-hood. It is this conception which receives name A.-B. The term *Svayambhu* (self-existent) is used synonym for A.-B. It has been suggested that this constitutes an approach to concept of a creator god, in that the A.-B. alone is held to be self-existent. Creative activity is not, however, a characteristic of A.-B.; he is not thought of as creating the five Buddhas, but as constituting their central principle. Other names by which A.-B. is known in Nepal support this view of the matter: *Adinatha*, or 'first protector' and *Svayambhulokanatha*, or 'self-existent protector of the world'; i.e., A.-B. is most characteristically *natha*, 'protector' rather than primeval creator-god. Linking of A.-B. and *Adinatha* may mean that for lay people A.-B. is assimilated to Hindu Shiva (since *Adinatha* is title of Shiva); but this still does not imply that A.-B. is thought of as a creator.

Earliest evidence of concept of A.-B. is found in the *Namasangiti,* a book dating poss. to 7th cent. CE, in which bodhisattva → *Manjusri* is ref. to as A.-B.

Eliot (*Hinduism and Buddhism,* III, 387) suggests that A.-B. concept developed as Buddh. Asia's attempt to come to terms with Islamic monotheism, and to show that monotheism was already contained in Buddh. thought.

D. Snellgrove, *Buddhist Himalaya* (1957); C. Eliot, *Hinduism and Buddhism* (1921, repr. 1957).

Adultery Adultery is mentioned in Buddh. texts as one of number of forms of similar sexual misconduct. Thus, a monk who is guilty of A. is to be excommunicated from Order; but this is so in any case of sexual intercourse in which a monk is wilfully involved, irrespective of whether woman is married or not. For laymen sexual intercourse is forbidden with any woman who is under any form of protection—whether that of parents, or guardians, or husband. However, in one of oldest texts, the → *Sutta-Nipata,* sexual intercourse with other men's wives is repr. as the most grave in series of examples of misconduct (*Sn.* 106–8). It is also regarded as serious cause of evil → karma, the effects of which would persist beyond present life and bring serious retribution (S. II:259).

Afghanistan Area known today as Afghanistan was formerly known by such names as Gandhāra, Kandahar, and Balkh. By beginning of Christ. era this was strongly Buddh. area: archaeological research in 20th cent. has demonstrated existence of a flourishing Buddh. culture which began to decline in 7th cent. CE; it had virtually ended by beginning of 10th cent., when Islam finally displaced it (→ Gandhāra).

Āgama A title used in Mahāyāna Buddhism for collection of scripture, roughly equivalent to term → *Nikaya* in Pali. There are 4 *Āgamas* in the Skt. canon, as there are 4 *Nikāyas* in → Pali canon. The names of 4 Skt. A.s are: *Dirghāgama, Madhyamāgama, Samyuktāgama, Ekottarikāgama.* As in Pali canon, these together constitute one of the three divisions of the → *Tripitaka,* namely, the *Sutta-Pitaka.* Different schools had their own A.s, and in 7th cent. CE there existed seven different collections. There is, now, no complete orig. Skt. Ā. text extant; they exist, however, in Chinese trans.

Ajantā An anc. Buddh. monastic site in Aurangabad dist. Bombay state, India. Neglected and forgotten for more than a thousand years, it was rediscovered in 1819. The monastic dwelling halls (→ *vihāra*) and shrine rooms (*chaitya*) are in form of caves, hewn from rock of valley-side to simulate wooden buildings of early Buddh. period; there are 30 altogether. The shrine rooms contain, as central feature, a sacred relic-mound or → *stupa.* Many of caves are decorated with paintings on walls, pillars and ceilings. In some there are also inscriptions in early Brāhmi script of 2nd cent. BC. Other of the paintings and inscriptions are of 5th–6th cents. CE. The scenes depicted illustrate stories of former lives of the Buddha, i.e., the → *Jātakas.* They thus deal with palace and court life, kings, queens and princesses; rural scenes which incl. wide range of animal and bird life—buffaloes, bulls, horses, elephants, lions, swans, geese, etc.; processions, dances, musicians, lovers—in fact an acutely observed panorama of Indian life in pre- and early Christ. era. There is also considerable sculptural work, a feature of which is the intense portrayal of human emotions. Besides illustrating the *Jātakas,* many of the most magnificent paintings and sculptures deal with life of historical Buddha as it is known from the *suttas:* the prince Siddhartha confronted by the three signs of old age, disease and death; the temptation by → *Māra;* and various other incidents of his life, together with final scene, the *parinirvāṇa.* The murals of A. are of importance to art historian, since development of styles over period of 1,000 years can be traced here.

Benjamin Rowland, *The Art and Architecture of India* (1959); Sukumar Dutt, *Buddhist Monks and Monasteries of India* (1962).

Ajātasattu King mentioned in Pali Buddh. scriptures, who reigned over the kingdom of → Magadha during last 8 years of the Buddha's life, and for 24 years after that. His name means 'enemy (*sattu*) while still unborn (*ajata*).' This is said to ref. to antenatal desire of his mother to drink blood from her husband's knee, interpreted by astrologers to mean that the child she was bearing would kill his father → Bimbisara, and seize the kingdom. An alternative explanation of name is 'he against whom there has arisen no foe.' A. is repr. as having been ambitious prince who could not wait for his father's death to inherit the kingdom, plotted to murder him. In this he had cooperation of → Devadatta, the Buddha's cousin, who through vain self-conceit wished to oust Buddha and become leader of the Sangha. Bimbisara was a supporter of Buddha., hence a double plot was formed: Devadatta was to murder Buddha, while A. murdered his father King Bimbisara. The plot was discovered; Bimbisara pardoned his son and abdicated in his favour. However, A., unsafe while his father was still alive, imprisoned him and starved him to death. One visit of A. to Buddha is recorded: the king recounts that he has visited six other ascetics and outlines their various doctrines; he then asks Buddha. concerning his doc. and its advantages, Buddha expounds to him advantages of the ascetic

Ālaya-Vijñāna

life. One further connection between A. and Buddha is of importance. His ambition as ruler led him to plan attack on the territory of the Vajjian confederacy of tribes; in connection with this he sent Vassakara, his brahman chief minister, to obtain Buddha's views on his chances of success. His reply concerning security of the → Vajjis is occasion for an import. piece of Buddh. teaching on virtues of democratic confederacy in general, and the Sangha's role as preserver of this form of organisation, which at that time was fast disappearing before advancing autocratic monarchy, such as that of A. (Mahā-Parinibbāna Su.). While there is no further evidence of any continued interest on the part of A. in teaching of Buddha, the trad. records that after Buddha's death, A. obtained share of his ashes and erected a stūpa over them in Rajagaha. (Mahā-Parinibbāna Su., pp. 164–6). Acc. to the → Mahāvastu, A. was then approached by members of the Sangha, who were planning a gen. council for reciting of entire teaching of Buddha, for the king's assistance. This was readily given, acc. to this Skt. source: the king ordered an enormous hall to be built, 'like the assembly-hall of the gods,' imposingly furnished with lofty seats for president and reciting monk. Acc. to trad., the Council of Rajagaha was then held, under patronage of king, and lasted seven months (→ Councils). Nevertheless, acc. to a Thv. recorded by → Buddhaghosa, A.'s evil deeds caused him to be reborn in hell, where he was to suffer torment for 60,000 years before rebirth as a → pacceka-buddha.

Malalasekera, DPPN, 'Ajatasattu'; Sacred Books of the Buddhists, vol. II (1899), pp. 56ff.; S.B.E., vol. II, pp. 131–4; vol. 19, p. 248; vol. 20, pp. 233–8, 241–3, 377; vol. 21, p. 6; vol. 22, pp. XIVff.; vol. 49 (II), pp. 161–4.

Ālaya-Vijñāna Term used by Buddh. school of → Yogācāra, usually trans. into Eng. as 'store-consciousness,' the basic consciousness or persisting element which is subject of successive births and deaths. This doc. was developed by → Asanga, the 4th cent. CE authority and exponent of the Yogacara school.

Alcohol (Buddhist attitude) One of the 5 moral rules (→

Eightfold Path) binding upon all Buddhists, monks and lay people, is the requirement to abstain from all intoxicating liquor; this incl. intoxicants and drugs of all kinds, whether made from grain, fruit, sugar, yeast or in any other way. The precept here, as in other four cases, takes form of voluntary vow of abstinence: 'I take upon me the vow to abstain from taking intoxicants and drugs such as wine, liquor, etc. since they lead to moral carelessness.'

Almsgiving → Dāna. Buddhism in China led to almost universal belief that great merit accrued to oneself and descendants by giving alms to the needy. This doctrine led to great increase in almsgiving, not only by Buddhists but by Confucians and Taoists. Giving alms to poor and needy, doing acts of public benefit, helping people in times of special need or trouble, all helped in producing honour in this world and merit for afterlife. It also resulted in making beggary an organized profession, at times so troublesome to the charitable that those desirous of distributing alms often arranged with a shop or temple to distribute relief tickets to the genuine poor. Since the Communist revolution in China organized beggary has been practically stamped out.

Buddhist influence in Japan resulted in charity being considered one of the three divine virtues; the bead for charity is one of the three insignia of the throne. Buddhism, with its teaching of charity and compassion to all living creatures, did much to foster almsgiving, and Buddhist monks were often active in organization of relief to the needy and destitute.

Alobha (Pali) 'Greedlessness': in Buddhism one of the three wholesome roots, or morally conditioning factors (→ *mūla*), which produce good → karma.

Altar, Japan In Buddhist temples, stands known as *kōdan* or *kodzukuya* (incense tables) were provided for burning of incense, whilst the domestic A.'s were in nature of shrines for image of Buddha.

Amarapura The Amarapura is one of the three major communities (*nikāya*) of Buddh. monkhood in → Ceylon. It takes its name from city of Amarapura, in Burma. In late 18th cent. it became difficult for Sinhalese who were not of

Amarāvatī

the *goigama* caste (→ Caste) to obtain higher ordination (*upasampadā*) (→ Ordination), owing to restrictive decree made by the king of Kandy, Kīrti Shrī Rājasiṃha. In 1799, Naṇavimalatissa, a monk of the *salāgama* caste, together with five novices, left Ceylon and in 1802 reached Amarapura, the Burmese capital, where they were received by Buddhist king, Bodawpaya, and given higher ordination by a Burmese *mahāthera*. Together with some Burmese monks, they returned to Ceylon and were able to give higher ordination to Sinhalese novices not of the *goigama* caste. From this beginning has grown present A. community of monkhood, divided into 18 sub-communities, numbering in 1959 more than 3,000 monks (Buddha Sāsana Commission Report, Government of Ceylon, 1959).

Amarāvatī Anc. city of S. India, once a great centre of Buddh. culture, now small village on S. bank of R. Krishna (Kistna), about 80 miles from coast. The city was the east. capital of the Sātavāhana rulers and was known as Dhānyakataka; the name A., 'habitation of the immortals,' seems to have been acquired in Buddh. times; its importance for Buddhists was on account of the Mahā Chaitya, the great shrine or → *stupa,* about ½ mile to E. of city, which, acc. to some Buddh. trad. contained relics of Buddha himself. The discovery of an Ashokan pillar-edict at A. has strengthened belief that the *stupa* was built by emperor → Asoka (third cent. BC). It was main object of veneration of the Mahāsanghika school, known as the Chaityakas; pilgrims are said to have come to it from as far as Pātaliputra (Patna). The Chinese pilgrim → Hsüan Tsang, in 7th cent. CE, recorded that there were about 20 flourishing Buddh. monasteries there, though there were others which had been deserted. The site was rediscovered at end of 18th cent.; the numerous sculptures which have survived provide valuable evidence of develop. of Buddh. art. The style is said to be partly derived from that of Mathurā and Sānchī, but with distinctively orig. features of S. Indian kind. It is a style that has evidently had a widespread influence, partic. the type of Buddha figure, evidence of which is found in Ceylon, Thailand and Indonesia.

Amida

D. E. Barrett, *Sculptures from Amaravati in the British Museum* (1954); Philippe Stern and Mireille Beniste, *Évolution du Style Indien d'Amaravati* (1961); D. Seckel, *The Art of Buddhism* (1964).

Amida Name used in Japan. Buddhism for Amita, a transcendental Buddha. In the → Mahāyāna of India, this transcendental Buddha was known both as *Amitayus* (external Life) and *Amitābha* (eternal Light). Main Mhy texts which ref. to Amita are greater and smaller *Sukhāvatīvyūha Sūtras* and *Amitāyur-dhyāna Sutra* (see *S.B.E.*, vol. 49). *Sukhāvatī* is 'the happy land' or paradise, to which Amita was believed to be able to bring his devotees. The worship of A. in Mahāyāna appears to be traceable back to just before time of → Nāgārjuna, i.e., to about begin. of 2nd cent. CE, since Nāgārjuna is said to have derived his knowledge of cult of A. from his teacher Saraha. The Greater *Sukhāvatīvyūha Sūtra*, which was trans. into Chinese about begin. of second half of 2nd cent. CE, relates story of Dharmākara, who is repres. as having lived many aeons ago, and who, although he could have entered into Buddhahood, chose not to do so, but made vow that he would wait until he could achieve such Buddhahood as would make him lord of a paradise (*sukhāvatī*), to which all who meditated upon this paradise ten times should be admitted. This he achieved as the Buddha Amitābha. The *Amitāyur-dhyāna Sūtra* describes series of sixteen meditations (*dhyāna*) upon *Amitāyus* which are said to lead to admission to his paradise. In Indian Mahāyāna, the cult of A. appears to have been of relatively minor importance, even though so eminent a figure as Nāgārjuna was among his devotees. In → Tibet and Nepal, A. is one among many Buddhas worshipped. By time of development of idea of the → *Adi-Buddha*, Amita had come to be regarded as one of the five principal Buddhas or Jinas, who are emanations of the Adi-Buddha. → Vasubandhu also composed a 'Discourse on Paradise' based on *Sukhāvatīvyūha Sūtra*; his discourse begins 'I take refuge single-heartedly in Amita and pray to be reborn in his Paradise.' It was in China and Japan, however, that the cult of Amita had its

Anāgāmin

greatest success and became one of predominant forms of Buddhism in those countries.

(Jap.): **Amitabha** (Skt.); **A-mi-t'o fo** (China) The → Buddha of infinite (*amita*) light (*ābhā*). Also known as Amitayus, i.e., of infinite (*amita*) life-span (*āyuh*). Personification or mode of manifestation of the primordial, self-existent Buddha (→ Adi-Buddha.), whose creative activity is symbolised under seven Dhyāna-Buddhas, of which A. is fourth. The cult of A. shows strong Iranian influence, and is only prominent in northern (Mahāyāna) Buddhism, being practically unknown in Siam (Thailand), Burma and Ceylon. It was introduced into China by Chih Ch'ien, of Indo-Scythian origin, by the trans. of the *A-mi-t'o ching* (*Sukhāvatīvyūha Sūtra*) in the period CE 220–52. By end of 4th cent., the cult was well established under the influence of → Hui Yüan.

As personification of infinite mercy, compassion, wisdom and love, figure of A. became the supreme object of devotion and faith in the → Pure Land sects which developed in China and Japan, → Jodo and → Shin. About middle of 7th cent. in China, A. superseded Shakyamuni and Maitreya as the supreme object of popular devotion. He was regarded as intermediary between Supreme Reality and mankind. Faith in him ensured rebirth in his Western Paradise (Sukhāvati). Associated with A. were the two great → bodhisattvas, → Mahāsthāmaprāpta and → Avalokitesvara (Kuan Yin).

E. Conze, *Buddhism* (1951); E. Zurcher, *The Buddhist Conquest of China* (1959); K. L. Reichelt, *Truth and Tradition in Chinese Buddhism* (1927); E. T. C. Werner, *Dictionary of Chinese Mythology* (1932).

Anāgāmin Term used in Buddhism for the 'non-returner,' i.e., one who has reached third stage of spiritual development: next stage before becoming an → *arahant*. The two previous stages of spiritual progress recognised in → Theravada are: the 'stream-enterer' (→ *Sotāpanna*), and the 'once-returner' (→ Sakadāgāmin). The non-returner is one who has gone beyond the spiritual attainments of the two earlier stages, having overcome the five 'fetters' which bind humans to sphere of senses, viz.: (1) belief in an enduring entity (2) doubt (3) belief in value of rules and rituals (4) sensuous desire (5) ill-will. He is thus free from the 'bond of craving' (*Kāma-yoga*), but has yet to become free of the 'bond of existence' (*bhava-yoga*). Existence for him will continue, but in a heavenly or supersensual sphere; it is to sphere of sensual existence that he is a non-returner. In the heavenly sphere (*deva-loka*), or, acc. to → Buddhaghosa (*Visuddhimagga*), in the 'Pure Abodes,' he will attain → Nibbāna. Attainment of the non-returner stage is often ref. to in the Pali canon, in words attr. to the Buddha. (*Itivuttaka* 39; 40; *AN.* V. 108; *SN.* V. 177, 178). In the *Mahā-Parinibbāna Su.* Buddha ref. to some Buddh. monks already deceased, who 'have all attained the state of non-returner and will attain *parinibbāna* without returning to this world again.' (*DN.* II, 92). The A. concept is found also among the → Sarvāstivādins; it is ref. to in the *Abhidharmakosasāstra* as third of four stages on the spiritual path, from which there is no return to sphere of sensuality. The concept thus passed into → Mahāyāna; but by Mahāyānists it is held that, if an A. wishes to return to help another being who is still in sphere of sensuality to attain Enlightenment he may do so by returning to sphere of sensuality in a 'spiritual' or 'blissful' body (→ *Sambhoga-Kāya*).

Anagārika Term used in anc. India for one who was not (*an*) a householder (*agārika*), i.e., one who had gone forth from home to homelessness, renouncing comforts of life to become a holy man, pursuing the holy life (*brahmacariya*). There were numerous groups or schools of such A.'s in anc. India, each having its own form of teaching or discipline. One of these was the Buddha → Sangha. Such groups of A.'s depended on householders or laymen for supply of food, and were thus sometimes in competition with one another; the Buddh. scriptures contain accounts of plots hatched against the Sangha by non-Buddh. groups, jealous of popularity enjoyed by the former (→ *Samyutta-Nikaya*, 1, p. 122).

Anagarika Dharmapala → Mahabodhi Society.

Ānanda One of foremost disciples of the Buddha. His name

Ānanda

means 'joy,' and he was so called acc. to commentary on the Theragāthā, because he brought joy to his kinsmen. A member of the Sākya clan and first cousin of Buddha, A. entered the Buddh. Order in second year after the Buddha had begun to preach his doc. From begin., A. was closely assoc. with Buddha; for the last 25 yrs. of his life was his personal attendant. This function A. agreed to perform on condition that he was to derive no personal benefits or comforts from his special position, so that none should say it was for these things that he ministered to the Buddha; his service was to be expression of personal devotion only. The great care with which he ministered, sparing no effort, and devoting himself tirelessly to Buddha's comfort and protection is emphasised in Pali canonical and commentarial lit. It was A. who foiled → Devadatta's plot to murder Buddha (→ Ajātasattu). A. was entrusted also by the Buddha with task of teaching the doc. Having given a short outline discourse, he would leave it to A. to provide for hearers of full exposition of what had been said. When the report of A.'s preaching reached Buddha, he praised A.'s perceptiveness and understanding. A. was a partic. close friend of Sariputta, Buddha's chief disciple. He was also champion of the women's cause. Buddha's stepmother, Pajāpati Gotamī, made request to him that women should be admitted to an Order. The Buddha at first firmly refused. A., finding the women weeping over the reply, then asked Buddha on their behalf that they should be admitted. When he maintained his refusal, A. asked him if women were capable of attaining the relig. goal of the Buddh. way. Buddha replied that they were; A. then repeated his plea that they be allowed to enter the Order, subject to special conditions. Buddha then agreed, although not without prediction that with admission of women the Buddh. Order would now last only half the time it would have lasted otherwise. A. is regarded in Buddh. trad. as having remained a *sekha,* that is not having achieved goal of → ara-hant-ship, until after Buddha's death, when by a great spiritual effort he at last attained that state. It was by A.

that the words of the Buddha's discourses are said to have been preserved with faultless accuracy. In first four → *Nikayas* of Pali canon, the phrase 'Thus have I heard' frequently occurs as an intro. to some words of Buddha. In this phrase, the 'I' is understood as being spoken by A.

After Buddha's death, A.'s last years were spent in teaching, preaching, encouraging and guiding younger monks. He was, however, at the Council of monks held immediately after Buddha's death, charged with certain previous faults, namely, that he had failed to ascertain from Buddha which were minor precepts only, which the monks could revoke if necessary (D. II, 154); that he had failed to request Buddha to live on for a further → *kalpa* (D. II, 115); that he had unnecessarily prevailed on Buddha to allow women to be admitted (Vin. II, 253). His reply was that he regarded these acts not as a fault, but would confess them as such out of respect for his fellow-monks. The Suttas of Pali canon which mention A., and together testify to his eminence, are listed by → Buddhaghosa as follows: the *Sekha, Bāhitiya, Āmanjasappāya, Gopaka-Moggallāna, Budhudatāka, Cūlasunnata, Mahāsunnata, Acchariyabbhuta, Bhaddekaratta, Mahānidāna, Mahāparinibbāna, Subha, Cūlaniyalokdhātu Suttas*. His death is not mentioned in Pali canon, but the Chinese pilgrim, → Fa Hsien, records anc. trad. that A.'s death took place in mid-river between domains of → Ajātasattu, King of Magadha, and the chiefs of Vesāli, and that both parties took a share of his ashes and built *cetiyas* for their enshrinement.

Anāthapindika Wealthy man of the Buddha's time who is remembered in Buddh. trad. for his great generosity. At great expense he purchased the Jetavana grove near Sāvatthi, and built there a monastery for the use of Buddha and his monks. For this, and other acts of generosity, he was remembered as the chief of alms-donors (A.I. 25). His name was Sudatta, but he was referred to as Anāthapindika (feeder of the poor) in recognition of his generosity. A number of suttas found in the *Anguttara-Nikaya* are addressed to A. One of these, the *Velāma Sutta*, consists of

Anatta

Buddha's words of encouragement to A., when as result of loss of his wealth, he was no longer able to provide food for the monks (A. IV, 392ff.).

Malalasekere, *DPPN,* vol. I, pp. 67–72.

Anatta (Pali) **Anātma** (Skt.) Buddh. doctrine that there is not (*an*) a permanent self (*atta*) within each individual being. This is third of the '3 characteristic marks of existence' (→ *ti-lakkhana*), and is a doc. entirely peculiar to Buddhism, distinguishing it from all other relig. and philosoph. schools of anc. India. Without proper appreciation of meaning of *anatta,* it is imposs. to understand Buddh. thought. The Buddha's teaching on this point was a denial of reality of a self or soul inhabiting the individual, a per-durable entity which is the agent of the individual's actions. Instead, the individual is seen as a temporary collocation of five → *khandhas,* or groups of constituent factors. The *khandhas* themselves are not enduring, but are series of momentary events; each such event standing in a causal relationship to next. While there is thus a flux of constantly changing factors in any given empirical 'individual,' there is also a certain continuity in the process—sufficient to give the appearance, both at physical and psychological levels, of individuality. The recognition of such continuity, and use of everyday terms and proper names to denote particular individuals, is allowed as concession and aid to economy of language. 'These are wordly usages, wordly language, wordly terms of communication, wordly descriptions by which a Tathāgata communicates without misapprehending them.' (D.I. 195f.). The doc. of A. is regarded in Buddh. trad. as the most difficult truth of all to apprehend, since the notion of a permanent 'self' is deeply rooted in everyday habits of thought. The idea of an individual self was re-introduced and affirmed by the → *pudgala-vādins,* whose views were not accepted as true by other Buddh. schools.

E. Conze, *Buddhist Thought in India* (1962).

Ancestor Cults Buddhism in China promoted A.-C. by practice of chanting masses for dead and in popular festival of Departed Spirits (Yü Lan P'ên Hui) held on the 15th of the

7th moon. Popular throughout China was the spring festival at the tombs, Ch'ing Ming at the end of the 2nd moon when the departed spirits were worshipped at the tombs.

Angel(s), China-Japan If by A. is meant a ministering spirit, a divine messenger, a spiritual being attendant upon a supreme deity, and ever-ready to do his bidding, A.'s are a constant theme in Chi. and Jap. mythology, folk-lore and Buddhist and Taoist religs. In the prevailing polytheism of the East they are classified as 'gods' (Chi. 'shên'), who occupy subordinate and inferior positions in a spiritual hierarchy. They are in close and constant relationship with human world. The → bodhisattvas of Buddhism, the 'immortals' of Taoism, the glorified saints and heroes of pop. relig. are conceived of, not only as enjoying felicity in spiritual world, but as agents of a supreme Being (Buddha or Yü Huang) in bringing healing, succour, guidance, and meting out rewards and punishments to men, or guiding souls of men to their appropr. destiny and judgement in underworld.

Anger In B. thought one of the three main morally unwholesome states, based on the mistaken notion of a 'self' within the individual. → Evil, in Buddhist thought.

Anguttara-Nikāya One of the five nikayas or collections of *suttas*, or discourses which together make up the Buddh. Pali → *Sutta-Pitaka*. The *A.-N.* is so arranged that first section deals with topics which occur in 'ones'; the next section of topics which occur in pairs; the next, topics in trios; the next, in fours; and so on up to topics which form groups of eleven, there being eleven sections in all to the *A.-N.* These eleven sections comprise some 2,308 suttas, or separate discourses, or by another reckoning 2,344; by yet another, that of the book itself, it contains 9,557 suttas. There is a good deal of overlap with other sections of the Pali canon; for instance, the description of 8 kinds of assembly is found here in the 'eights' section; it occurs also in the *Mahā-Parinibbāna Sutta* of the → *Dīgha-Nikaya*. The scheme used in the *A.-N.*, of progressive numerical classification is one which in a later and more developed form is basis of the → Abhidhamma lit.

Anicca

W. Geiger, *Pali Literature and Language* (1956); B. C. Law, *A History of Pali Literature* (1933); F. L. Woodward and E. M. Hare (trs.), *The Book of the Gradual Sayings*, 5 vols. (1932–6, repr. 1953–65).

Anicca Buddh. doc. of the impermanence of all things; the first of the '3 characteristic marks of existence' (→ *Ti-Lakkhana*). It is a feature of all mundane existence; it is empirically observable at the physical levels in human body, whose constituent elements are in constant flux, quite apart from the more obvious bodily impermanence observable in difference between infancy, childhood, youth, maturity and old age. Even more impermanent, however, in the Buddh. view, is cognisance, mind, or consciousness, which arises and ceases from moment to moment. (S. II:94–5). Whereas impermanence of physical things is readily observable empirically, impermanence of consciousness is not so readily discerned, until it is pointed out (i.e., in the course of Buddh. teaching). 'The characteristic of impermanence does not become apparent because, when rise and fall are not given attention, it is concealed by continuity. . . . However, when continuity is disrupted by discerning rise and fall, the characteristic of impermanence becomes apparent in its true nature' (*Vism.* XXI:3). It is the notion of 'rise and fall,' or coming into being followed by dissolution, which is at root of notion of impermanence. Body and mind are alike regarded as scenes of events, bodily or mental. Each moment of consciousness is regarded as being formed from cause and condition and as being unstable, and therefore immediately dissolving. The analogy of the sound of a lute is used: this does not come from any 'store' of sounds, nor does it go anywhere' when it has ceased; rather, from not having been, it is brought into existence by the lute and the player's effort, and then, having been, it vanishes (S. IV:197). So with all material and mental events: they come to be, and having been, vanish.

This inevitable dissolution of whatever is brought into being, or *anicca*, provides subject matter for contemplation for Buddhists: *aniccānupassanā* or 'contemplation of impermanency' is one of three major ways in Buddh. meditation to achieve insight (→ *vipassanā*). The others are contemplation of → *dukkha*, and contemplation of → *anatta*.

Annam → Vietnam.

Annihilation Term sometimes mistakenly used in West in connection with the Buddh. *Nirvāna*. The Buddha expressly rejected notion of 'annihilationism' (*uccheda-ditthi*) as a false or misleading idea, since its use presupposes existence of an individual entity which can be annihilated; a supposition which is contrary to the basic. Buddh. tenet of → *anatta* (→→ Nibbāna; Uccheda-Vāda).

Anuruddha (1) A prominent monk of the Buddh. → Sangha in time of Buddha, mentioned many times in the Pali canon and in the → *Mahāvastu*. A. appears as close and loyal comrade of Buddha. He was present at his death, and was active in strengthening and exhorting the other monks. To him is attr. the reciting and preserving of the → *Anguttara-Nikaya*.

Malalasekere, *D.P.P.P.N.*, vol. I, pp. 85–90; *Vinaya-Pitaka*, II, pp. 180–3, *Mahāvastu*, iii, 177f.; *D.N.*, II, pp. 156–7; Thag. 908.

(2) Author of the Pali work, → *Abhidhammattha-Sangaha*, who is believed to have been incumbent of the Sinhalese *Mūlasoma-vihāra* (monastery). Little else is known of him. His name appears in list of saintly men of S. India; and he is believed to have composed at Kāñcipura (Conjevaram) another learned Buddh. work, the *Paramattha-vinicchaya*. His dates are not known with certainty: prob. after 8th and before 12th cent. CE.

Anurādhapura Anc. capital of Ceylon until 10th cent. CE, where was situated the Great Monastery (*Mahāvihāra*) which had been stronghold of → Theravada Buddhism in Ceylon, since its intro. in 3rd cent. BC. Also in A. was the rival Abhayaggiri Vihāra, a centre of liberal Buddhism of the Mahāyāna type. When capital was moved to Polonnaruwa, A. was abandoned and its many temples, monasteries and pagodas fell into ruins. Rediscovered in 19th cent., it is now recognised as valuable repository of early Sinhalese Buddh. art and architecture (→ Ceylon).

Anussati

Anussati Pali Buddh. term for 'recollection.' The conventional list of six objects of recollection, each recommended as a form of meditational exercise, consists of: recollection of the Buddha (*buddhānussati*); of his doctrine (*dhammānussati*); his community (*sanghānussati*); morality (*silānussati*); detachment (*cāgānussati*); the heavenly sphere (*devānussati*). Any of these types of recollection is regarded as effective in bringing the meditator to → Access-Concentration (*upacāra-samādhi*).

Arahant Term used in Pali Buddhism for one who reached final stage of spiritual progress; lit. 'the worthy.' The word A. was used gen. in anc. India to indic. respect, not unlike the Eng. usage 'his worship.' In the *Rg-veda* the term is used of the god Agni (II, 3.3). It was also used as an epithet of → Mahāvira, the founder of the Jain community. It was applied to the Buddha also by his contemporaries. Later it came to have a specialised meaning in Buddh. usage. Four stages of spiritual attainment were distinguished: first that of the → *sotāpanna,* or 'stream-enterer'; the → *sakadāgāmi,* or 'once-returner'; the → *anāgāmī* or 'non-returner'; and, finally, the *arahant*. The A. was regarded as one in whom all the → *āsavas,* or 'influxes,' which produced further → karma and thus continuance of existence in the sensuous sphere, had been extinguished. While attainment of first 3 stages was poss. for lay people, attainment of 4th by a layman was regarded as very unusual and extremely difficult. This view is expressed, e.g. in the → *Milinda-Pañha* (*SBE*.36, p. 56). Among Ceylon Buddhists it is held that a layman who attains arahantship should immediately enter the monastic Order (*sangha*). Acc. to the Buddha, women were equally capable with men of becoming A.'s. Many examples of nuns (*therīs*) who attained A.ship are given in the → Therīgāthā. In time of Buddha and immediately after, A.'s were neither expected nor encouraged to withdraw from human society, as is clear from Buddha's own example. The trad. of Indian asceticism was, however, strongly in favour of withdrawal, and early Buddhism provides examples of the solitary A. Normally, the A. continued to live disinterestedly within human society.

Architecture

Among → Theravadins the A. tended to be regarded with
great reverence; the → Mahāsanghika school, however,
criticised this exaltation of the A., and maintained that
some who were held to be A.'s in fact exhibited various
imperfections. This criticism was voiced by Mahādeva.
Criticism of A. ideal was continued by the Mahāyāna
schools, on ground that the *nirvāna* which the A.'s reached
was merely cessation of the *āsavas* and not full enlightenment (*sambodhi*). Superior to the A. ideal was, according
to Mahāyāna Buddhists, the → *bodhisattva* ideal. The
Mahāyāna work *Saddharma-pundarīka*, e.g., maintains that
A.'s, having extinguished the *āsavas,* must go on to seek supreme enlightenment, i.e., become a Buddha.
Kindred Sayings (PTS) III, 68ff.; V. 170; 181ff.; E. Lamotte,
Histoire du Bouddhisme Indien, pp. 300ff.; E. Conze, *Buddhist Thought in India* (1962), pp. 166–9; 234–6.

Ārāma Term used in anc. India for a park or grove, and partic.
for such places when set aside for use of Buddh. monks as
places of quiet retreat, and, eventually of residence.
(→ Monasteries).

Architecture (Religious) Jap. secular architecture and the
great Buddhist temples and monasteries were, in the first
place, almost wholly dependent on Chinese influence and
inspiration. In Nara period (CE 710–782) Chi. T'ang Dynasty
A. was meticulously copied as to design and construction.
(*Vide* the Hōryūji temple at Nara.) It was only during the
Heian Period (CE 782–1068) that there occurred in A. a re-
surgence of Jap. national taste. In the great mountain monasteries of → Tendai and → Shingon the formal Chinese
layout was impossible, whilst the needs of large lay con-
gregations and tantric rituals led to development of great
individual halls of worship. These demanded experiments
in new forms of A., and the development in Japan of temple constructions less dependent on traditional Chinese
patterns. Nevertheless, throughout Jap. hist. the influence
of China on A. has been immense. → Art, Sacred.
E.R.E., I, p. 773; R. T. Paine and A. Soper, *The Art and Architecture of Japan* (1955); Jean Herbert, *Shinto* (1967), pp.
92ff.

Ariya-Sacca

Ariya-Sacca (Pali); **Arya-Satya** (Skt.) → Four Holy Truths.

Art, Sacred Much of the art of Buddh. countries has been directly inspired by Buddh. ideas and practices, although very little (unless lit. is incl.) has been work of Buddh. monks: the production of works of art has been primarily done by Buddh. laymen. Sculpture, painting and architecture are the major fields; music is not encouraged in Buddh. devotional contexts and is not used by monks, whose corporate chanting of suttas in devotional services bears some slight similarity to European plain-chant but is basically a reciting aloud. In field of sculpture, however, Buddhism has a rich record, partic. in develop. of the → *rupa,* or Buddha-statue, from early beginnings in N.W. India to its mod. forms in S.E. Asian countries, notably in Thailand. The painting of murals on walls of monasteries and temples has also had a long develop. and has produced many different styles; the principal subjects have been, and still are, scenes from life of Buddha, and from → Jātaka stories. In field of architecture the → *stupa* has provided ample scope for rich develop., culminating in such structures as the pagodas of S.E. Asia, notably the Shway Dagon, in Rangoon; monasteries and temples have also provided outlet for rich creative skills, the results of which are to be seen throughout Buddh. Asia from Ceylon to Japan. The subject is a vast one; the reader must be ref. to specialist works on subject, a few of which are mentioned below (→→ Ajanta: Gandhara).

B. Rowland, *The Art and Architecture of India* (1959); A. K. Coomeraswamy, *Elements of Buddhist Iconography* (1935); S. Kramrisch, *The Art of India* (1954); H. Zimmer, *The Art of Indian Asia,* 2 vols. (1955); R. Le May, *Buddhist Art in Siam* (1967); R. T. Paine and A. Soper, *The Art and Architecture of Japan* (1955); D. Seckel, *The Art of Buddhism* (1964).

Arūpa-Loka (or -Dhātu, or -Bhava) → Cosmology.

Āryadeva Younger contemporary and pupil of → Nāgārjuna, who was founder of the Mādhyamika Buddh. → Mādhyamika system. A. is sometimes ref. to simply as Deva; sometimes as Bodhisattva Deva. His activity as an exponent of Mādhyamika should prob. be dated during 1st half

Āryadeva

of 3rd cent. CE. The sources of information for his life are: the biography trans. into Chinese by → Kumārajīva (4th–5th cent. CE); the Chinese pilgrim → Hsüan Tsang's travel diary, and two Tibetan histories, those of → Bu-Ston and Taranatha. A great deal of the material in these sources is, however, legendary. Acc. to Hsüan Tsang, A. was one of the 'four suns' who illumined the world, the other 3 being → Asvaghosa, Nāgārjuna, and Kumāralabhda. Hsüan Tsang records also that he was a native of Ceylon. This is confirmed by 6th cent. CE writer Candrakīrti, in his commentary on A.'s. Catuḥśataka. A. left Ceylon for S. India, poss. because the Mahāyānist trend of thought, to which he was attracted, had more congenial environment in S. India than in predominantly → Theravādin Ceylon. There were close contacts at that time between these 2 areas, espec. between Ceylon and Nāgārjunikonda, the centre of Nāgārjuna's teaching activity. Nāgārjuna and A. are trad. connected also with → Nālanda, the great monastic centre of learning in N.E. India.

A.'s principal written work is the Catuḥśataka, the '400' treatise (i.e. the treatise of 400 verses), the complete text of which is preserved in Tibetan trans. the Skt. orig. surviving only in fragments. The Skt. text has been reconstructed from the Tibetan by V. S. Bhattacharya (Vishva Bharati Series, 1931). The 1st half of work deals with the Madhyamika system of thought and its discipline; the 2nd half is devoted to refutation of the → Abhidharma, and of 2 of the six Indian (non-Buddhist) philosophical systems, the Saṃkhya and Vaiseṣika. Other works attr. to A. are: the Akṣara Śatakam, a treatise expounding some 20 propositions of Mādhyamika philosophy; and the Hasta-vāla-prakaraṇa (the Hand Treatise), a summary of Mādhyamika doc. A restored Skt. text of this was pub. by F. W. Thomas in J.R.A.S., 1918 (pp. 267–310).

A. was not only an import. literary exponent of the Mādhyamika school; he was also a powerful debater. Adherents of other contemporary schools of thought are said to have been frequently defeated in public debate with him. Acc. to Chinese sources this brought about his death:

Asanga

he was murdered by a disciple of a non-Buddh. teacher who had been worsted in debate.

T. R. V. Murti, *The Central Philosophy of Buddhism* (1955), pp. 92–5; H. Winternitz, *Hist. of Indian Literature*, vol. 2; E. Obermiller (tr.) *Bu-Ston's History of Buddhism in India and Tibet*; V. S. Bhattacharya, *The Catuḥśataka of Aryadeva* (1931).

Asanga Indian Buddh. philosopher of 4th cent. CE, founder of the → Yogācāra or Vijñāna-vāda school. His most import. work was the *Yogācārabbhūmi-Śāstra*. It is held that A. had no human teacher (hence his name: A-sanga, 'unattached'), but had received his doc., that of Yogācāra, direct from the heavenly Buddha → Maitreya. This 'supernatural' teacher has, however, been identified by some mod. scholars with a human preceptor, an hist. personage named Maitreya-natha, regarded as orig. author of the *Yogācārabhūmi-Śāstra*. Others, notably Demiéville, have rejected this identification, on grounds that attempt to find in Maitreya a human teacher is due to a 'manie historiciste introduite de l'Occident,' and a basic misunderstanding of relig. psychology, espec. that of → Mahāyāna Buddhism, where it is customary to attr. doctrines to supernatural inspiration, often that of Maitreya. Not all mod. scholars are convinced by Demiéville's objections: T. R. V. Murti maintains that Maitreya-natha's historicity is now firmly estab. S. Dutt takes a similar view. A. is gen. held to have been eldest of three brothers, born in Purusapura (mod. Peshawar, in W. Pakistan). The second brother was → Vasubandhu; the third was Viriñcivatsa, of whom little is known, except that he became an → arahant. Acc. to Paramartha's *Life of Vasubandhu*, main source of information about A., Vasubandhu's criticism of Mahāyāna doctrines grieved A.; but when these were properly expounded to Vasubandhu by his brother, he was converted from the → Sarvāstivāda school, and became a Mahāyānist. In order to compensate for his earlier criticisms, he then began, at instigation of A., to devote himself to an acute and skilful exposition of the Yogācāra doctrines.

A.'s own works expounding Yogācāra are, principally,

Asceticism, Buddhist

the *Mahāyāna-Saṇgraha,* the *Yogācārabhūmi-Śāstra* (unless this is attr. to an hist. Maitreya-natha), and the *Mahāyānasūtrālankāra.* The second of these sets out the 17 stages, or → bhumi, by which the → Bodhisattva achieves Buddhahood. These, acc. to A., consist of intellectual and spiritual attainments; these 17 *bhūmis* taken together are called *'Yogācārabhūmi.'* The first part of text has been ed. by V. S. Sastri (*The Yogācāra-Bhūmi of Acarya Asanga,* Calcutta University, 1957). The *Mahāyānasūtrālankāra* has been ed. by Sylvain Levi, and trans. into French. Levi notes that there is in this work an element of Manichean and neo-Platonic thought. The area in which A. lived, namely → Gandhāra, had been one of strong Graeco-Roman influence since time of Alexander the Great. Another work, which has been connected with A.'s name, is the Tantric Buddh. work, *Guhya Samāja Tantra.* If the connection is accepted, A. is seen as an important leader of the Tantra, or → *Vajrayāna.*

G. Tucci, *On Some Aspects of the Doctrines of Maitreya* (*nātha*) *and Asanga* (1930); E. Frauwallner, *On the Date of the Buddhist Master of the Law Vasubandhu* (Serie Orientale Roma III) (1951); P. Demiéville, La Yogācārabhūmi de Sangharaksa, in *Bulletin de l'École Française d'Extrême Orient,* XLIV, fasc. 2 (1954).

Āsava (Pali); **Āsrava** (Skt.) The 'influxes' or 'taints,' 4 in number, which in Buddh. thought are regarded as intoxicating the human mind and preventing spiritual progress. The 4 influxes are *kāmāsava,* sensuality; *bhav-ā.,* lust for life (rebirth); *ditth-ā.,* false view or speculation; *avijj-ā.,* ignorance. The 4 together are frequently mentioned in the → *Sutta-Pitaka.* In some cases 3 only are mentioned, *ditth-ā.* being omitted. This may represent earlier usage, *ditth-ā.* having been added later. The extinction of the A.'s was held to constitute arahantship, hence a syn. for the → arahant is *anāsava,* i.e., one in whom there is no (*an-*) *asāva.* Another such syn. is *khīnāsava,* i.e., one whose A.'s are destroyed (*khīna*). The A.'s are ref. to also as 'floods' (*ogha*) and as 'yokes' (*yoga*).

Asceticism, Buddhist The practice of physical austerities was

29

Aśoka

a familiar feature of India in the Buddha's time. Contemporary ascetics are ref. to in the Pali canon by various names. In the *Mahāsihanāda Sutta* (MN. I.77ff.), Buddha tells Sariputta of his own experience as an ascetic during period before his enlightenment. He had engaged in bodily self-mortification as means to spiritual attainment; but gaining no spiritual benefit he abandoned these practices. (→→ Buddha, Gotama). In gen., therefore, the Buddh. attitude towards A. is to avoid this extreme, and, avoiding also opposite extreme of hedonism, to follow the Middle Way between the two. The life of the Buddh. monk, as prescribed in the → *Vinaya*, is one of self-discipline; extreme asceticism is forbidden. A list of some 13 practices of self-humbling kind, mentioned separately at various places in Pali canon, is given in the → *Visuddhimagga* II; these are recommended as helping to promote right attitudes of mind. They are as follows: (1) wearing patched up robes; (2) wearing no more than minimum of 3 robes; (3) going for alms-food; (4) not discriminating between houses on alms-food round; (5) eating one meal only each day; (6) eating from alms bowl only; (7) declining further offers of food; (8) living in the forest; (9) living at the foot of tree; (10) living under open sky; (11) living in a graveyard; (12) being satisfied with one's dwelling; (13) sleeping in sitting position rather than lying down. Even in following such practices, however, it is emphasised that monk must do so for sake of frugality, contentedness, purity etc., rather than for praise; otherwise they will be of no value: mere external performance is not real self-discipline. (*Puggala-paññatti*, P.T.S. 1883, 275–84).
Buddhism, imported into China and Japan, taught a strict discipline of body and mind, and certain sects not only forbade eating of meat but all forms of self-indulgence. Many monks in Buddhist monasteries practised A. along with intense meditation.

Aśoka (Ashoka) Ruler of Mauryan empire of N. India in 3rd cent. BC who, after conquest of Kalinga, became a Buddhist. The founder of the Maurya dynasty, Chandragupta, in wake of Alexander the Great's invasion of N.W. India, had extended the Magadhan kingdom into W. half of N. India. His son, Bindusāra, extended it yet further; Ashoka, by his conquest of Kalinga gave it a S.E. seaboard, so that it extended across India from sea to sea. This last campaign, with its terrible bloodshed, produced in Ashoka a psychological crisis. He embraced the faith which had made its appearance in Magadha 2 centuries earlier, that of the Buddha; in his own words, there was heard thenceforth in his domains no longer the sound of the drum, but the sound of the Dhamma (Dhammaghosa). The main sources of information about A. are 2-fold: (1) Pali chronicles produced by Buddh. monks, which portray him as a Buddh. emperor; (2) archaeological evidence in form of rock- and pillar-edicts and epigraphs, for which A. himself was responsible. Whereas the Pali chronicles repr. A.'s empire as Buddh., and A. himself as a missionary enthusiast seeking to propagate the Buddh. faith outside his realm, the edicts reveal a monarch who, while he himself a Buddhist, with personal contacts with the → Sangha, nevertheless encouraged and patronised various relig. communities as natural part of his duty as an Indian ruler. The edicts frequently mention the → Dhamma, which A. wished his subjects to follow and to practise. But it is not certain that this word, of widespread use in anc. India before it was given a special meaning by Buddhists, here denotes the Buddha-Dhamma.

G. P. Malalasekere, *D.P.P.N.*, vol. I, pp. 216–9; V. Smith, *Asoka* (3rd edn. 1920); S. Dutt, *Buddhist Monks and Monasteries of India* (1962), pp. 107–14; E. Lamotte, *Histoire du Bouddhisme Indien* (1958); A. Sen, *Asoka's Edicts* (1956).

Asuras Common term for demons in anc. India, *asuras* are mentioned almost always collectively in Pali canon as a spirit-host, hostile to all forces of goodness. The word A. is cognate with *ahura* in Iranian, where, however, it denotes a good spirit. In Pali canon A.'s are usually mentioned in assoc. with their counterparts, the → *devas*, or heavenly beings, with whom they wage continual war. A.'s are incl.

within whole range of living being subject to renewed existence; but are regarded as very low in the scale, being one of the four forms of evil rebirth poss. to human beings. The lord of the A.'s (*asurinda*) is Rāhu (AN. II, 17). Another name for this 'lord' is Vepacitti (SN, IV, 202).

Aśvaghosha Name of a Buddh. writer, or writers. To an A. of 1st/2nd cent. CE is attributed authorship of → *Buddha Carita, Saundarānanda,* and *Śariputra-Prakarana.* The Mhy. work, *'The Awakening of Faith'* (*Śraddhotpāda Śāstra*), preserved in Chinese, has also been attr. to this A.; but Murti considers that ideas elaborated in this work are post-Nāgārjuna (4th cent. CE), and therefore work of another A., of 5th cent. CE. S. Dutt has suggested that on grounds of style, manner, and contents the works commonly attr. to A. may be ascribed to 3 diff. authors. *'The Awakening of Faith'* is title of a trans. by D. T. Suzuki and T. Richard of the *Śraddhotpāda*; in this summary of Chinese and Tibetan, legends concerning A. are given, one of which speaks of no less than 6 A.'s who flourished at various times. A. thus seems likely to have been a name assumed by, or applied to, a number of different authors of various periods. Acc. to Tibetan trad., a man of this name was a leading figure at first Mhy. Council, convened by emperor → Kanishka, and was called upon to give precise formulation of doctrines agreed by the Council.

Atthakathā Pali term meaning 'a commentary' on Buddhist canonical scriptures. Acc. to → Buddhaghosa, there was in existence in → Ceylon in his day an anc. A. which, acc. to trad., had been brought from India by → Mahinda when Buddhism was intro. into island, and which he used as basis of his own work. He mentions that the version he received was in Sinhalese, and that he trans. it into Pali. Nothing is known to have been directly preserved of this ancient A., which may have existed in several sections, since Buddhaghosa refers to the 'composers' of the A. (*Atthakathācariyā*). The hist. portions of the A. provided the basic source for the later compilation known as the → *Dipavamsa* ('The Island Chronicle'), or hist. of Ceylon. There is evidence that the old A. was in existence in Ceylon as late as 12th cent. CE.

W. Geiger, *Pali Literature and Language,* 2nd edn. (1956), pp. 25f.

Atthasālini Name of commentary in Pali by → Buddhaghosa on the → Dhamma-Sangani, first book of the → Abhidhamma-Pitaka, of Buddh. Pali canon. It is gen. held to have been composed in Ceylon, and may have been based on an earlier commentary by same writer and bearing same title, written while he was in India. The A. has itself been subject of further commentaries (*Tikā*) by Ceylonese and Burmese Buddh. writers from 12th cent. CE onwards.

Avadāna Type of Buddh. literature which repr. transitional stage between lit. of → Hinayāna schools and that of the → Mahāyāna. A notable feature is its tendency to glorification of the → Bodhisattva ideal. The word A. means 'a noteworthy deed,' gen. in a good sense (though occasionally the reverse also), to indic. a relig. meritorious feat, such as sacrifice of one's life for others, or giving of something very precious for erection of a Buddh. sanctuary. The general theme of the A. lit. is to show that 'black deeds bear black fruits, while white deeds bear white fruits,' and is thus homiletic in intention. The stories, which bear such morals, are usually intro. as though told by the Buddha (in stylised manner like that used in the → *Jātakas*). Stories of this type occur throughout the canonical scriptures; but they are also collected together into anthologies in the A. lit. Among such anthologies are, e.g., the *Avadana-Sataka,* 'the 100 A.'s' which was trans. into Chinese in 1st half of 3rd cent. CE. (→ Divyāvadāna).

M. Winternitz, *Hist. of Indian Literature* (1933), vol. 2, pp. 284ff.

Avalokiteśvara One of most prominent → Bodhisattvas in Mhy. Buddhism. The name may be regarded as being formed from two Skt. words: *Avalokita,* he who looks down upon human world, i.e., with compassion, and *Isvara,* the Lord (a common word for God in Indian relig.). This 'looking down' in compassion is from the Tusita

Āvāsa

heaven where A. is regarded as dwelling. It is equally poss. however that *avalokita* means 'he who is looked to' (for help). A. thus repres. one of two major aspects of the Buddha-nature, viz. compassion (→ *karunā*), the other being wisdom (→ *prajñā*); the latter is repres. in Mhy. mythology by the Bodhisattva → Mañjuśrī. One of A.'s epithets is *Mahākarunā*—the great Compassion. With A.'s compassion is linked, in Mhy. thought, his miraculous power to help human beings, when they call upon him in times of difficulty or distress. In his cosmic aspect A. is sovereign lord of universe; hence he possesses absolute power to protect men from natural disasters such as storms; on the other hand, to grant fertility to childless women. This cult of A. has been described as 'the Buddhism of Faith,' in contrast to earlier doc. of human self-reliance and disavowal of heavenly aid. In his final development, in → Vajrayāna Buddhism, A. becomes magician, who works by means of *mantras* or spells. In accordance with notion that the great Buddh. ruler is an incarnation of a Bodhisattva, it is held that ruler of → Tibet, the Dalai Lama, is an incarnation of A. The various transformations of which A. is capable, in order to guide and help men, are described in the Mhy. Skt. treatise, the → *Saddharma-Pundarīka Sūtra* (Eng. trsl. by H. Kern, *S.B.E.*, vol. 21).

C. Eliot, *Japanese Buddhism* (1935), pp. 117–24; *Hinduism and Buddhism,* vol. 2 (1921), pp. 13–9.

Āvāsa Name used in anc. India for Buddh. monks' dwelling place during rainy season. (→ Monasteries).

Avidyā (Skt.); **Avijjā** (Pali), Ignorance, in the Buddh. view, is failure to see true nature of things, and is a primary root of ordinary man's unsatisfactory condition. It is one of the → *āsavas,* and in the cycle of renewed mundane existence is one of critical 'links' where whole process may poss. be interrupted, by following of the Buddh. way. Ignorance is also called *moha,* delusion, one of basic 3 roots of evil, the other two being *lobha* (greed) and *dosa* (hate).

Āyatana Term used in Buddhism for basis of a sensation, these bases being arranged in 6 pairs: eye and visible object; ear and sound; nose and odour; tongue and tastable object; body and tactile object; mind and mental object. The *āyatanas* together thus constitute a preliminary classification of factors involved in sensual existence, as basis for further analysis.

B

Bala Buddh. term meaning 'power' (Skt. plur. *balāni*). In →
Pali canon a frequent group of 5 moral powers are: faith
(*saddhā*), energy (*viriya*), mindfulness (*sati*), concentration
(*samādhi*) and wisdom (*paññā*). Other 'powers,' e.g., moral
shame, and moral dread, etc., are mentioned in Pali texts,
singly or in groups. In Mhy. Buddhism there is a conventional list of ten 'powers' with which a → Bodhisattva is
said to be endowed. They are: *āsayabala*, having mind
strongly turned away from worldliness; *adhyāsaya°*, having
faith growing ever stronger; *prayoga°*, power of disciplin-
ing oneself in exercises of Bodhisattvahood; *prajñā°*, intuitive power of understanding minds of all beings; *prani-
dhāna°*, power of having every prayer fulfilled; *carya°*,
power of working until end of time; *yāna°*, power of creating varieties of vehicles (*yana*) of salvation, while remaining true to Mhy.; *vikurvana°*, power to make a pure
world in every pore of skin; *bodi°*, power of awakening
every being to enlightenment; *dharmacakrapravartana°*,
power of uttering one phrase of universal appeal.

Banāras (Benares) The most holy city in India and import. in
Buddhism (Buddha having preached first sermon in Sarnath, on outskirts); sometimes spelt *Benares,* it is also
known by names Vārānasī and Kāśī. It has immemorially
been centre of pilgrimage, and has been long import. for
Sanskrit learning. It owes its preeminence partly from situation on the Ganges (it is held to lie at intersection of the
heavenly Ganges, i.e., the milky way, the earthly Ganges,
and the invisible underground Ganges). It contains large
numbers of temples, but few are old, because of repressive
policy of Aurangzeb, who built a large mosque now domi-

nating sky line, beside the stump of a pillar erected by →
Asoka. The river front is lined with bathing steps or *ghats*,
among which are numbered the *Dasasvamedha Ghat*
(where anciently a ten-horse-sacrifice was performed,
asvamedha) and the Tulsi Das Ghat, named after poet who
rendered the Ramayana into Hindi. Among import. relig.
teachers orig. in B. was Kabir. The river itself is focus of import. pilgrimages, as well as daily ablutions; the ghats are
occupied by relig. teachers and the pious, incl. many wid-
ows. The area round B. is also sacred; the circuit of fifty
miles along the *panchkosi* road, starting and ending in B.
itself, is an esp. meritorious pilgrimage. Also in B. is the B.
Hindu University, whose foundation owed something to
Annie Besant, the Theosophist, and expresses Hindu trad.
in a mod. manner.

Bhūmi (Skt.) Lit. 'earth': term occurs in cpd. form *bhūmispar-
shamudrā*—the earth-touching gesture of certain → *Bud-
dha-rūpas*. Used also in specialised sense in Mhy. Buddhism as 'stage,' in upward spiritual progress of a →
Bodhisattva; there are conventionally 10 such 'stages.'

Bimbisāra A king of → Magadha at time of the Buddha, and 5
yrs. his junior. At age of 30, B. is said to have heard Buddha
preach and have become a Buddh. lay adherent and supporter. For remaining years of life he piously observed duties of a layman and used his power in support of Buddha
and his community. His death was brought about by his
son → Ajātasattu, in whose favour B. had already abdicated, and at instigation of Devadatta, the notorious
enemy of Buddha.

Malalasekere, *D.P.P.N.*, vol. II, pp. 285–9.

Bodhi Indian term used espec. in Buddhism, meaning 'enlightenment' or 'awakening,' from *budh:* to awake, become conscious. B. is held to be of 3 kinds, that of the disciple, or hearer of the Buddha, that of an isolated enlightened one, or → *Pacceka-Buddha,* which is independently
gained; and that of the universal Buddha, the *samma-sam-
buddha*, which is independently gained, but also proclaimed to others. → Buddha (as a generic title).

Bodhidharma (c. CE 470–543). In Chinese = Ta Mo. An Indian

Bodhisatta

Buddhist monk who went to China and is credited with the estab. of → Ch'an or the Meditation Sch. of Buddhism. The date of his arrival in China is generally given as CE 520, and he soon acquired an outstanding influence. The accounts of his life are largely legendary. He based his teachings on the *Lankāvatāra Sūtra* (E.T. by D. T. Suzuki, London, 1932), and his message was summarised in the famous stanzas:

A special transmission outside the Scriptures,
No dependence upon words or letters,
Direct pointing at the soul of man,
Seeing into one's own nature and attainment of Buddhahood.

E. Wood, *Zen Dictionary* (1962).

Bodhisatta (Pali); **Bodhisattva** (Skt.) Term used in Buddhism for one who aspires to → *Bodhi* (enlightenment), i.e., one who is a Buddha-to-be. Orig. term appears to have been used to denote → Gotama the Buddha's state prior to becoming a Buddha: cf. phrase found in Pali texts such as *Mahāpadāna Sutta* (DN. ii. 13), 'in the days before my Enlightenment when I was as yet only a Bodhisatta . . .' Interest in 'previous lives' of Buddha thus developed, and stories concerning the B. Gotama were brought together in the → *Jātakas*. Speculation concerning state of life of a B. is also discernible in → Pali canon; acc. to the *AN.* (iv, 127; viii, 70), the B., before being born on earth in his last existence, i.e., as a Buddha, dwells in place of bliss, the *Tusita* heaven, where he may live as long as 6 million years. As speculation developed further, so concept of the B. became further conventionalised: his career as a B. was held to begin with his making a formal resolution to become a Buddha, for welfare of all beings. This was the B.'s *abhinīhāra,* and its ultimate realisation depended on fulfilling of 8 conditions, viz. that the aspirant (1) was a human (2) male (3) able to become an → *arahant* during existence in which resolution was made (4) a recluse, (5) declared his resolution to a Buddha (6) was able to attain state of → *jhāna* (7) was prepared for absolute self-sacrifice (8) was unswerving in his resolve (*Buddhavamsa* ii, 59).

Bodhisatta

The concept of B. received a greatly increased importance in Mhy., where it replaced *arahant* ideal as goal of Buddh. life. In Har Dayal's classic work, *The Bodhisattva Doctrine,* it is argued that the B. ideal was revival of the orig. genius of Buddhism, which had become obscured by too self-centred attitude of monks who were seeking lesser goal of arahantship. The distinction made by Mahāyānists is that the B. aims at enlightenment of all beings without distinction of 'self' and 'not-self'; whereas the *arahant* aimed only at self-enlightenment. The quality of compassion is emphasised equally with wisdom in the Mhy., whereas the → Hīnayāna had emphasised wisdom more than compassion. The B. ideal was thus of a universalist character. The question when one can justifiably be called a B. was answered by → Nāgārjuna (1st cent. CE) as follows: 'This change from an ordinary being to a Bodhisattva takes place when his mind has reached the stage when it can no longer turn back on enlightenment. Also, he has by then gained five advantages: he is no more reborn in the States of woe, but always among gods and men; he is never again born in poor or low-class families; he is always a male and never a woman; he is always well-built, and free from physical defects; he can remember his past lives, and no more forgets them again.' (*Mahāprajñā-paramitā-sāstra* 86.C–89.C; Conze's trans., *Buddhist Scriptures,* pp. 30f.). Acc. to the *Lankāvatāra Su,* an important work of → Yogācāra school, the B. is characterised by 9 endeavours: (1) to rid himself of all perverted views of existence; (2) thereby to liberate himself from fetters of conventional concepts; (3) to penetrate unreality of a so-called external world of particulars; (4) to attain position where → *samsāra* and → *nirvāna* are understood as 2 aspects of one and the same reality; (5) to cultivate a compassionate heart and skilful means; (6) to perform effortless deeds; (7) to cultivate contemplation (*samādhi*) which sees beyond all forms; (8) to have perfect wisdom (*prajñā*); (9) finally, to manifest the Buddha-body. When these all have been achieved, the B. will have come to Buddhahood.

Since this is a path open to all, acc. to Mhy., the concept

of B. implies poss. of existence within world of many B.'s. Those who were regarded as having reached penultimate stage of existence in the *Tusita* heaven, were thought of as heavenly beings, upon whom ordinary mortals could call for help, confident that the compassionate B. would not fail them. In such terms were regarded the major B.'s, such as →→ Avalokitesvara, Manjusri and Maitreya. In this way the Mhy. philosophy was able to provide what in Mhy. Buddh. view was a respectable rationale for a popular cult.

The term B. was not, however, confined to 'celestial' beings. Great teachers, e.g., →→ Nagarjuna and Asanga, were referred to as B.'s. It was also a convention of Buddhists in S. E. Asia to regard their kings as B.'s, since they were beings whose great efforts were directed towards securing welfare of the many → Kings.

Malalasekere, *D.P.P.N.*, vol. II, pp. 322–9; Conze, *B. Thought in India* (1962), pp. 234ff.; Eliot, *H.B.*, II, ch. XXVII; H. Sarkisyanz, *The Buddhist Backgrounds of the Burmese Revolution* (1965); Pe Maung Tin, *B. Devotion and Meditation* (1964), pp. 56–8.

Bodhi-Tree (Bodhirukkha) The *aśvattha* (*ficus religiosus*) tree under which, acc. to Buddh. trad., the Buddha attained enlightenment, at Uruvelā, on bank of the Neranjara River, near modern Gāya. The Pali texts recount propagation of other *bodhi* trees from this parent one. The people of Sāvatthī are said to have asked Buddha's disciple, Ānanda, for provision of a shrine where they might make their offerings of flowers and incense in honour of Buddha at times when he was absent from the place. After consulting him, Ānanda is said to have obtained a seed of the *Bodhi*-tree of Uruvelā, and to have planted it in front of the Jetavana monastery which Anāthapindika had built at Sāvatthi for Buddha and his disciples. The tree, which sprang from the seed, was hallowed by Buddha's spending a night beneath it in meditation. From its planting by Ānanda, this second b. tree became known as the *Ānanda bodhi*. Another descendant of the Uruvelā B.-T. is said to be that at Anurādhapura in → Ceylon. Acc. to Pali chronicle (*Mahāvamsa* XVII, pp. 46f.), a cutting was taken to Ceylon in reign of →

Devanampiya Tissa and planted there with royal ceremony. From the seed saplings are said to have been raised at various other places in Ceylon.

It has been suggested that the connection of the *aśvattha* tree with Buddha's enlightenment has no hist. foundation, since the most continuous and detailed account of events surrounding the enlightenment, viz., the *Mahāsaccaka Sutta* (*MN.* 36), does not mention the matter of the tree. (S. Dutt, *Buddha and 5 After Centuries,* pp. 40ff.). The veneration of sacred trees was a common feature of anc. Indian life, long before time of Buddha; this primitive tree-cult may have made its way into Buddh. trad. The veneration of *aśvattha* tree was perhaps provided by Buddh. piety with a legendary connection with Buddha enlightenment; an actual *aśvattha* tree at Uruvelā was then identified with tree of legend.

Malalasekere, *D.P.P.N.,* vol. I, p. 275; vol. II, pp. 319–22; S. Dutt, *Buddha and 5 After Centuries* (1957).

Bodies of the Buddha → Buddha-Kāya.

Bon and Tibetan Pre-Buddh. Relig. Pre-Buddh. relig. in Tibet is ref. to in earliest texts simply as the 'sacred conventions' (*lha-chos*) or the 'pattern of heaven and earth' (*gnam sa'i lugs*). Relig. officiants were known as *Bon* ('invokers') and as *gShen* ('sacrificers'). It was only later on, when early indigenous relig. began to be permeated with Buddhism, that the relig. itself came to be known as Bon, and the practisers of this new composite relig. known as *Bonpo.* Retrospectively all pre-Buddh. beliefs and rites were called Bon; this causes some confusion.

A special feature of the early relig. was cult of the royal dead, who were entombed under mounds together with certain possessions and even accompanied by close companions, who were seemingly bound under oath to die with king. By 7th cent. this practice was sufficiently humanised to permit officials concerned to live at the tomb but keeping out of contact with other living men and women. Acc. to often recited myths, king was conceived of as divine being descended from celestial spheres. Orig. kings were supposed to have returned to zenith by means of celestial cord, thus not leaving bodies behind on earth. It is told in legend how cord came to be cut, and from then on kings had tombs on earth. In Yarlung Valley, east of Lhasa, there is group of ten royal tombs dating from 7th and 8th cents. CE. Until Buddhism taught otherwise, there is no suggestion of another life in heavens or hells. Deceased belonged to realm of dead, prob. rather like a kind of Hades. In gen. pre-Buddh. relig. in Tibet, like so much of the relig. of simple people throughout whole Buddh. period, was primarily concerned with affairs of this life. Its purpose was to discover by means of sortilege or astrological calculation, causes of human misfortunes, and then prescribe suitable cures. Main causes of misfortune were local gods, demons and sprites of various kinds; usual ways of counteracting their attacks were by ransom offerings. Such practices were soon taken over by Buddh. in Tibet in order to win lay support from already entrenched indigenous priests. There was an import. cult of powerful local gods, often conceived of as mighty warriors with host of fighting attendants. Some were explicitly connected with certain mountains; one may note that first king of Tibet was thought of as having descended from heavens onto mountain known as Yar-lha-sham-po. Ransom offerings took the form in early period of sacrificial victims, and acc. to Chinese reports, even human beings were once sacrificed. But from the hist. period (7th cent. CE onwards) there is no proof of this. Like early kinds of sortilege and rites, many local divinities were accepted by Buddh. clergy as protecting divinities who had sworn to defend the new Buddh. relig. This whole class of local 'converted' gods were known as *dam-can,* the 'oath-bound'; from now on they began to receive their offerings as part of elaborate Buddh. rituals. Special sacrificial cakes made of barley-flour, but shaped and coloured to look like flesh-offerings, were offered to them; this continues right up to 20th cent. While Buddhs. were adopting non-Buddh. practices, priests of old relig. grad. organised themselves into a new relig. order, incorporating all they could of Buddh. docs. and practices. They began to build temples and later mon-

Bon and Tibetan Pre-Buddh. Relig.

asteries on Buddh. pattern. Writing was intro. into Tibet from 7th cent. as part of limited court interest in Buddhism; hence nearly all lit. intro. and trans. was Buddh. in inspiration. No other philosophy was known in Tibet; the Bonpos, as they were now called, developed their own sets of philosophical works, which they took over from Buddh. with occasional changes of terminology. They developed their own sets of tantras, interesting since they centre on Bon divinities; but in content and intention they correspond with Buddh. tantras. They developed systems of yoga and meditation, and produced their own treatises and manuals. Thus by 14th cent. they were fully organised as special kind of Buddhism, unorthodox in that they persisted in claiming that their teachings had not come orig. from India, but from W. Tibet (known by old name of Shang-shung), and orig. from even further west, from land of *sTag-gzigs* (modern Tadzhig?) identified vaguely with pre-Muslim Persia. The founder of their relig., Mi-bo gShen-rab, was supposed to have come from there; an elaborate biography was grad. put together from early mythological materials, but shaped on model of the historical or quasi-historical biography of Shākyamuni. In their conventional set of 'Nine Ways of Bon' they grouped their early teachings on prognostics, ransom-offerings, placating gods and demons together with tantric rituals, → stūpa-worship, practice of the ten (Buddh.) virtues, relig. asceticism, higher tantric practice of using mystic circles as means towards spiritual integration, and finally highest reaches of yoga, where all theories and methods are transcended. Later they copied the dGe-lugs-pas in a new insistence on strictness of monastic life, in the study of philosophy and logic, and even in awarding the degree of *dGe-bshes* (a kind of doctorate) for skill in logical and philosophical debate. In this they even went beyond the older orders of → Tibetan Buddhism, who do not seem to have followed dGe-lugs-pas in this. Some writers have referred to Bon as 'shamanism'; but, although pre-Buddh. relig. in Tibet may have had certain features vaguely classifiable under such heading, it comprised very much else besides; in its subsequent develop., it loses any shamanistic affiliations it might once have had, becoming merely a special kind of Tibetan Buddhism.

Helmut Hoffmann, *The Religions of Tibet* (E.T. 1961); D. L. Snellgrove, *Nine Ways of Bon* (1967).

Brahma-Cariya In Buddh. usage this term denotes 'holy living,' i.e., life of the monk, with enlightenment as ultimate goal. It can be applied also to relig. life of the lay Buddh., who undertakes to observe not the 5 moral precepts (*pañcasila*) only, but the additional three, and undertakes to refrain from sexual misconduct in lieu of vow of complete chastity.

Brahma-Vihāra 'The Spiritual Abodes,' or 'Heavenly Abodes,' are, in B. thought, the four universal virtues: loving kindness (*metta*); compassion (*karunā*); sympathetic or altruistic joy (*muditā*); equanimity (*upekkha*). They are fully expounded by → Buddhaghosa in his *Visuddhimagga,* ch. IX. The Buddh. is exhorted frequently, in the Suttas, to cultivate these virtues in such a way as to embrace all beings in every direction throughout world. For this reason, these 4 virtues are known also as 'Illimitables.'

S.B.E., vol. XI, pp. 201ff., 272ff.

Buddha (as generic title) In Buddh. thought, 'an enlightened one' or 'awakened one,' and thus a man distinguished from all others by his knowledge of the Truth (*Dhamma*). As P.T.S. Dictionary points out, Buddha is an appellative, not a proper name. In Buddh. theory, the perfect knowledge, made known by a Buddha, eventually becomes lost to world, and has then to await emergence of a new Buddha, in order to be known and proclaimed again. Such a being is ref. to more precisely as *Sammā-sambuddha,* a universal, perfectly enlightened being. It is the same doc. which is proclaimed by all these successive Buddhas, namely, the 4 holy truths proclaimed and expounded by → Gotama the *Buddha.* A being who is enlightened and discovers the truth, and is thus *buddha,* but who does not proclaim it, is termed an isolated or 'private' Buddha (→ *Pacceka-Buddha;* Skt. *pratyeka-*). Related to concept of a Buddha is that of the → *Bodhisattva,* a state of being which precedes final state of Buddhahood. Once this final state has been reached, the Buddha endures as such only as long as his physical life lasts; after that he has no further relations with world of space and time, acc. to → Theravādin thought. But in the → Mhy., Buddhas are held to be transcendental beings to whom appeal for help can be made by mortal men.

(Gotama) (Gautama-Skt.) Concerning dates and life story of Gotama, the Buddha, there is no hist. certainty. Not until → Asvaghosa, in 1st/2nd cent. CE, composed his → *Buddhacarita* (*Acts of the Buddha*) was a comprehensive account of his life produced. Evidence of earlier kind is found in many biographical references to Buddha in the Pali canon of scripture, both the → *Vinaya-Pitaka,* and in various scattered details in the 5 *Nikayas* of the → *Sutta-Pitaka.* Acc. to the → Theravāda school of Burma and Ceylon, the dates of Buddha's life are 623–543 BC; in Cambodia, Laos and Thailand, 624–544. The → Mhy. and most mod. scholars prefer the dates *ca.* 566–486, or 563–483. It will be seen that all these give a life-span of 80 years. From biographical details provided by Pali literature, an outline of Buddha's life emerges as follows. A member of the Sakya tribe, who inhabited the Himalayan foothills and were subjects of the Kosalan king, G. was the son of Suddhodana, ruler of → *Kapilavatthu,* and his chief consort Mahā Māya. He was of the Gotama-clan, and his personal name was Siddhattha (same as that of 16th of the 24 preceding Buddhas → Buddhas (other than Gotama). Thus he was known, by personal and clan name together, as Siddhattha Gotama (Skt. Siddhattha Gautama). He was known also as the 'sage' (*muni*) of the *Sakya* tribe, i.e., *Sakyamuni.* His birth is regarded in the trad. as having been surrounded by miraculous features. Without at the time having marital relations with her husband, Mahā Māya had a dream of the → Bodhisatta (Buddha-to-be), as a white elephant, entering her womb; she then ceased to have any desire for sexual pleasure. The birth, which took place in consequence, is thus properly described as parthenogenitic (but not necessarily a virgin birth). The birth occurred in the → *Lum-*

Buddha

binī grove, while Mahā Māya was journeying between Kapilavatthu and her parents' home. The courtiers attending her, escorted mother and child back to Kapilavatthu; Mahā Māya died seven days later. Acc. to trad., Gotama lived an easy and protected life in childhood and youth, married and had a son; then, at the age of 29, he renounced home and comforts and adopted the ascetic life. Certain incidents had provoked dissatisfaction with his old life of ease: the sight of a man suffering from extreme old age; a sick man; a corpse being carried out to burning ghat. On the full-moon day he saw also a holy man, and became convinced of virtues of ascetic life. He himself, after the Renunciation or going forth (*pabbajjā*), i.e., from home, spent six years engaging in the most austere of ascetic practices and was brought to point of death, without deriving spiritual benefit. He then decided to abandon extreme asceticism, and, on the full-moon day of *Vesākha* (May), he sat down in meditation at foot of the → Bodhi-tree, at Uruvelā, beside river Neranjarā (tributary of the Ganges), near modern Gaya; he determined to remain there until he had attained Enlightenment. The trads. tell of efforts made by → *Māra*, the Evil One, to deflect him from his purpose, but to no avail. The night was spent in deep meditation; at dawn his Enlightenment came. The truth, which he had supernaturally perceived, he then sought to teach to others. His first discourse was addressed to certain ascetics who had formerly been his companions; it is known as the 'Discourse of the Setting in Motion of the Wheel of *Dhamma*' (→ *Dhamma-Cakkappavattana Sutta*) (*SN.* V. 420). This sermon certainly contains some of fundamental principles of early Buddh. thought and practice; in its present form, it is a product of later times. Acc. to trad., it was delivered in the Deer Park of Banares. Grad. the Buddha, as he now was, began to gain disciples and the → *Sangha* or assembly (i.e., of monks) was formed. For next 20 yrs. some kind of chronology can be worked out on basis of the Pali texts; it has been done, e.g. by G. P. Malalasekere in his *D.P.P.N.* (Gotama). These years were spent by Buddha and his monks in various places of middle Ganges basin of N.E.

Buddha

India: → Banares, Uruvelā, → Rājagaha, → Vesālī, Sāvatthi, Kosambī, and → Kapilavatthu. The 3 months of rainy season each year were spent in a rains-retreat, often a monastic shelter provided by wealthy supporters; the remainder of year was devoted to travelling from village to village, staying a little while in each, and preaching to all and sundry and engaging in discussion with Brahmins and with other relig. communities. For last 25 years of the Buddha's life no consecutive chronology can be constructed. Devadatta's plot to kill him appears to belong to 8th year before his decease (→→ Ajatasuttu; Devadatta). A fairly full account of last year of Buddha's life is given in the → *Mahā-Parinibbāna Sutta,* which describes the events leading up to his decease at Kusinārā and his entry into *parinibbāna* at the age of 80. Acc. to trad., Buddha's last words to disciples were: 'Decay is inherent in all compounded things; work out your salvation with diligence.' The cremation was carried out seven days after the decease, and was accompanied by highly honorific ceremonies. After the cremation, the relics of Buddha were divided among eight claimant parties; these were then carried off and → *stupas* were built over them in various places (→ Funerary Rites).

Malalasekere, *D.P.P.N.* ('Gotama'); Sukumar Dutt, *The Buddha and Five After-Centuries* (1957), pp. 1–56; Ashvaghosha, *Buddhacarita,* trans., *S.B.E.,* vol. 49, and by E. H. Johnston, *Acta Orientalia* (1937); E. J. Thomas, *The Life of Buddha as Legend and History,* 3rd edn. (1949); H. Oldenberg, *Buddha, sein Leben, seine Lehre, seine Gemeinde,* 9th edn. (1921, E.T. 1882); E. Lamotte, *Histoire du Bouddhisme Indien* (1958).

(Gotama) (Historicity) Since mid. of 19th cent. orientalists have assessed in varying ways the evidence for the historicity of Gotama, the Buddha. Some have considered the data provided by Buddh. trad., both Pali and Skt., to be largely legendary. H. H. Wilson, in 1856, suggested that the life of the B. in the trad. accounts was an allegory of Indian philosophical school of *Sāmkhya,* of which Buddhism was seen by him as a variant derivative form. E. Senart of Paris and H. Kern of Leyden regarded the trad. life as a solar

Buddhacarita

myth, seeing in the 'turning of the wheel of the Law' (*Dhamma-Cakkappavattana Sutta*) (*DN.* V. 420), a solar symbol of the universal monarch. Senart's theory, propounded in 1875, was challenged by H. Oldenberg in 1882, in his *Life of the Buddha,* based on Pali sources, from which he maintained that it was poss. to reconstruct an authentic hist. account. While Kern did not deny that some such hist. personage as Gotama may have existed, he argued that all trad. stories about him are mythological descriptions belonging to a corpus of solar myths. A mythological interpretation has recently been reargued by Paul Levy. Edward Conze, a European Buddhist, has affirmed that the hist. existence of Gotama as an individual is a matter of no importance, although he does not deny his hist. existence. The B., he says, is 'a kind of archetype which manifests itself in the world at different periods, in different personalities, whose individual particularities are of no account whatsoever' (*Buddhism,* pp. 34f.). Similarly, Murti: 'though Gotama is a hist. person he is not the only B. . . . The Mahayana religion escapes the predicament of having to depend on any particular hist. person as the founder. . . .'

The gen. opinion nowadays is, as A. Bareau points out, that there really existed a man to whom may be att. the founding of Buddhism, an hist. personage, the principal features of whose life and personality can be retraced, thanks to mod. critical appreciation of the data.

H. H. Wilson, *Buddha and Buddhism, J.R.A.S.,* t. XVI (1856), pp. 248ff.; E. Senart, *Essai sur la Légende du Buddha* (1875); H. Oldenberg, *Buddha, sein Leben, seine Lehre, seine Gemeinde* (1881); E. Conze, *Buddhism,* 3rd edn. (1957), pp. 34ff.; P. Levy, *Buddhism, A Mystery Religion?* (1957); A. Bareau, *Les Religions de l'Inde* (1966).

Buddhacarita A Mhy. Buddh. work in Skt. by 1st/2nd cent. CE poet → Aśvaghosha. The title may be trans. 'Acts of the Buddha.' Earliest known consecutive life-story of the Buddha Gotama. Of the orig. 28 cantos only 17 are preserved in Skt.; poss. only 13 of these authentic. Exists in Tibetan trans. in 28 cantos. The Chinese Buddh. pilgrims to India of

Buddhaghosa

7th cent. CE recorded that it was then widely read or sung throughout India. Acc. to Murti, it reflects a trend in 1st cent. India towards 'Buddha-bhakti,' or the glorification of Buddha as a cult figure, and thus towards greater popularisation of Buddhism. (*Central Philosophy of Buddhism*, pp. 79f.)

Buddhadatta Thv. Buddh. monk-scholar, native of Uragapura in S. India, contemporary with → Buddhaghosa; like latter an important commentarial writer. Acc. to Pali trad., he met Buddhaghosa, and like him lived and studied in Great Monastery (Mahāvihāra) at Anurādhapura in Ceylon. His two principal works are the *Vinaya-Vinicchaya* and the *Abhidhammāvatāra*, being commentaries on the → *Vin.* and → *Abh. Pitakas* respectively.

Buddha-Gaya A location in N.E. India, sacred to Buddh. → Gaya.

Buddhaghosa → Theravāda Buddh. monk-scholar of Ceylon of 4th/5th cents. CE, famous for commentaries on Pali canon of scripture, esp. his great compendium of Buddh. thought and practice, the → *Visuddhimagga* (the Path of Purification). In Thv. countries B. is regarded as greatest exponent and interpreter of canonical scriptures; emphasis is laid on fact that his name means 'the voice of the Buddha.' Nothing is known with certainty of date or place of his birth. The Sinhalese trad., contained in 2 Pali works, the → *Culavamsa* and the *Buddha-ghosuppatti* (a collection of legends about the great man), is that he was a native of → *Magadha* in N. India, a brahman by birth who was early attracted to Buddhism by contact with a learned Buddh. monk named Revata; he was ordained into the → Sangha, and travelled to Ceylon, settling in Great Monastery (Mahāvihāra) or Anurādhapura, where he spent most of life in study of scriptures and writing; he returned at end of life to his native Magadha and died at Gaya. Burmese trad. claims him as a native of Burma, who, having studied in Ceylon and there composed his great work, the *Visuddhimagga*, intro. this and complete Pali canon of scripture into Burma, thus inaugurating what Burmese regard as a new era in Buddhism of their country. Mod. research, using in-

Buddha-Kāya

ternal evidence of his works and archaeological evidence, suggests Andhra, in S. India, as his place of birth. B.'s writings reveal close familiarity with the Andhra of that time, whereas his refs. to N. India contain inaccuracies difficult to reconcile with theory of his Magadhan origin (e.g., his ref. to Patna (Pātaliputta) as seaport). Beside the *Visuddhimagga*, B. wrote commentaries on (1) the → *Vinaya-Pitaka*, (2) → *Sutta-Pitaka*, and (3) → *Abhidhamma-Pitaka*. These are as follows: (1) on the *Vinaya; Samantapāsādikā* and *Kankhāvitarani;* (2) on *Sutta-Pitaka; Sumangalavilāsini* (on the *DN*), *Papañcasūdanī* (on the *MN*), *Sāratthapakāsinī* (on the *SN*), *Manorathapurāni* (on the *AN*), *Paramatthajotika* (on the *KN*); (3) on → *Abh. Pitaka; Atthasālinī, Sammohavinodani,* and *Pancappakaranaṭṭha-katha*. His great achievements were: the new status he gave Pali scholarship at time when Skt. in India had become the prestige language among Buddh., as well as among brahmans; the develop. of a coherent and systematic Theravāda school of philosophy.

The *Culavamsa*, E.T., C. Mabel Rickmers, 2 vols. (1953); B. C. Law, *The Life and Work of Buddhaghosa* (1923) (new edn. 1946); Nyanoponika, *The Path of Purification* (1964); S. Dutt, *Buddhist Monks and Monasteries of India* (1962), pp. 249–60.

Buddha-Kāya in Buddh. thought, since the Buddha is equated with the → Absolute, as well as being one who is concerned with welfare of world, the conception of the three *Buddha-kāya,* or Buddha-bodies, has been developed to express relationship of one aspect of the Buddha-nature to the other. The 'three-bodies' doc. (*Tri-kāya*) affirms that Buddha exists as (1) *Dharma-kāya;* (2) *Sambhoga-kāya;* (3) *Nirmāna-kāya*. The *Dharma-kāya,* Dharma-body, or Truth-body, is also known as *sva-bhāva-kāya,* or 'self-being-body,' because it is self-existent; it is the Dharma, or reality, remaining within its own nature. It is in this sense, says Suzuki, 'the absolute aspect' of the Buddha-nature (*op. cit.,* 308). (2) The *Sambhoga-kāya,* or 'Bliss-body,' is the celestial manifestation of the Buddha-nature, i.e., as it is perceived by celestial, or non-mortal beings.

Buddhas

There is also in this term the sense of 'Enjoyment-body,' i.e., that which is 'enjoyed' by the Awakened One (Buddha); a well-deserved 'enjoyment' of fruit of spiritual discipline. These two notions converge in another poss. trans. of *Sambhoga-kāya*—viz, 'Glorious-body' or 'body of glory.' It is, says Murti, 'the concrete manifestation to himself and to the elect (of) the power and splendour' of the Buddha-nature. (3) the *Nirmāna-kāya* is the 'Assumed-body.' This body is necessitated, says Suzuki, because 'the Dharma-kāya is too exalted a body for ordinary mortals to come into any conscious contact with. As it transcends all forms of limitations, it cannot become an object of sense or intel-lect. . . . The essence of Buddhahood is the Dharmakāya, but as long as the Buddha remains such, there is no hope for the salvation of a world of particulars. The Buddha has to abandon his original abode, and must take upon himself such forms as are conceivable and acceptable to the inhab-itants of this earth' (*op. cit.,* 310). The *Nirmāna-kāya* is thus the hist. manifestation of the Buddha-nature as a man, e.g., as → Gotama. This doc. of the Triple-Body of Buddha is a late development in → Mhy. Buddhism, although the germs of doc. were present long before it was thus given systematic form. The formal affirmation of the doc. is assoc. with the crystallising of the → *Yogācara* philosophy into a system by → Asanga and his disciples in the 4th cent. CE. D. T. Suzuki, *Studies in the Lankāvatāra Sutra* (1930), pp. 308–38; T. R. V. Murti, *The Central Philosophy of Buddhism* (1955), pp. 284–7.

Buddhas (other than Gotama) The Buddh. idea that, when truth (*dhamma*) is lost to men, it needs to be reproclaimed by a new Buddha, is reflected in belief that there had been earlier Buddhas in the world before appearance of Gotama the Buddha. The Pali canon, in its → *Khuddaka-Nikaya,* incl. a book entitled *Buddha-vaṃsa,* or the Buddha-line-age. This gives accounts of lives of 24 Buddhas prior to Go-tama, and incl. him as the 25th. Of these 24, the last seven are mentioned in earlier works found in Pali canon, viz. in the *Dīgha-Nikaya* (II, pp. 5ff.), the *Samyutta-Nikaya* (II, pp. 5f.), and *Vinaya-Pitaka* (II, p. 110). These seven are Vipassi,

Buddha-Sāsana

Sikhi, Vessabhu, Kakusandha, Konagamana, Kassapa and Gotama. (On these, see further, *Mahāpadāna Sutta.*) These 7 are incl. in the *Buddha-vamsa,* together with the preceding 18 (Dipankara, Kondanna, Mangala, Sumana, Revata, Sobhita, Anomadassi, Paduma, Narada, Padumuttara, Sumedha, Sujata, Piyadassi, Atthadassi, Dhammadassi, Siddhattha, Tissa and Phussa). The 27th ch. of this book mentions a further 3, who preceded Dipankara, viz. Tanhankara, Medhankara and Saranankara. In the Skt. literature of the Mhy., the number is further increased: the → *Lalitavistara* has a list of 54, and the *Mahāvastu* of over a hundred. It should be noted, to avoid confusion, that the names given above are not exclusively those of previous Buddhas, but are frequently used by other individuals, and are often taken as the 'religious' names assumed by Buddh. monks, in a fashion similar to that by which Catholic children are given names of saints.

In addition to Gotama, and Buddhas who preceded him, the *DN* of the Pali canon mentions also those Buddhas who will follow him, i.e., those who are yet to come, after the present Buddha-era. Ten of these are named in the *Cakkavatti-Sihanāda Sutta* (*DN,* III, pp. 75ff.): Metteya, Uttama, Rama, Pasenadi, Kosala, Abhibhu, Dighasoni, Sankacca, Subbha, Todeyya, and Nalagiripalaleyya. Of these the most important in Buddh. thought is the next successor to Gotama, the coming Buddha, → Metteyya. Acc. to Pali trad. the Buddha is born only in Jambudīpa (India), one of the 4 great continents in Indian → cosmology and only in the *Majjhima-desa* region of that land, i.e., the 'middle-country,' approx. the region where Buddhism orig. and developed historically. Not only does every Buddha preach the truth (*dhamma*) which has been lost by men; he also founds an Order (→ *Sangha*) and does not pass into → *nibbāna* until the relig. (*sāsana*) is well-estab. (*DN,* III, p. 122).

Buddha-Sāsana Term commonly used in Asian countries for the 'religion' of the Buddha (lit. 'the Buddha-discipline'). The term implies whole scheme of moral precepts, devotional practices, meditation, and social relationships which

is regarded as owing its origin to Buddha. A more specialised meaning is that of the ninefold Buddha-S. (*navanga
Buddha-sāsana*) in → Thv. Buddhism, by which is meant
nine forms in which teaching of Buddha is found, discourse (*sutta*); mixed prose (*geyya*); exegesis (*veyyāka-
rana*); verse (*gātha*); solemn utterance (*udāna*); sayings
(*itivuttaka*); previous-birth-stories (*jātaka*); marvels (*ab-
huta-dhamma*); analysis (*vedalla*).

Buddha-Vamsa 'The Buddha-lineage,' a Buddh. canonical text
of the Pali canon (→ Buddhas, other than Gotama).

Buddhism, General Survey Buddhism is the West. name for
what in Asia is gen. known as the *Buddha-Sāsana,* i.e., the
relig., or, lit., 'discipleship' of the Buddha, or Awakened
One (→ Buddha, as generic title). The relig. thus named
orig. in N.E. India, in region now known as Bihar, in 6th
cent. BC, as result of experience of Gotama (or Gautama), a
young 'prince,' or more exactly, son of a ruler of the →
Sakya tribe. His home was in → Kapilavatthu, in the foothills of the Himālayas; but his 'awakening' or 'enlightenment' occurred at a place now known as Budh-Gaya, on
banks of one of the south tributaries of the Ganges (→
Buddha-Gaya). The doc. which he then began to preach is
known as the → Dhamma (or Dharma); it consists of an
analysis of the human situation, of nature of human existence, and structure of human personality, and a setting
forth of means whereby the suffering and mortality, which
is common lot of mankind, may be transcended and a new
state of being achieved (→→ Dukkha; Anicca; Anatta; Four
Holy Truths; Nibbana). Acc. to Buddh. trad., the first proclamation of this doc. was at Sarnath; the discourse has
come to be known as the → Dhamma-Cakkappavattana
Sutta. The Buddha's personality and preaching attracted
disciples, who were subsequently organised into community of those who followed the way of Buddha, and known
collectively as the → Sangha. The doc. was independent of
any belief in a supreme creator god (→ Creation), and of
priestly rites or functions. It was regarded by contemporary
brahman priests as heretical; in many discourses (→ Sutta)
the Buddha is repr. as engaging in controversy with brah-

Buddhism, General Survey

mans. The new community of the Sangha was an egalitarian society in which caste differences were entirely disregarded. (→ Caste, Buddh. attitude). The doc. gained for Buddha and his community the sympathy and support of the king of → Magadha, viz., → Bimbisara. By time of Buddha's death at age of 80 (→ Kushinagara), the Buddhs., i.e., both members of Sangha, and lay-followers, had become a large and growing body, drawn mainly from land-owning, merchant, and labouring classes; a few brahmans had also become Buddh. Among principal disciples of Buddha was → Ananda, who is credited with having had responsibility of preserving the orig. form of a number of most import. discourses of Buddha, which now form the → Digha-Nikaya, one of main sections of the → Pali canon of scripture (→ Tipitaka). The suttas, together with rules for monastic order (i.e., the Sangha), later codified in the → Vinaya-Pitaka, were rehearsed and their correctness endorsed at council held immediately after Buddha's death, at → Rajagaha (→ Councils). Differences of opinion among monks concerning keeping of these rules developed about a cent. after Buddha's death and were reason for convening of second council, at → Vesali. A further difference of opinion, this time on matters of doc., developed in 3rd cent. BC, during reign of emperor → Asoka, who had by this time become a Buddh. (in revulsion against violent campaigns he had waged earlier). A third council was held to deal with these doc. differences, at imperial capital of Pataliputta (Patna). As result of this, a section of monks who held the → Sarvāstivāda view, as against trad. view of the elders or Sthaviras (→ Buddh. Schools of Thought) moved away from lower Ganges plain N.W.-wards towards Madhura, which became their stronghold. Out of these differences, and criticisms of lowered spiritual standards of traditionalists, a new movement within Buddhism eventually emerged, which called itself the 'Great Means' to salvation (→ Mahāyāna); by this was meant the wider scope of their concern for salvation of men, as this was understood by Buddhs. They gave older school the name → Hīnayāna, or 'Lesser Means' to salvation (→ Yāna). The

54

strength of new Mhy. school was in N.W. of India, in area that was influenced by Graeco-Roman culture, through Greek Bactrian Kingdom on N.W. borders of India (→ Gandhāra). The new school's much greater emphasis on virtue of compassion, as well as on wisdom (which had been principally emphasised by Hīnayāna School) has led to suggestion that Christian influences may have had some part in development of the Mhy., since at that time trade between India and Roman world was also a vehicle for traffic of ideas, eastwards and westwards. Another feature of the Mhy. school was their new emphasis on the → Bodhisattva (or Buddha-to-be) as one whose function towards men in gen. was virtually that of a saviour. It was this form of Buddhism which spread northwards into C. Asia in 1st cent. CE, and in 2nd cent. from there onwards into China, where also it began, from end of 2nd cent. CE to meet with increasing acceptance. A feature of the Mhy. was use of → Sanskrit, language of the brahman Hindu priests; in this prestige-language many new writings of the Mhy. Buddhism were composed. In India the 2nd cent. CE saw development of further stage in unfolding of the analytical principles of Buddh. thought, viz. the emergence of the → Madhyamika school, with its doc. of *śūnyā*, in which Buddh. logical analysis reached its ultimate and most highly sophisticated form. The founders of this school, which is regarded by some as climax of develop. of Mahāyāna, were → Aryadeva and → Nagarjuna. Its oversophistication brought about a certain reaction, or turning away from the extreme intellectualism and logical analysis which characterised Madhyamika, towards greater emphasis on direct apprehension of spiritual truth through cleansing and clarifying of consciousness; this new develop., led by → Asanga and his brother → Vasubandhu in 4th cent. CE was known as → Yogacara, so far as its practical emphasis on methods of meditation (*yoga*) were concerned, or as Vijnāna-Vāda, so far as its doc. of the permanent and supreme reality of consciousness (*vijñāna*) was concerned. The final stage of develop. in Mhy. was that of the absorbing of much non-Buddh. material in the way of *man-*

tras, symbols, and cultic practices of various kinds in a process which in gen. was characterised by aim of spiritual enlightenment through use of these various devices and practices, and was known, first as → Mantrayana and later as → Vajrayana, or Tantra. It made its way to China as the Chenyen, and to Japan as → Shingon, and in 9th and 11th cents. CE to Tibet, where it persisted as dominant form of Buddhism. Meanwhile Buddhism had spread, by agency of missionary monks, over much of rest of India, first the Deccan and west. side of subcontinent, then the S.; in time of Asoka, in Hīnayāna form it had travelled to → Ceylon. Its spread eastwards across Bay of Bengal to → Burma and what is now → Thailand also took place during early cents. of CE; at first in the Mhy. form; later this was displaced by Pali or → Theravada form from Ceylon. The Theravāda was one of 18 schools into which the Hīnayāna had developed; it is only school which has persisted to mod. times. From Ceylon, and Thailand, Theravāda Buddhism spread to Cambodia and Laos, in 13th and 14th cents. CE, while from China the Mhy. form travelled into Vietnam (→ Buddhism in Southeast Asia). In India the Tantric or Vajrayāna form of Buddhism (*vide supra*) was followed by gradual decline in strength of the Buddh. community, and eventually it was displaced at popular level by various Hindu bhakti and Tantric cults. The → Monasteries declined, and finally, by 13th cent., Buddhism had virtually disappeared from India, except for a few pockets of survival on N.E. frontiers, notably in the Chittagong area of E. Bengal. In Ceylon, however, about 60% of population still adhere to Buddhism; in Burma, Thailand, Laos and Cambodia about 90%. From Ceylon knowledge of Buddhism, in its Pali form, came to Europe and America in 19th cent. Since then interest in the docs. and way of life of the Buddha has increased grad. and steadily in West. countries, notably England, Germany and U.S.A.; Buddh. monks from Ceylon, Thailand, Burma and Tibet are now found living in these countries; Buddh. societies of West. lay people are also increasing in number from year to year; some West. nationals have also taken → ordination in Sangha. Another feature of mod. hist. of Buddhism has been its revival in India, land of its origin; this has taken 2 forms: (1) increased interest on part of Indian intellectuals in this feature of their own heritage, esp. among those dissatisfied with Hindu relig.; (2) a mass movement to Buddhism among the Scheduled Classes (the former 'untouchables') led by conversion to Buddhism of their leader, Dr. B. R. Ambedkar, Minister of Law in Govt. of India, in 1956. (→ Cambodia–Laos.)

(in China) Chinese B. is usually classified as belonging to the Northern or → Mahāyāna form of B.; but from its inception Hīnayānist texts, trans. from Sanskrit, exerted considerable influence, espec. on monastic discipline through the Vinaya, and in the Dhyāna or meditation schools. B. infiltrated along the central Asian silk roads about beginning of CE, and till close of Han Dynasty (c. CE 220) was largely confined to scattered groups of foreigners. Influence on court circles about middle of 2nd cent. CE is recorded. At first Taoist scholars assisted as translators, Taoist terms were used to trans. B. ideas, and similarities between the two religs. were emphasised. Early Chinese B. was an urban phenomenon, and till end of 3rd cent. CE the hist. of Chinese B. is largely that of translators whose work gave the literati access to speculative ideas of Mahāyāna. Weakness and disunity consequent on downfall of Han Dynasty led to invasion of N. China by non-Chinese peoples, who controlled vast areas during ensuing 300 years. The ruling princes of the N. looked favourably on B. relig. and B. monks became diplomatic, military and political advisers. They also gained great reputation among populace for thaumaturgical and magical practices. Fo T'u-têng (d. 349) and other indefatigable B. preachers converted nearly whole of N. China to B., whilst a famous school of translators under → Kumarajiva (CE 344–413) worked at the capital, Ch'ang-an. The minds of Chinese scholars were thus opened to great ideas of the Indian masters of Mahāyāna.

In CE 399, Fa Hsien left Ch'ang-an on his famous pilgrimage to India, inaugurating a pilgrim movement to centres of Indian B., which proved a source of perennial inspira-

Buddhism, General Survey

tion. In S. China, the 4th cent. witnessed penetration of B. into 'gentry' circles. Educated and wealthy lay patrons assisted the → Sangha, helped to pay for trans. work, founded monasteries and temples, and accepted the five rules of B. morality. Two trends developed in S. China; the dhyāna school of meditation, control of the mind and suppression of passions, Hīnayānist in inspiration; the prajñā school, interested in questions of ultimate reality, in trans. of the great Mahāyāna sūtras, and in fostering close connection between the sangha and the literati.

In this period of B. development in China, the central figures were Tao An (312–85), → Hui Yüan (344–416) and Tao Shêng (360–434). Under their influence, great monastic foundations were estab., the Vinaya rules translated, and the speculative ideas of Mahāyāna widely disseminated. In works of these great Chinese B. masters we see germ of ideas which developed into the distinctive Mahāyānist schools of the Sui and T'ang dynasties. The teachings of Confucian and Taoist classics were wedded to the Mahāyāna B. of Ashvaghosha, Nagarjuna, Vasubandhu and Asanga, and thus led to a distinctive Chinese B. trad. This flowered espec. in the T'ien T'ai, Pure Land, Hua Yen and Ch'an schools, which reached their maturity in the T'ang Dynasty. It is estimated that by c. CE 420 there were 1,786 temples and some 24,000 B. monks and nuns in China. The growing wealth and court influence of the B. clergy, together with doctrines which seemed to undermine stability of family and Confucian morality, gave rise to acute criticism, and outbreaks of persecution.

In the T'ang Dynasty (CE 618–907), B. in China reached its maturity. The dynasty was on the whole favourable to B. Contacts opened up with central Asia and India brought many foreigners into China. When → Hsüan Tsang (c. 596–664), the famous B. scholar and pilgrim, returned to China from 13 years spent in India, he received a hero's welcome. He exerted immense influence, and left behind a prodigious work of trans. By middle of 9th cent. Chinese B. had reached peak of its influence. The power, wealth, influence and splendour of its monastic establishments, inevitably leading to corruption, finally provoked great persecution of B. under emperor Wu-tsung (CE 845), a persecution from which Chinese B. never recovered. It is estimated that some 4,000 temples were sequestered or destroyed, and some 250,000 monks and nuns forced back into secular life. Priceless B. treasures of art, and extensive libraries perished in the flames of destruction. During the T'ang Dynasty some eight or ten major schools of B. flourished in China; but gradually a process of syncretism obliterated salient features of doctrine and practice, so that by the Sung Dynasty only the Pure Land and Ch'an schools remained active.

With estab. of Mongol (Yüan) Dynasty, Tibetan or Lama Buddhism became prominent in China; but for past 700 years, apart from monks confined to ascetic life in monasteries, B. became largely absorbed in a popular relig., in which Buddh. and Taoist elements combined. This popular relig. of the masses was tolerated by the literati, but despised as a mass of crude superstitions.

The late 19th cent. and early 20th cent. brought an intellectual awakening and moral reform to Chinese B., notably under T'ai Hsü (1890–1947). But with rise of militant Communism, B. is once more under a cloud. → also Fa Hsien; Hsüan Tsang; Hua Yen School; Hui Yüan; I Tsing; Tien T'ai School; Ch'an; Hui Nêng; Tun Huang; Amida; Bodhidharma. For the Chinese Buddhist Canon → Tripitaka, Chinese.

D. H. Smith, *Chinese Religions* (1968), ch. 10; E. Zurcher, *The Buddhist Conquest of China* (1959); A. F. Wright, *Buddhism in Chinese History* (1959); K. L. Reichelt, *Truth and Tradition in Chinese Buddhism* (1927); K. K. Ch'en, *Buddhism in China* (1964).

(in Southeast Asia) While the Buddhism of Burma, Thailand, Cambodia and Laos has, in each case, been shaped to some extent by hist. of country concerned, certain features of the relig. are common to these Buddh. countries of continental S.E. Asia. In each case the early form appears to have been much more strongly of the → Mahāyāna trad. than is case now; often there were considerable → Tantric elements. The influence of the Sinhalese form of Theravāda Buddhism has, however, become so strong thāt it is this form which provides ecumenical framework of Buddhism in S.E. Asia: all four countries use same → Pali canon of scriptures, their monks are of Theravāda order, adhering closely to rules of the → Vinaya; they can pass from monasteries of one country to those of another with greatest ease (except where political conditions at present provide barrier), and Pali is their common language. Each country has in course of its hist. been a monarchy, whose ruler was trad. a Theravādin Buddh., and in each case there developed the office of chief monk, or supervisor of whole monastic order throughout country (*Sangharāja*, in Burma *Thathanabaing*). Moreover, in each country there has been accommodation to local indigenous forms of relig., notably belief in → spirits who must be placated, and in astrology and numerology. These local beliefs have, in each case, been fused with Buddhism at popular level to produce distinctive national amalgams which should properly be described as Burmese Buddhism; Thai Buddhism, etc. (→→ Burma; Cambodia; Laos; Festivals; Holy Days, Buddhist; Thailand).

(Political Power) In hist. of Buddhism four patterns of relationship with State can be distinguished: (i) easy co-existence between Buddhism and the State; (ii) State patronage of Buddhism; (iii) identity of Buddh. → Sangha with State; (iv) persecution of Buddhism by State. Examples of (i) occurred during lifetime of Buddha and reign of → Bimbisara, king of Magadha, in certain periods in hist. of Chinese and Japanese Buddhism, and present situation in → Ceylon. Examples of (ii) are → Asoka in anc. India; Medieval Ceylon, Burma, Thailand and Cambodia, under such kings as Parakamma, Bahu, and Anawratha; mod. → Thailand and Cambodia. Tibet until time of Chinese invasion in 1950 provides almost only example of (iii); from 1950 the same country provides a clear example of (iv); Chinese Buddhism also provides examples of State persecution, notably that which occurred in early part of 7th cent. CE under first emperor of T'ang Dynasty, Kao Tsu, and the more severe persecution of CE 845, ordered by emperor Wu-Tsung, who commanded that some 45,000 temples and small shrines should be destroyed and a quarter of million monks and nuns ejected from monastic life → Buddhism (in China). The experience of Buddh. Sangha in those Asian countries which fell under European imperial domination from 16th cent. onwards was in some cases that of direct persecution, as in Ceylon under Portuguese in 16th cent., and in other cases disablement, due to indirect attack or to social, economic or legal discrimination, as in cases of Ceylon and Burma. It was largely because of such disablement that Buddh. monks in Burma and Ceylon under British rule became allies of those of their compatriots who were agitating for freedom from foreign rule. Even in medieval Burma, however, under conditions of State patronage of Buddhism, Burmese monks did not hesitate to reject or oppose decisions or actions of king if they considered these to be contrary to spirit of the Buddha-Dhamma. An attitude of protest against a secular government hostile to Buddhism is seen in the → self-immolation of monks and nuns in Vietnam in recent times.

Buddhist (Pali) Literature Buddh. Pali lit. falls into 2 categories: (a) canonical, (b) non-canonical. (a) *Canonical lit.:* this consists of the Ti-pitaka, or '3-baskets,' viz. Vinaya-Pitaka, Sutta-Pitaka and Abhidhamma-Pitaka. (→ Tipitaka). To these is added, in Ceylon, as part of canon, a supplement known as the *Paritta* (Sinhalese *pirit*), a collection of canonical chants used in certain popular rituals, such as building of new house, at funerals, in times of sickness, etc. These are used in Burma also in ceremonies and rituals for lay people.

(b) *Non-canonical lit.:* this consists of (1) chronicles, (2) commentaries on canonical texts, (3) compositions based on canonical texts and presented as compendiums or manuals of Buddh. life or philosophy. The chronicles are → *Dipavamsa,* i.e. 'the Island Chronicle' (the island being Ceylon); this is oldest of the chronicles; → *Mahāvamsa,* 'the Great Chronicle'; → *Culavamsa,* 'the Little Chronicle'; → *Mahābodhivamsa,* 'the Chronicle of the Bodhi-Tree'; →

Buddhist Schools of Thought

Thupavamsa, 'the Chronicle of the Stupa'; *Dathavamsa,* 'the Chronicle of the Sacred Relic' (i.e. the Buddha's Tooth); → *Sāsanavamsa,* 'the Chronicle of the Religion,' a work composed in 19th cent. in Burma. The commentaries are far too numerous to list, these being not only commentaries upon various books of Tipitaka, but also commentaries and sub-commentaries upon the commentaries. Some of the more import. of these may be noted, viz. those composed by → Buddhaghosa: on the Vinaya-Pitaka, *Samantapāsādikā;* on the Digha-Nikaya, *Sumangala-vilāsini;* on the *Dhamma-Sangani* (1st book of the Abh.-Pitaka, *Atthasālinī.* The third type of non-canonical lit., the compendiums or manuals, incl. import. works such as Buddhaghosa's → *Visuddhimagga;* the *Malindapanha;* the → *Abhidhammattha-Sangaha.*
Trans. into Eng. of many of these non-canonical texts may be noted: *The Great Chronicle of Ceylon* (Mahavamsa) (1912, repr. 1964); *Minor Chronicles of Ceylon* (Culavamsa), 2 vols. (1929–30); *The Sāsanavamsa* (1952); *The Expositor* (Buddhaghosa's Atthasālinī), 2 vols. (1920–1, repr. 1958); *The Path of Purification* (Visuddhimagga) (1964); *Compendium of Philosophy* (Abhidhammattha-Sangaha) (1910, repr. 1963); *Inception of Discipline* (intro. to Samanta-pāsādikā) (1962); *Milinda's Questions* (Milinda-Panha), 2 vols. (1963–4).

Buddhist Schools of Thought The first major division in the Buddh. → Sangha is trad. connected with the Council of Vesali (→ Councils, Buddh.), approx. 100 years after decease of the Buddha (*c.* 383 BC). Disagreement arose concerning degree of strictness with which monastic discipline (→ Vinaya-Pitaka) was to be observed. The dissentient body, who disagreed with the stricter, more conservative *Sthaviras* or Elders, henceforth became known as the → *Mahāsanghikas,* i.e., the Great Sangha Party, since they claimed a greater following for their more liberal interpretation of the rules. The *Sthaviras* subsequently divided into 18 schools, among the more important of which were the → Pudgala-Vādins, Vibhajyavādins, → Sarvāstivādins, and Theravādins (→ Theravāda).

Burma, Buddhism in

The *Mahāsanghikas* also divided into number of separate schools, among whom the more import. were the Lokottaravādins (→ Mahāvastu), Prajñaptivādins and the Caitiyas. The develop. of the → Mahāyāna from within the Mahāsanghika trad. is, as Conze says, 'wrapped in obscurity' (*Buddhist Thought in India,* 1962, pp. 198f.). The 2 principal Mahāyāna schools in India were the → Mādhyamikas and the → *Yogācaras.* In China and Japan, Mahāyāna developed into a number of schools peculiar to those countries, notably the T'ien-t'ai or →→ Tendai, Ch'an or Zen, Chen-yen or Shingon, the Pure Land, and the Nichiren → Buddhism (in China).

Buddhist Scriptures → *Tipitaka.*

Burma, Buddhism in as elsewhere in S.E. Asia, has two aspects: monastic and lay; these two aspects are organically connected, and neither could exist apart from other. The Buddhism of the monasteries is predominately of kind which looks to Pali canonical and commentarial lit. (→ Buddhist, Pali Literature) for its norms and standards, and is known as → Theravāda. There are, however, a few very small, isolated monasteries adhering to the → Mahāyāna; these are supported by, and minister to, local Gurkha and Chinese communities; the former in some hill areas of north, and the Shan States of E. Burma; the latter in Rangoon.

Historically the Mahāyāna has lost ground in Burma. Archaeological evidence indic. that in earlier period Skt. Buddhism, both Mahāyāna and → Sarvāstivādin, had considerable influence. B. of some kind may have existed in Burma as early as 3rd cent. ᴄᴇ, if evidence of an early Chinese source can be accepted. Certainly from 5th cent. ᴄᴇ there is epigraphical and other archaeological evidence of a fairly flourishing Buddh. life, which appears to have been closely connected with N.E. India, and poss. also with Andhra, on east coast of S. India. Fragments of the Buddh. Pali canon have been discovered at Prome, dating poss. from as early as 5th cent. ᴄᴇ. By 7th cent., for which evidence is available in accounts given by Chinese pilgrims, both the Theravāda

63

and Sarvāstivāda forms existed. From 8th and 9th cents. CE the Mahāyāna form appears to have existed in lower Burma, notably at Prome, where it was intro. from N.E. India (Bengal). Before long this had followed the Indian course of develop., and became markedly Tantric (→ Vajrayāna). A new era for Burmese B. began in 11th cent. CE with coming of a ruler of Pagan named An-aw-ra-hta (the Burmese form of *Aniruddha*), who became king of upper Burma in 1044. Converted to Theravāda B. by a monk, he set out to reform the relig. from extreme form of → Tantrism into which it had developed under control of the *Aris* (or Aryas), a corrupt Tantric priesthood which dominated upper Burma. Having extended domain eastwards to Thaton, he opened up Burmese Kingdom to strong Theravāda influence emanating from the Mons who at that time inhabited S.E. Burma. It is from this time that Theravāda became dominant form of B. practised by Burmese of the central river valley regions; from this, says Coedès, sprang the civilisation, lit. and art of the Burmese, which have persisted to mod. times. The Aris, however, were not completely suppressed; they managed to maintain their corrupt form of B. (incl. the eating of meat, drinking of spirits, use of spells, and sexual licence) until as late as 18th cent. Nor did Theravāda B., though it had royal patronage, succeed at once in transforming the earlier indigenous worship of spirits, or Nats; it grad. made its way, transforming local beliefs and practices and producing through the cents. the amalgam of Theravāda B. and local trad. which is peculiar to Burma, and to which the name Burmese B. must be given. When this was first discovered by Europeans, it was declared to be a thin veneer of Buddhism covering the 'real' religion of Burma, viz. nature-worship. More recently, however, it has been argued (by E. M. Mendelson and others) that Burmese B. is properly understood as a spectrum, at one end of which are the indigenous cults and beliefs, at the other the authentic Theravāda B. of the Pali canonical scriptures practised in the monasteries; between these two extremes is a continuum in which the transition from one to the other is made, with a steady growth of the authentic

Theravāda element. At this level there has been communication with other Theravāda countries, notably → Ceylon, from time to time. Burma has become noted for its → Abhidhamma studies, and in recent centuries has attracted monks from Ceylon to the monasteries where this is specially studied. The British conquest of Burma in 19th cent. and imposition of Brit. imperial rule seriously damaged trad. structure of → Sangha organisation; when Burma achieved independence in 1947, the task of recovering a great deal of lost ground confronted the Sangha. U Nu, prime minister of independent Burma until 1962, attempted to fill the role of the Buddh. kings of precolonial days in acting as protector of B. In 1956, the 2500th anniversary (acc. to Theravāda chronology) of the Buddha's entry into *nibbāna* was celebrated by holding of a great 'Buddh. Council,' with reciting and revision by monks of entire text of the → Tipitaka, in a vast cave-auditorium outside Rangoon specially constructed for purpose from public funds. In 1961 a measure was passed in the Rangoon Parliament making B. the official relig., but without discrimination against other religs., which together account for the approx. 20% non-Buddh. portion of pop. of Burma. This was subsequently rescinded by military government under Gen. Ne Win, who took over control of Burma in March 1962.

Burma has many monasteries. Through the heartland of Burmese civilisation (the river valleys) they are to be found in almost all small towns and villages, where they provide centres of influence, moral and educational, for the local people. Burma, like other Theravāda countries of Asia, has a high rate of literacy. The → pagodas, built and furnished by kings and lay people, are found attached to monasteries in most towns; some of the more magnificent of these, such as the pagodas of Mandalay and the *Shwe Dagon Pagoda* at Rangoon, covered with gold leaf donated by Buddh.-laypeople, are famous as centres of pilgrimage, and provide places of assembly for vast crowds on festival days. G. Coedès, *Les Peuples de la Peninsule Indochinoise* (1962); *Les États Hindouisés d'Indochine et d'Indonésie*

Bu-Ston

(new ed., 1964); N. R. Ray, *Sanskrit Buddhism in Burma* (1936); E. Sarkisyanz, *The Buddhist Backgrounds of the Burmese Revolution* (1965); E. M. Mendelson, 'Religion and Authority in Modern Burma,' in *The World Today* (March, 1960), 'Buddhism and the Buddhist Establishment,' in *Archives de Sociologie des Religions,* 1964, No. 17.

Bu-Ston Tibetan Buddh. scholar and historian: b. CE 1290; d. CE 1322, who is credited with collection and arrangement of Buddh. Tibetan canon; author of commentaries on import. Buddh. treatises. Best known for *History of Buddhism,* in two parts, trans. by E. Obermiller (Heidelberg, 1931–2).

C

Cakkappavattana → Dhamma-Cakkappavattana Sutta.
Cambodia and Laos (Buddhism in) Like other countries of
S.E. Asia, Cambodian relig. was, in earlier period of medieval history a mixture of Brahmanism and Mhy. Buddhism.
The Khmer kingdom, of which mod. Cambodia is survival,
with its centre at Angkor, was in former times of great influence and importance in the Indo-Chinese peninsula and
was strongly Hindu in culture. The description of Cambodian affairs in years 1296–7 given by a Chinese envoy, Chao
Ta-Kuan (French trans. by P. Pelliot, *Bulletin de l'École
Française d'Extrême Orient*, II, 123), shows at end of 13th
cent. Theravāda Buddh. monks were one of 3 principal
relig. groups in country (the others being Hindu brahmans
and Saivites). In 14th cent., as result of growing influence
of the Thais, who had now estab. Ayudhaya (see Thailand,
Buddhism in) as capital, and accepted the Sinhalese, →
Theravāda form of Bhm., Cambodia became more predominantly Theravādin and has continued so until present.
From Cambodia, Ther. Bhm. was intro. into newly founded
state of Laos in 14th cent. A Thai prince, brought up by a
Buddh. monk in old Cambodian capital at Angkor, and
himself son-in-law of king of Cambodia, proclaimed himself king at Lan Ch'ang (modern Luang Prabang) in 1353; he
founded the state of Laos, which also, since 14th cent.,
been a predominantly Ther. Buddh. country, having strong
links with the Buddh. Order in neighbouring Thailand (the
Lao people themselves being of same ethnic group as
Thais).
G. Coedès, *Les États Hindouisés d'Indochine et d'Indonésie* (1964); *The Making of South-East Asia* (1966); D. Dey-

dier, *Introduction à la Connaissance du Laos* (1952); M. L. Manich, *History of Laos* (1967).

Canon of Scripture → Tipitaka.

Caste (Buddhist attitude) Caste, of Indian type, has strictly no place in Buddh. social structure. In rejecting role of brahmans as guardians and transmitters of sacrificial system, the Buddha implicitly rejected their claim to pre-eminent social status, and ritual hierarchical structure of Indian society of which brahman supremacy was key-stone. Early disciples of Buddha were from various social strata: a few brahmans, some kshatriyas ('landed gentry'), a large number from vaishya (merchant) class, and some from shudra or labourer class. In becoming a disciple of Buddha, one shed former hereditary lineage (*gotra*) and became member of (spiritual) lineage of Buddha. (*Vis. IV:* 74). Within the early → *Sangha* there were no distinctions on grounds of former caste membership; honour was accorded to those who were spiritually advanced, or who were seniors, or 'elders' → *Thera,* in terms of years of membership of Sangha. This attitude to caste distinctions continued to characterise Sangha throughout most of its hist.; in Ceylon, however, a caste-system exists among Buddhists, both of cen. Kandyan highlands, and of lowlands. The highest and most numerous caste is the Goigama; the caste incl. not only Buddhist laymen, but also monks whose family are of this caste. The tendency of Goigama to separate themselves from others even in matters of Buddh. devotion at local temple is, however, even by them occasionally seen to be basically inconsistent with Buddh. principles (Cf. Ryan, *op. cit.,* pp. 121ff.).

D. D. Kosambi, *The Culture and Civilization of Ancient India* (1965), ch. 5; Nyanamoli, *The Path of Purification* (1964), pp. 142ff.; R. Pieris, *Sinhalese Social Organisation* (1956); B. Ryan, *Caste in Modern Ceylon* (1953), *Sinhalese Village* (1958); Nur Halman, 'The Flexibility of Caste Principles in a Kandyan Community,' in E. R. Leach (ed.), *Aspects of Caste in S. India, Ceylon, and N.W. Pakistan* (1960).

Causation, Chain of, in Buddhist thought → *Paticca-Samuppada.*

Cetiya Earthen mound or tumulus, reverenced as cult-object in pre-Buddh. India. → Stupa. The name survives in Siamese name for a Buddh. pagoda, viz. *'chedi,'* or more properly *'Phra Chedi,'* (*Phra* being a term of respect) → *Pagoda.*

Ceylon, Buddhism in Acc. to the *Mahāvamsa,* 5th cent. CE Pali chronicle, the → Buddha made three visits to island of Ceylon. Once he went to the top of Sumanakata (now known as Adam's Peak), and there left his footprint. The story has no historical basis; but the footprint remains one of the great centres of pilgrimage in C., and is a potent symbol of popular belief that C. is the *dhammadipa,* the island which is the guardian of Buddha's teaching.

The hist. advent of Buddhism in Ceylon was result of embassy sent by Tissa, king of C., to Indian emperor → Ashoka. In his reply, Ashoka commended the Buddh. relig. and arranged for his son, the *bhikkhu* (→ Ord. Bhd.) Mahinda, to visit C. and instruct Tissa. This is the *Mahāvamsa's* account, which is confirmed in part by Ashokan inscriptions. In these Ashoka claims to be supreme over many countries, incl. Tambapanni (Ceylon), and to have sent embassies to estab. Buddhism in all his dominions. The *Mahāvamsa* account surrounds embassy of Mahinda with various legendary elements, but behind them a kernel of hist. truth may be discerned. Tissa accepted the new relig.; with Mahinda, he arranged for a *vihāra* to be built in the capital city, Anurādhapura. Here were accommodated members of the → sangha who had arrived in C. with Mahinda. This community of *bhikkhus* was forerunner of the Mahāvihāra which for many cents. was leading sect in C. The ruins of Anurādhapura have recently been uncovered, incl. one of most striking moments of the Mahāvihāra, the Ruwanvali *dāgaba,* built prob. by king Dutthagāmani in 1st cent. BC. The fame of the Mahāvihāra is confirmed by → Buddhaghosa, who came to C. in 5th cent. CE and lived as member of Mahāvihāra community. He rewrote in Pali the Sinhalese commentaries on the → Tripitaka; and these works, together with his comprehensive summary of Buddh. teaching and practice, the *Visuddhimagga,* have been of great import. in shaping the → Theravāda trad. found in C.

Ceylon, Buddhism in

The close connection between rulers of C. and the sangha goes back to time of Mahinda and Tissa. From advent of Buddhism to occupation of Kandy by British in 1815, it was required that ruler of country should be Buddhist. It may have been the close relationship between court and sangha, and custom of court gifts to sangha, which was responsible for growth of different sects. A king of 1st cent. BC arranged for a gift to be made, not to the Mahāvihāra, but to an individual *bhikkhu,* and from this beginning sprang the Abhayagiri sect. Although there was at first no difference in teaching or discipline, the new *vihāra* became centre of foreign influence. The Mahāvihāra *bhikkhus* were conservative guardians of Theravādin orthodoxy; the Theravāda Tripitaka had been committed to writing in 1st cent. BC before rise of the Abhayagiri. The new sect welcomed ideas from abroad, and studied both Theravāda and → Mahāyāna teaching. The link between Abhayagiri and Buddhism in India is confirmed by fact that when the Tooth relic was brought from Kalinga to C. in 3rd cent. CE it was given into custody of Abhayagiri *bhikkhus.* From this time dates the cultus of the Tooth (claimed to be a left eye-tooth of Buddha). The Chinese pilgrim → Fa Hsien, who visited C. at beginning of 5th cent. CE described in detail the Anurādhapura of this period, giving a picture in which the Abhayagiri and cultus of Tooth relic overshadow the Mahāvihāra.

A third sect, the Jetavana, was formed in much the same way as the Abhayagiri, and finally seceded from them in 3rd cent. CE. These three sects remained foundation of sangha during succeeding cents. in which period there was a great deal of S. Indian and Hindu influence. An 8th cent. CE king is said to have repaired many old *devālayas* (temples of Hindu gods); temples to Visnu and Siva have been found at Polonnaruwa, dating from 11th or 12th cent. CE. A great revival of national independence and Buddhism was begun by 11th cent. CE king Vijaya, and carried to completion in next cent. by Parākrama Bāhu. Under Vijaya the various sects of sangha were united into one group, accepting orthodox Theravādin teaching. Parākrama Bāhu stressed importance of Tooth relic for well-being of C., together with another relic, the alms-bowl of Buddha which has now been lost. During succeeding cents. the Tooth relic moved with capital and court. The Portuguese claimed to have captured and destroyed it in 16th cent. CE; but Sinhalese maintain that this was a replica, and that original was eventually taken to Kandy, where it is still housed today.

Popular Buddhism in C. is centred on the *vihāras* which are both dwelling places for *bhikkhus* and shrines for Buddh. devotees. The first *vihāras* on C. consisted of *bhikkhus'* living quarters, together with *dāgaba* in which a relic was buried. Usually a bo-tree was grown also. The bo-tree, which still stands in Anuradhapura, is said to have been grown from cutting of tree at → Buddha-Gaya under which Buddha attained enlightenment, and brought to C. by sister of Mahinda. From 4th cent. CE onwards, image-houses became regular feature; together with the *dāgaba* and bo-tree, it forms part of most *vihāras* in C. today. One further development in the *vihāra* took place from 12th cent. CE onwards, when the *devālayas* came to be more closely assoc. with the *vihāras*. By the 15th cent. CE *devālayas* were being constructed in same building as the image-house. The gods who are besought in the *devālayas* incl. pre-Buddh. deities such as Sumana, guardian of Adam's Peak, and Hindu deities such as Bishnu. In popular imagination, propitiation of such deities is often of greater importance than reverence paid to Buddha.

The popular relig. of Ceylonese people incl. pre-Buddh. practices such as use of devil-dancers to cure sick and of *kattādiyas* or exorcisers to cast off spells. Much use is also made of astrologers, another pre-Buddh. practice. Some of Buddh. customs betray pre-Buddh. background, such as *pirit*, the chanting of suttas from Tripitaka to ward off evil spirits. More firmly Buddh. is customs of *dāna*, the giving of food to *bhikkhus*, by which means much merit accrues to donor.

Buddh. festivals enjoy great popular support, esp. festival of Wesak, which commemorates three great events in life of Buddha—the renunciation, enlightenment, and entry into *parinibbāna*. Even more powerful in popular imagination is annual *perahara* held in Kandy, during which Tooth relic is carried in procession. This procession also incl. the representatives of four of the popular deities worshipped in the *devālayas*. Once in 10 yrs. the relic itself, normally carried in casket, is exposed; multitudes of pilgrims pass through the *Māligāva* where relic is housed.

The sangha today is divided into three major communities or *nikāyas*, in add. to which there are some smaller communities. The leading community, the Siam Nikāya (so-called because it received its authority from Siam in 18th cent. CE) is distinguished chiefly by caste, only members of highest Ceylonese caste being admitted. The Amarapura Nikāya incl. members of other castes, while the Rāmanya Nikāya is distinguished by slightly stricter discipline. There is no difference in teaching between the *nikāyas*.

Although sangha maintained its numbers during occupation of C. by Portuguese, Dutch and British, during this period Buddhism fell to low ebb. It was revived only towards end of 19th cent. Since visit to C. of theosophist Col. Olcott, there has been steady increase in Buddh. study and learning. The two Buddh. universities of Vidyalankāra and Vidyodaya were founded to stimulate Buddh. education. Since independence of country in 1947, there has been growing sense of cultural and national identity linked with revival of Buddhism. The Buddh. missions estab. by C. in Europe and America bear witness to C.'s self-conscious role as the *dhammadipa*, the country which is bearer of Buddha's message to mod. world.

W. Geiger (tr.), *The Mahavamsa* (1912); R. S. Copleston, *Buddhism Primitive and Present in Magadha and Ceylon* (1892); E. W. Adikaram, *Early Hist. of Buddhism in Ceylon* (1946); W. Rahula, *Hist. of Buddhism in Ceylon* (1956); E. F. C. Ludowyck, *The Footprint of the Buddha* (1958).

Ch'an (→ Zen) A school of Chinese Buddhism and undoubtedly one of most distinctive and original products of the Chinese mind. The character *'ch'an'* is derived from the Sanskrit *dhyāna*, and hence the school was designated the

Ch'an

Meditation School. It aims at an immediate awareness of Reality in which subjective and objective are transcended; a state of being in which there is no duality. This goal is referred to as *prajnā, nirvāna, bodhi,* etc. Ch'an taught that the only reality is the Buddha-mind, which cannot be apprehended by philos, or relig. thought, meditation or practice of ritual or magic. It cannot be taught, or transmitted by books or teachers. Ch'an stressed 'realisation' by a kind of spiritual illumination which comes when thought and sense-perception have ceased, everything being a manifestation of the Buddha-mind; → *samsāra is* → *nirvāna,* my mind *is* the Buddha-mind, pure consciousness *is* wisdom.

Ch'an has affinities with Tibetan Mahāmudra. Tao-an and → Hui Yüan had early emphasised the importance of dhyāna exercises; but the beginnings of Ch'an are attributed to → Bodhidharma (*c.* CE 520), whose teaching is summed up in the lines:

A special transmission outside the scripture.
No dependence upon words or letter.
Direct pointing to the soul of man.
Seeing into nature and attainment of Buddhahood.

Bodhidharma emphasised the teachings of the → *Lankāvatāra Sūtra.*

With Hung-jên (CE 601–74), the 5th patriarch, and his two outstanding disciples, Shên-hsiu (605–706) and Hui-nêng (638–713), Ch'an began to develop divergent tendencies concerned with interpretation and method. Whereas Shên-hsiu and the N. school distinguished between pure and false mind, and taught the need to eliminate all false thinking and gradually reach the point of absolute quietude, Hui-nêng and the S. school refused to make this distinction and sought realisation in sudden awareness of Absolute Truth.

Hui-nêng is credited with authorship of the only Chinese Buddhist writing to be honoured with the rank of *sūtra* (*ching*), the famous *Platform Sūtra* of Hui-nêng, which became a basic text of Ch'an. Soon after Hui-nêng's death (CE 713), the meditation hall came into use in Ch'an monasteries. At the same time Buddhist laymen and lay

73

Chinese Religions

women were encouraged to practise Ch'an meditation in their homes. By 10th cent. CE the Kung-an (→ Koan) came to be recognised and used extensively as a device for attainment of enlightenment.

Ch'an did not object to conceptual knowledge as such, but to the clinging to intellectualization. Nor did Ch'an meditation preclude vigorous and creative physical activity. The search for direct communication with the inner nature of things and the vision of a world beyond all opposites led to a great outpouring of creative art in China and Japan. Ch'an also had a profound influence on the neo-Confucian movement of the Sung Dynasty, and as → Zen in Japan it exerted untold influence on Japanese civilisation.

W. T. Chan, *Source Book in Chinese Philosophy* (1963), ch. 26; Fung Yu-lan, *Hist. of Chinese Philosophy,* vol. 2 (1953), pp. 386ff.

Chinese Religions It has been customary to speak of the three religs. of China as Confucianism, Taoism and Buddhism. Though in the past these three great systems of belief, ritual practices and organisational relationships designed to deal with ultimate matters of human life have exercised a profound influence, as definite relig. systems they have, for several centuries, had only a historical interest.

In anc. China relig. was a political function conducted by officially appointed shaman-diviners, and contained four leading elements: the cult of ancestors; the worship of Heaven and its subordinate nature-deities; divination; and sacrifice. With the estab. of empire, an ethicopolitical Confucian orthodoxy was linked to the anc. cult, and Confucian scholars, versed in tradition, ritual and customary law, became under the emperor the 'priests' of the cult. This 'official' relig. continued throughout history till the fall of the Chinese monarchy.

It was only with the rise of relig. Taoism (2nd cent. CE) and the intro. of Buddhism into China (from 1st cent. CE) that for the first time (except perhaps for Mohism) membership in a consciously organised relig. was based on conversion and the voluntary choice of the individual believer. Through several centuries Taoism and Buddhism developed as distinct religs., with trained priests, vast monastic foundations, numerous temples and millions of adherents. They lacked, however, centralised authority and cohesive national organisation. Syncretistic and eclectic tendencies, and mutual borrowings characterised Chi. religs. From the Sung Dynasty (CE 980–1279) onwards the three religs., Confucianism, Taoism and Buddhism, were in large measure merged into a Popular Relig., permeating almost every aspect of Chi. life, which for the past 700 years has been the relig. of the majority of the Chi. people.

Though there are millions of Chi. who might be correctly labelled Confucian, Buddhist or Taoist (together with some 15 million Muslims and 3 million Christians), for the vast majority of Chi. a popular relig. suffices, grounded in an anc. nature-worship linked to a cult of → ancestors, and borrowing various features from all three religs., such as Confucian ethics, the Buddhist belief in transmigration and concern for the after-life, the Taoist pantheon with its supreme deity and a host of deified saints and heroes, its belief in divination, magic and sorcery, and faith-healing. The popular relig., weak in formal organisation, is catered for by a host of Buddhist monks and Taoist priests and sorcerers, and exercises a diffused and pervasive influence in every major aspect of Chi. social life.

The permeation of Chi. society by the popular relig. is everywhere evidenced: by the number and variety of temples and wide range of functions which they serve; by festivals, → pilgrimages, ceremonies etc. of a relig. character; by the spirit-tablets, images and pictures of deities to be found in every traditional Chi. home; and by the rituals of relig. brought to bear on every major event of social or family life. Belief in the supernatural is an outstanding mark of Chi. popular relig., but its main concern is to seek the help of these supernatural agencies, whether they be gods, Buddhas, immortals or mere tutelary and nature spirits, to avoid or overcome the ills of life, and guarantee a happier existence in the future. Yet, through a combina-

Ching

tion of Confucian ethics, Taoist mysticism, Buddhist discipline and techniques of meditation, relig. has proved to be a most potent factor in the development of Chi. civilisation.

W. E. Soothill, *The Three Religions of China* (1923); E. R.–K. Hughes, *Religion in China* (1950); K. L. Reichelt, *Religion in Chinese Garment* (1951); C. K. Yang, *Religion in Chinese Society* (1961); D. H. Smith, *Chinese Religions* (1968).

Ching Chinese character used for classic books; e.g. *Wu Ching*—the five books that make up the Confucian Canon; *Hsin Ching*—the *Heart Sūtra* (Buddhist); *Shêng Ching*—the Holy Bible (Chr.).

Ching T'u → Pure Land School.

Citta An import. term in the Buddh. analysis of human existence; sometimes trans. as 'consciousness', sometimes as 'mind.' It is regarded as a characteritic of all beings above level of plant life. C. is used as collective term for whole stream or series of momentary mental states (somewhat after manner of the individual 'frames' in a film, which, when shown quickly and successively, give impression of continuous action). The systematic analysis of the → *Abhidhamma* distinguishes in all phenomena three elements: *citta;* the quality of the citta, or that which 'accompanies' it (*cetisakā*); the material shape or corporeality (*rūpa*).

Every C., or individual momentary state of consciousness, is characterised by pain, pleasure or indifference; sensation of sight, hearing, taste, etc.; whether morally wholesome or unwholesome, etc. C.s. are distinguished also acc. to whether they are 'states of consciousness' in the material-sensory world (*kāma-loka*), the world of pure form (*rūpa-loka*), world of formlessness (*arūpa-loka*), or transcendental world. Acc. to the → Thv. *Abhidhamma* there are altogether 121 different types of C.s. Each of these is capable of occurring in combination with any of 52 mental properties or concomitants (*cetasikā*), thus making poss. a great variety of poss. mental events.

In → Mahāyāna Buddhism, C. is identified by the → Yogācārins with the 'store-consciousness' or → *ālaya-vijñāna*. It is thus, acc. to the → *Lankāvatāra Sutra,* that which 'gath-

Conception, in Buddh. thought

ers up *karma*'; '*karma* is gathered up by *citta.*' In gen., in Buddh. usage, C. is virtually a synonym of → *Vijñāna,* also trans. 'consciousness.'

S. Z. Aung, *Compendium of Philosophy,* PTS. 1910 (repr. 1956); D. T. Suzuki, *Studies in the Lankāvatāra Sutra* (1930), pp. 176, 180ff., 398–402.

Compassion One of the 4 'illimitable' or universal virtues in Buddh. thought, described also by Conze as the 'social emotions' (*Buddh. Thought in India,* 1962, ch. 6). C. (*karunā*) follows loving kindness, i.e. it is a resultant of cultivation of attitude of loving kindness; and in the Buddh. order it precedes 'sympathetic joy.' In → Mhy. Buddhism, compassion is elevated to place of importance equal to that of wisdom (*prajñā*); in → Hīnayāna Buddhism, compassion was subordinate to wisdom. In the Mhy. the term *karunā* denotes partic. the 'infinite grace of the Buddhas and Bodhisattvas for beings' (Murti, *Central Philosophy of Buddhism,* 1955) → Brahma-Vihara.

Conceit In Buddh. thought, 3 types of conceit (*māna*) are distinguished: 'superiority-conceit'; 'equality-conceit'; 'inferiority-conceit'. In Buddh. view, it is characteristic of those who believe in a permanent, enduring → ego to entertain such conceits. All those who rely on idea of a permanent individual self imagine, 'Better am I', or 'Equal am I', or 'Worse am I'; all these imagine thus through not understanding reality (SN.XII:49). C. is thus a 'fetter,' which is broken only at attainment of → Arahantship.

Conception, in Buddh. thought (1) The conception by mind of an object, in Buddh. thought, is result of operation of 3 distinguishable mental properties, or *cetasika: vitakka* (directing of attention to object); *vicāra* (sustaining of attention upon object); *adhimokkha* (decision to go on attending to that one object out of many presented to the consciousness). (2) Physical conception in womb of mother, acc. to B. thought, takes place when three conditions are fulfilled: (a) when intercourse has taken place (b) when time is auspicious for mother (c) when some *karma*-energy (i.e. from some previous existence) is ready to enter upon a new life. When these 3 conditions are fulfilled an embryo is produced; this is known as *okkanti* (lit. 'descent'). In B. countries, it is usual to reckon age of child from time of conception, which is regarded as re-beginning of life-process (*jāti*), rather than from time of birth. In some S.E. Asian B. countries, e.g. Thailand, concep. is gen. welcomed, since it is regarded as a blessing from the Buddha.

Consciousness → Citta.

Cosmogony, Japan From 6th cent. CE → Buddhism influenced Jap. C. ideas. In particular, the world of forms was believed to be constituted from emanations proceeding from the Dhyani-Buddha, Vairochana, with whom, in Ryobu-Shinto, the sun-goddess, Amaterasu, was identified as a temporal manifestation (→ Creation).

D. C. Holtom, *The National Faith of Japan* (1938), pp. 21, 101ff.; J. Hackin (ed.), *The Mythology of Modern Japan* (1932, 1963), p. 415; E. Dale Saunders in *M.A.W.*, pp. 411ff.

Cosmology Not all schools of Buddhism have concern with cosmology: the → *Mādhyamika*, e.g., with its view of unreality of external world and exclusive concern with questions of ontology, had relatively little interest in cosmological schemes. Among 3 schools, where there was interest in phenomenology, a broadly similar C. was (and is) affirmed. These 3 are (1) the → Theravādin (2) the → Sarvāstivādin (3) the → Yogācāra. In many respects this C. was that of brahmans of anc. India, in which an infinite number of worlds was affirmed, the cosmography of each being basically similar to that of this world, which had as central point a huge mountain, Mt. Meru, on 4 sides of which were 4 territories, each ruled over by a Great King, or guardian. The southern territory or continent was called Jambūdvipa; it was this which the anc. Indians believed they inhabited. Since there were unlimited numbers of similarly structured worlds, a scheme of classification of these worlds was developed. In B. cosmology, the entire universe is divided into 3 spheres, or *dhātus: Kāma-dhātu* ('sensual' sphere); *Rūpa-dhātu* ('sphre of form' only); *Arūpa-dhātu* (sphere of 'formlessness'). The word *loka* (world) may occur in these 3 compounds instead of *dhātu*.

Cosmology

Another syn. for *dhātu* is *bhava* (existence); this term occurs most frequently in the *Suttas* of Pali canon, where considerable ref. is made to this 3-fold cosmology. The lowest of the 3 spheres is the *Kāma-dhātu* (or *K-loka,* or *K-bhava*), the sensual world. This ranges from, at very lowest, a vast number of hells, upwards through the realms of ghosts (*pretas*), of animals, and of men, to realm of the inferior 'deities', the → *asuras,* on to the heavens of superior 'deities', the *devas,* at highest point of sensual-world. The whole of this world is inhabited by beings with six senses —sight, hearing, taste, smell, touch, and mental impression (the last name is regularly regarded in B. thought as one of 6 senses). In the various hells are beings who are suffering in various degrees of previous wickedness. Some hells are dark, some cold, some hot; each type has eight grades in rank-order from bad to worst (in the hottest hell, e.g. there is no intermission of pain whatsoever). The surface of earth is realm of animals and mankind. The *asuras* belong partly to surface of earth, partly to upper regions. The *devas* inhabit highest plane of sensual-world, viz., the heavens above summit of Mt. Meru. Here is the Heaven of the Thirty Three Gods (*Trayastrimsa*); the Heaven of → Yāma, where it is never night; the Tusita Heaven, where resides → Metteyya, the Buddha-to-be; and the two highest heavens where even a wish or a thought (without action) can generate new *karma;* the highest heaven is the abode of → Māra, the Evil One, who is thus supreme over whole sensual-world. A notable feature of the *deva*-heavens is that no women are there; rebirth there is always as male. The second world, the *Rūpa-dhātu* (or *R-loka,* or *R-bhava*) (sometimes trans. 'Fine-material world') is characterised by absence of 3 senses of taste, smell and touch; here there is only sight, hearing and mental impression. The inhabitants of this world still have shape, or form (*rūpa*), which at this level is still indispensable to their existence. The *Rūpa*-world is divided into a number of heavens: 17 acc. to the → *Abh.-Kosa* of Vasubandhu; 16 acc. to the Thv. and 18 acc. to the Yogācāra. Connected with these heavens are various stages of Jhāna → (Dhyāna), or contemplation: the

Cosmology

practice of the 1st Jhāna gives access to the 1st 3 *Rūpa*-heavens (sometimes called *Brahma-loka* or Brahma-world); the practice of 2nd Jhāna, the next 3; the 3rd Jhāna to next 3; the final Jhāna to last 8. Above the *Rūpa*-world is the third major division of the cosmos, the *Arūpa-dhātu* (°*loka*, or °*bhava*). In this 'formless' or 'immaterial' world, sight and sound are absent; there is only mental impression, or, in Yogācāra terms, consciousness-only. All schools agree in a list of 4 heavens in the Formless World: the heavens of boundless space; of infinite consciousness; of nothingness or nonexistence; of neither consciousness nor unconsciousness. To these heavens come beings, whose rebirth follows meditation on one of the 4 illimitables or → Brahma-vihāra. These two upper worlds (the Fine material (*Rūpa-dhātu*), and the Immaterial (*Arūpa-dh.*)) are sometimes ref. to collectively as the *Brahma-loka*, or spiritual world, although, as already mentioned, this term is sometimes used in a more partic. sense of the 3 heavens of the *Rūpa-dh.*

The → Hinayāna and → Mhy. cosmologies are approx. the same up to this point. But beyond the 3 worlds *Kāma*, *Rūpa*, and *Arūpa*, the Mhy. points existence of yet another realm, the *Buddha-Ksetras* (lit. the 'Buddha-fields'). Each is field of influence of a supremely Enlightened One (or Buddha → *Buddhas other than Gotama*); each Buddha is regarded by Mahayanists as able to secure rebirth in his own heaven of all men who call on his name in perfect faith. Women also may be reborn there, but it will be as men; just as only male beings inhabit the *deva* heavens of *Kāma-dhātu* (see above). In Mhy. Buddhism, espec. in China and Japan, rebirth in the Buddha-land becomes for lay people the real relig. goal, displacing → *nirvāna* as the ultimate hope (→ Creation, Buddh.).

The lit. sources in which the C., outlined above, is most prominent are: (1) for Theravadin school, certain Abh. works, notably the *Vibhanga* (last chapter) and *Dhamma Sanganī*; there are cosmological refs. in the *Kathā-vathu*; beyond the canonical lit., Buddhaghosa's *Visuddhimagga* is on this, as on other import. B. topics, the standard authy.

Councils

(2) the Sarvāstivādin views are repr. in the *Abh.-Kosa* of Vasubandhu (3) the Yogācārin system is repr. in the *Vidyāmātra Siddhi* of → Dhammapada.

R. Spence Hardy, *Manual of Buddhism* (1853; 1st Indian edn. 1967); Nyanamoli, *The Path of Purification* (1964); W. M. McGovern, *A Manual of Buddhist Philosophy*, vol. I, *Cosmology* (1923).

Councils Acc. to Buddh. trad., there have been, in the course of Buddh. hist., a number of councils: the number accepted as authentic varies from country to country. Ceylon and Burma, e.g. acknowledge 6; the 6th having been held in Rangoon in CE 1956. Thailand acknowledges 10, the Rangoon C. in this case being reckoned as 10th. All, however, are agreed on first 3. These are (1) at Rajagrha (Rājagaha), in monsoon season following Buddha's decease, c. 483 BC (2) at Vesāli, about a cent. later (3) at Pātaliputra (Patna) during reign of emperor → Ashoka, poss. c. 250 BC. These are all locations within India, in the lower Ganges valley. A 4th C. was held in N.W. India, under auspices of the Kushan emperor → Kanishka. The date of this C. is uncertain, as K's own dates are matter of controversy. The Pali chronicles of the Thv. school do not take this 4th C. into account, although it is not certain that Thv. monks did not take part. It was held, acc. to some authorities, at Jālandhar; acc. to others, in Kashmir. The Thai Buddh. trad. reckons the 4th C. to have been one held at → Anuradhapura in Ceylon, convened by King of Ceylon, Devanam Piyatissa c. 220 BC. Burmese and Sinhalese trads., however, reckon as the 4th the C. held at the Aloka Vihara in Ceylon, convened by King Vatthagāmini c. CE 90. Acc. to Thai trad., the 6th and 7th C.'s were also held in Ceylon, in 27 BC and CE 1044 respectively; the latter being convened by the great king Parakrama, at Pulatthi-nagara. Thai trad. claims that 8th and 9th were held in Thailand, in CE 1477 at Chiengmai (N. Thailand) and CE 1788 at Bangkok, respectively; the latter being convened by Rāma I, King of Thailand. Acc. to Sinhalese trad. the 5th C. was held in CE 1865 at Ratnapura in Ceylon, the royal patron being Basnayaka Nilama. Acc. to Burmese trad. (which at this point only differs from the

Councils

Sinhalese), the 5th was the C. held at Mandalay in CE 1871, convened by Min-don-min, King of Upper Burma.

The occasion for assembling of these C.'s was gen. a need to agree upon text of the Buddh. scriptures, or commentaries thereon. Thus the 1st C., acc. to unanimous trad. of all Buddh. schools, met to estab. text of the → Vinaya-Pitaka and → Sutta-Pitaka. Mahākassapa is held to have presided, and a monk named Upali to have supplied the definitive version of the Vinaya, and → Anānda that of the Sutta-Pitaka. The text thus agreed was recited in chorus; hence the Pali name for the assembly, 'sangīti,' a 'singing-together'; this word is repr. in Eng. as 'council.' The historicity of this 1st C. has been challenged by mod. scholars, notably by Oldenberg, and is still held by some to be purely legendary; however, a considerable body of scholarly opinion, in both East and West, supports the view that such an assembly did take place shortly after the Buddha's decease. Acc. to Buddh. trads., the 1st C. was held in a large cavern in a hillside, near Rajgrha (the mod. Rajgir), though the site has not been identified. The trads. agree that 500 monks took part. The basic account of 1st C. is found in the → Cullavagga, which is followed in the Pali extra-canonical lit. of the → Dipavamsa and Mahāvamsa. Other accounts are those of the → Mahāvastu (the Vinaya of the Lokuttara-vadins) of → Ashvaghosha, and the Tibetan Dulva. Other accounts such as → Buddhaghosa's Samantapāsādikā and that of Chinese pilgrim → Hsüan Tsang, though much later compositions, may embody anc. trads.

The 2nd C., held at Vesali, was occasioned by growth of irregular practices among certain monks in that area. A highly venerable monk named Yasa, disciple of Ānanda, reproached them with ten breaches of Buddh. monastic discipline. They replied with counter-accusations against Yasa. Another highly respected and venerable monk, Revata, of great repute for learning and piety, was appealed to by all concerned. He gave his verdict in support of Yasa, and at his suggestion a C. of 700 monks was convened at Vesali to settle the dispute. This C. appointed a committee of 8 monks, 4 from the 'western territory' and 4 from the 'eastern territory.' The committee reported unanimously in condemnation of practices of monks of Vesali. Acc. to Pali trad. of Buddhaghosa, this was followed by recital by all the monks of a new arrangement of the *Vinaya* and *Suttas*. The royal patron of this 2nd C. is held to have been Kālāsoka, a descendent of King Ajātasattu. This C. is last event in hist. of Buddhism which is commonly recorded in all the various versions of the *Vinaya-Pitaka,* i.e. both Pali and Skt. The accounts of 2nd C., like 1st, were regarded by Oldenberg as unhistorical; but majority of mod. scholars accept historicity of 2nd C. more readily than that of 1st.

The 3rd C. is assoc. with name of the great Mauryan emperor, Ashoka. The emperor himself had become a Buddh. in revulsion against carnage involved in his early conquests; as ruler, his primary concern was not partisan, but rather maintenance of harmony among his subjects and discouragement of sectarian quarrels. The → Theravādin trad., which repr. him as actively promoting harmony by agreeing to convening of a C. to deal with a variant form of Buddh. teaching, whose exponents were called → Sarvāstivādins, has therefore a large element of hist. authenticity. The Sarvāstivādin doc., that not only present states of mind (→ *citta*) are real but also past and future states, was repudiated by the orthodox, who called themselves *Vibhajyavādins,* 'those who make distinctions' (between present, and past/future states?). The growth of the Sarvāstivādin view was apparently causing dissension in the → Sangha, and at instigation of the venerable → Moggalliputta Tissa, a defender of orthodoxy of those who adhered to teaching of the Elders (the *Sthaviras,* as the orthodox were also known), Ashoka agreed to convene a C. of a thousand monks at Patna, capital city of the Mauryan empire. At this 3rd C., Tissa is said to have recited the → Kathā-Vathu, a work composed by him in refutation of various heresies; it subsequently became part of Theravādin → *Abh.-Pitaka.* Ashoka is reputed to have favoured Tissa and the Vibhajyavādins; in consequence the Sarvāstivādin groups withdrew from region of Patna northwestwards, and made first Ma-

Councils

thura and then Kashmir their strongholds. Acc. to Thv. chroni. 80,000 heretical monks wer expelled from the Patna region after the Ashokan C., because of their refusal to subscribe to Vibhajya-vādin doc. Certain rock edicts of Ashoka, condemning monks who were guilty of causing dissensions and therefore expelled, are held to provide epigraphical evidence in support of the Thv. trad. (J. Bloch, *Les Inscriptions d'Asoka,* Paris 1950, pp. 152f.).

Of the 4 C.'s held in Ceylon and reckoned by Thai Buddhists as the 4th, 5th, 6th and 7th C.'s, only that of 90 BC at Aloka-Vihara is reckoned by Ceylon Buddhists. The 5th by Thai reckoning, it is known in Ceylon as 4th C. (that of Kanishka in N.W. India being disregarded by the Thv.). This 4th C. was for purpose of revising commentaries on the → *Tipitaka.* At end of C., the entire *Tipitaka,* with its commentaries, are said to have been committed to writing: they were inscribed on palm-leaves and submitted to extensive checking and counter-checking. The other 3 Ceylon C.'s (by Thai reckoning) were not C.'s in the true sense, but concerned only with revision of commentaries.

Five C.'s belong to the period of mod. history: that of 1477 at Chiengmai, N. Thailand (then the Thai capital), lasted for a year; it was convened by Thai King to estab. Buddhism more firmly in that country; that of 1788 also in Thailand, at newly estab. capital of Bangkok under King Rāma I, was prelude to a purification of the Sangha and a revival of Buddhism in Thailand; the Ceylon C. of 1865 at Ratnapura, which lasted for 5 months, is reckoned by Sinhalese as 5th C., whereas that of 1868–71 at Mandalay, when the entire *Tipitaka* was recited and subsequently inscribed on 729 marble tablets, is reckoned by Burmese as the 5th. The occasion for the so-called '6th' C. in 1956 in Rangoon was celebration of 2500th anniversary (acc. to Thv. chronology) of the Buddha's entry into *pari-nibbāna* in 543 BC. It was held under patronage of the Buddh. prime minister of Burma, U Nu. 500 Burmese monks, with collaboration of learned monks from India, Ceylon, Nepal, Cambodia, Thailand, Laos and Pakistan, were charged with task of revising text of the *Tipitaka.* Greetings to the C. in warmest terms were received from the President of India, and from the prime minister of India, Jawaharlal Nehru. At end of C., the entire text of the Pali *Tipitaka,* and its commentarial literature, was recited by assembled monks in the vast auditorium built to simulate the cave-assembly of anc. India. The revised edition of text was subsequently published (in Burmese characters) by the Burmese authorities.

E. Lamotte, *Histoire du Bouddhisme Indien* (1958); M. Hofinger, *Étude sur le Concile de Vaisāli* (1946); A. Bareau, *Les Premiers Conciles Bouddhiques* (1955); N. R. Ray, *Theravāda Buddhism in Burma* (1946), pp. 245–9; P. V. Bapat (ed.), 2500 *years of Buddhism* (1956), ch. IV.
Bapat (ed.), *2500 Years of Buddhism* (1956), ch. IV.

Craving (*Tanhā,* Pali; *Tṛṣṇā,* Skt.) Acc. to the 2nd of the Buddh. → Holy Truths, craving is the root of all suffering entailed in mortal existence. C. (or lit. 'thirst') is closely linked, in Buddh. analysis, with → Ignorance (*avijjā*), and Karma, as forces which perpetuate sorrowful existence, i.e. continue the cycle of rebirth. In the Buddha's first sermon (*SN,* V, pp. 420ff.; *Vin,* 1:10), it is proclaimed that C. must be got rid of, if → *nibbāna* is to be attained. Three kinds of C. are distinguished: (1) for sensuous pleasure (2) for rebirth (3) for no further rebirth. Thus, even so long as *nibbāna* is the object of C., it cannot be attained; all C. of any kind whatsoever is regarded as a sign of imperfection. In some passages in Buddh. scripture, C. is spoken of as having another 3 aims: C. for sensual existence (*kāma*); for fine-material existence (*rūpa*); for non-material existence (*a-rūpa*). In Buddh. mythology C. is the 4th member of → Māra, the Evil One's army. C. has a 6-fold source: it arises in connection with visible objects, sounds, odours, tastes, bodily contacts and mental impressions. The term is used more extensively in passages where language is popular, picturesque or poetic; is less often used in passages of philosophical analysis, although C. is mentioned in famous formula of Chain of Causation (→ *Paticca-Samuppāda*). The most common syn. for C. in the Buddh. *Suttas* is greed (*rāga* or *lobha*).

Creation

Piyadassi Thera, *The Buddha's Ancient Path* (1964), ch. 4.

Creation (Buddh. view) The doc. of a personal God who created the universe *ex nihilo* is not found in Buddhism. Such a being is neither explicitly affirmed nor denied. In so far as Brahmanic theology asserted a doc. of creation by Brahma, and that Brahma was proud of his achievement, this was met by the Buddh. counter-assertion that such a being, victim of self-conceit, must be morally inferior to the Buddha. But on larger question of how universe originated the Buddh. attitude is one of agnosticism. The Buddhist views the attempt to answer question as futile, and having no relig. importance in comparison with prior task confronting men, i.e. of spiritual progress and elimination of moral evil, acc. to way opened up by the Buddha. Buddhist thought is positive in emphasising that world has existed for such an incredibly long duration as to make it tantamount to being datum from which human knowledge starts; consequently the question: 'How did the universe begin?' is virtually ruled out as beyond scope of proper human concern. Buddh. thought conceives of world-history in terms of *kalpas* (Skt.) or *kappas* (Pali), each of which is, to all intents and purposes, an eternity; of such world-periods there have already been many hundred thousands. 'Inconceivable, O Monks,' said Buddha, 'is this → *Samsāra*; not to be discovered is any first beginning of beings' (*SN.* XV. pp. 5) (→ Cosmogony; Cosmology, Buddh.).

Creed The nearest Buddh. approach to a formal creed in Christ. sense is the 3-fold affirmation, 'I go to the Buddha for refuge; I go to the Dhamma (Doctrine) for refuge; I go to the Sangha (Order of monks) for refuge.' This is the most widely used devotional formula among Buddhs., and forms preliminary invocation to daily recital of the *Pansil,* or affirmation of five basic moral precepts by laymen and monks alike. Apart from this, no formal statement of faith is binding upon Buddh. In → Theravādin countries of S.E. Asia, there is tacit acceptance of the Doctrine (→ *Dhamma*) of the Buddha, as this is contained in the Pali canon; but even this is to be accepted on authority only tentatively as first step towards experimental verification of

Cullavagga

its truth. Without intention of practical verification, intellectual acceptance of doc. is not regarded as in itself of any ultimate value. The *Kālāma Sutta* teaches that there should be no acceptance of propositions on authoritative grounds alone (→ Faith, Buddh.).

K. N. Jayatilleke, *Early Buddhist Theory of Knowledge* (1963), ch. VIII.

Cremation → Funerary Rites.

Culavamsa 'The Short Chronicle,' a continuation of 'Great Chronicle' (→ *Mahāvaṃsa*), or Buddh. history of Ceylon. The titles 'Mahāvaṃsa' and 'C.' are not found in work itself: they were intro. by W. Geiger, who edited Pali text of whole chronicle; his terminology has been adopted by other western writers. The Sinhalese use only the title *Mahāvaṃsa* for whole history, from intro. of Buddhism to Ceylon in 3rd cent. BC to arrival of authorship at ch. 37.51 (point at which the *'Culavaṃsa'*, acc. to Geiger, begins). The earlier chapters of *Mahāvaṃsa* (1–37.50) are attr. to a monk called Mahānāma, who lived at Anurādhapura *c.* 5th cent. CE. The section beginning at ch. 37.51 is attr. to a monk of 13th cent. CE, named Dhammakitta, who prob. lived at Polonnaruwa. The chs. dealing with period after 13th to 18th cents. (90–100) are gen. held to have been added in latter part of 18th cent.; ch. 101, dealing with arrival of British, is a yet later addition (→ Ceylon).

Culavaṃsa (Pali text, 2 vols., ed. by W. Geiger, with German trans. 1935; E.T. by Mrs. C. Mabel Rickmers, 1953); W. Geiger, *Pali Literature and Language* (2nd edn. 1956); Walpola Rahula, *History of Buddhism in Ceylon: the Anurādha Period* (1956).

Cullavagga → *Vinaya-Pitaka.*

D

Dāgaba Name used, espec. in Ceylon, for a Buddh. reliquary mound. The word is a compound of → *dhātu* (element, essence, and hence 'a sacred relic') and *garbha* (a chamber, or cavern); thus a chamber for a sacred relic. The D. usually has the architectural form of → *Stupa* or memorial-mound, though the two words are not, as sometimes assumed, completely interchangeable. Not all *stupas* are D.'s, i.e., they do not all contain a relic chamber. A secondary meaning which has been seen in word D. is derived from usage of *dhātu,* to mean element in the sense of 'seed,' and *gharbha* in sense of 'womb': a D. is thus a place of sacred potential, the seed in the womb. The word 'pagoda' may possibly be a Europeanisation (Portuguese and Eng.) of *dāgaba,* though this is uncertain (→ Pagoda).

Daibutsu (Great Buddha) Name given to several large images of → Buddhas and → bodhisattvas in Japan, usually made of bronze, in a sitting or standing posture. The three most important D. are at Nara, Kyoto and Kamakura. The colossal D. at Nara was erected under patronage of zealous Buddh. emperor, Shōmu Tennō (CE 724–48) to be perpetual memorial of successful attempt to plant Buddhism in Japan and to ally it with the native Shinto. It was completed in CE 754. The image, in a sitting posture 53 ft high, stands in the Todaiji temple at Nara. The Kyoto D., a sitting figure of Lochana-Buddha $58\frac{1}{2}$ ft in height, was begun for self-glorification by Hideyoshi and completed early in 17th cent. by his son Hideyori. It was destroyed by earthquake in 1662; the copper used for coinage. The present Kyoto D. dates from 1801. The D. at Kamakura, though smaller than that at Nara, is better known. It is an image of → Amida Buddha 49 ft. 7

in. in height. Erected in 1252, it marks the success of the great Amidist (Pure Land) sects. Originally it was housed in a temple, twice destroyed in 1369 and 1494 and since then never rebuilt.

D. Lloyd in *E.R.E.*, IV, pp. 389–90.

Dainichi Japanese name for Mahā-Vairochana Buddha, the Great Illuminator whose body was deemed to comprise the whole cosmos, and whose body, speech and thought make up the life of the universe. Acc. to → Shingon, all deities and demons of Buddhist pantheon are but manifestations of D.

M. Anesaki, *Hist. of Japanese Buddhism* (1930), pp. 125ff.

Dalai Lama → Tibet.

Dāna The Pali word D. means lit. 'giving'; this is one of the major B. virtues. Generosity is encouraged as an essential B. attitude, and as best way of offsetting human tendency to individualistic self-centredness. It is also regarded as a form of renunciation, open to all, laymen as well as monks, and hence is first of three major ways of making merit (*puñña*); the other two, in ascending order of value, being observance of moral precepts (*sila*) and meditation (*bhāvanā*) (DN.33; Itivuttaka 60). For the monk, if he is a hermit-ascetic, such as are found in some places in Ceylon, he has no possessions whatever to give; if he is a village-monk, however, as are vast majority in Ceylon and S.E. Asia, 'giving' for him means giving of time and service to village community in form of teaching, counselling, etc. For the layman, practice of generosity has been cast in certain routine forms since earliest days of Buddhism, and consists largely in economic reciprocation of monks' services to villagers. Thus, merit is gained by the layman in giving food to monks, either daily when the monks make their almsround, or on special occasions when monks are invited to ceremonial meal; it is gained also in giving of robes, money (often to head of monastery, for the community's needs), and sometimes land, or materials, or labour, for building of new monastery or pagoda. In some B. countries (e.g. Burma) there is a recognised hierarchy of merit-making by D., as follows (in descending order of

Dead, State of

value): (1) to build a new pagoda (2) act as sponsor for a novice-monk (3) build and donate a monastery (4) donate a well to a monastery (5) feed a group of monks on a special occasion (6) feed monks in normal way (7) give hospitality to laymen.

M. M. Ames, 'Magical Animism and Buddhism: a Structural Analysis of the Sinhalese Religious System,' in *J.A.S.* (1964); Manning Nash, *The Golden Road to Modernity* (1965), ch. 4.

Dead, State of In Buddh. lit. unhappy spirits of departed, who are unable to find rebirth in embodied form, are ref. to by anc. Indian term *preta* (Pali, *peta*). Their wretched existence is regarded as enduring until their evil *karma* is exhausted, when they will achieve further, poss. more happy, rebirth. They are held to inhabit region immediately below surface of earth; sometimes they are found on surface; but certainly in a situation somewhat superior to that of inhabitants of the various hells, in bowels of the earth (→→ Cosmology, Petavatthu).

Death (Buddh. recollection of) In Buddhism one of the four Recollections (→ Anussati), which are sometimes added in B. lists to the 6 basic R.'s described in the *Suttas* (the other 3 are the Body, Breathing, Peace). The recollection of D. consists in monk's frequent calling to mind, every evening and every dawn, the many risks which surround human life, and thus how easily D. may come upon him. He must then consider unsubdued evil states within him, which could lead to prolonged future suffering should he die thus. 'If he understands that this is the case, he should use his utmost resolution, energy, effort, endeavour, steadfastness, attentiveness and clear-mindedness in order to overcome these evil unwholesome things.'
(*A.N.,* VIII, p. 78).

(Buddh. view of) Acc. to Buddhism, the death of any living being is inherent in its nature as a compounded entity: it is the dissociation of the constituent elements of a being. 'For the born there is no such thing as not dying' (*S.N.,* II). D. is thus a natural function of the ongoing process of life. For just as a birth leads inevitably to a death, so a death leads inevitably to a birth. Of the five → *khandhas,* the most import. is consciousness. At death of an individual these five khandhas contract, so to speak, to a zero-point; the momentum of life itself, however, carries the constituent elements on beyond this zero-point, to open out into new life; thus consciousness becomes assoc. yet again with another *rupa,* or form, another series of feelings, perceptions, etc. For this reason, the last state of consciousness of one 'life' is held to be of great import. for first state of consciousness of the ensuing one; if it was wholesome (*kusala*), this will produce a 'wholesome' inauguration of new life. Similarly, if it was *akusala,* unwholesome, the ensuing new life will be unwholesomely inaugurated. It is not this last state only which determines the character of the new life; the whole previous life has produced a momentum of a wholesome or unwholesome kind, in varying degrees, which will inevitably have effects upon the ongoing course of life.

Death, Personification of → Māra, the Evil One.

Defilement, in Buddh. thought There is in the Buddh. system no conception of *ritual* defilement which needs ritual cleansing, as there is in some relig. systems. The practice of the Buddh. way of life is, however, described as purification (*visuddhi*); this implies a condition from which men need to be purified. In Buddh. thought this is a condition of mind; the natural man is at mercy of influxes (→ *Asava*) which have to be overcome by insight, sense-control, avoidance of occasion of their arising, right use of food, sleep, etc. More commonly the → *Kilesas* are trans. by Eng. word 'defilements.' These are the morally defiling passions, the extinction of which constitutes → *Arahantship* or the attainment of holiness. The extinction of these defilements is first aspect of → *nibbāna,* and is sometimes ref. to as *Kilesa-nibbana.*

Demons Belief in demons does not constitute a primary or essential feature of Buddh. thought. Such beliefs were, however, common in anc. India at time of the rise of Buddhism and were accepted by early Buddh. as part of cosmic 'scenery'; refs. to demons of various kinds are not un-

Dengyō Daishi

common in B. sacred texts, where they have approx. same doctrinal status (or lack of it) as refs. to demons in early Christ. texts. One of more prominent roles of the demons, such as → *yakkhas,* → *pisacas,* etc., was their supposed activity of causing distraction to B. monks (and nuns) in their meditation, by causing loud or frightening noises, often by assuming guise of some wild bird or beast. Demons are thought of in early Buddhism as beings whose doleful and malevolent condition is due to bad *karma* of some previous existence. Wherever Buddhism has spread, it has accommod. itself to indigenous popular demonology in a gen. tolerant spirit, not openly denying existence or function of demons, but by its own characteristic docs. directing focus of attention away from such conceptions to moral and psychological roots of human evils; B. thought is not tied to such demonology; and can easily dispense with it (→→ Mara, the Evil One; Asuras).

J. Masson, *La Religion Populaire dans le Canon Bouddhique Pali* (1942); T. O. Ling, *Buddhism and the Mythology of Evil* (1962).

Dengyō Daishi (CE 767–822). Posthumous name of great and learned Buddh. priest Saichō, who, having studied in China the idealistic teachings of T'ien T'ai, formulated by Chih-i (536–97), intro. them into Japan as → Tendai. Tendai became a unifying force in Japanese → Buddhism, teaching that supreme object of all mysteries, virtues and wisdom is to realise Buddhahood in one's own consciousness. Though not distinguished as an original thinker, D. D. expounded the *Lotus Sūtra* (*Saddharma-Pundarika*), and made its idealistic teachings the basis of a practical relig. system, influential for centuries. D. D. had great influence at court, and built a monastery on Mt. Hiei near Nara, a centre of Buddh. learning and ecclesiastical power. He and Kōbō Daishi were the two most influential Buddh. of the Heian period.

Desire (Tanhā/Trsnā), in Buddh. thought → Craving (Buddh.).

Determinism (rejection) The B. view that human existence is a continuous psycho-physical stream, in which birth of any

92

one so-called 'individual' is conditioned by previous human actions and attitudes, might be thought to imply a closed determinism with regard to human conduct. In fact, this is not so. The deterministic view was known in early Buddhism as *Niyativāda;* it is explicitly rejected by Buddha at several places in the canonical scriptures. Thus, in the *A.N.* ('Book of the Threes,' §61) Buddha examines view, held and taught by some recluses and brahmans, who say that 'whatever weal or woe or neutral feeling is experienced, all that is due to some previous action.' His reply to them is that for those who hold such a view there is no motive for desiring or striving to do any action or for abstaining from that action, and that they have in fact no logical reason at all for the pursuit of life of a recluse: 'they live in a state of bewilderment' (*A.N.,* III:173). The view that all that happens to a man is 'due to what was previously done,' is examined in the *Devadaha Sutta* also (*M.N.,* II:214–28), where again it is rejected by Buddha on ground that such a view of the human situation leaves out of account the real effect of present 'effort and striving.' In the → *Jataka,* the view of the Non-Causationists is rejected: if human action has no element of free choice, then there is also no human responsibility for evils suffered. It is rejected on ground that it is untrue to say that human action has in it no element of moral choice (*Jat.,* V:237). It is because the B. analysis begins from premise that conscious beings have freedom of moral choice that deterministic views are rejected. Starting from same premise, Buddhists reject also any doc. of divine predestination of life of man (→ *Predestination*). The Buddha rejected both the view called Determinism—that the course of human events is unalterably fixed and determined by antecedent factors, and that of complete Indeterminism—that all which man suffers occurs as matter of chance without causal connection with antecedent moral choices.

K. N. Jayatilleke, *Early Buddhist Theory of Knowledge* (1963), pp. 410–1, 444–6, 469; Piyadassi Thera, *The Buddha's Ancient Path* (1964), pp. 62–4; I. B. Horner, *The Middle Length Sayings* (1959), vol. 3, pp. 3–14; E. M. Hare, *The Book*

Deva

of the Gradual Sayings (repr. 1953), vol. 3, pt. III, ch. VII, 'The Great Chapter.'

Deva Pali and Skt. term meaning 'a heavenly being' or lit. 'a shining one' (rel. to Lat. *deus*). Used in B. cosmology for beings who inhabit the heavenly sphere, invisible to mortals. D.'s are not strictly 'gods' in any absolute sense, since they are not 'eternal,' but are subject, together with all other sentient beings, to law of rebirth. Acc. to B. → Cosmology, D.'s are found in all three realms into which universe is divided: *Kāma-dhātu; Rūpa-dh.* and *Arūpa-dh.;* although they are most usually thought of as inhabiting highest level of first of these, i.e. the sensual world, or *Kāma-dhātu.* They are opposed by the → *Asuras,* disembodied spirits gen. of an evil or hostile disposition. Acc. to the B. *Suttas,* when the hosts of D.'s increase and the hosts of Asuras decrease, this is a happy situation for mortal men, just as it is inauspicious when reverse occurs (→ Demons).
J. Masson, *La Religion Populaire dans la Canon Bouddhique Pali* (1942); T. O. Ling, *Buddhism and the Mythology of Evil* (1962).

Devadatta A cousin of the → Buddha who, hearing him discourse on his return to Kapilavatthu after his Enlightenment, was converted and joined the → Sangha. He became a highly honoured member of Sangha, but about 8 years before Buddha's death he grew jealous of him, and won over the King of Magadha, → Ajatasattu, as his ally in conspiring to bring about his death: three attempts were made, once with a gang of assassins, who were overcome by Buddha's presence and converted; once by D.'s hurling a stone at him of which only a splinter struck his foot; once by letting loose a wild elephant, which was calmed and subdued by the Buddha. D. then set about causing dissension in the Sangha; he advocated a more strict asceticism than Buddha favoured, who replied that those who wished might follow such rules but he would not make them binding upon all monks. D. then began to proclaim that Buddha was not a true ascetic, and was given to luxurious living; he thus succeeded in drawing away 500 newly

ordained Vajjian monks from Vesālī. D. died of an internal injury which caused blood to come from his mouth; acc. to the commentaries, in his last moment he declared that his only refuge was the Buddha. Acc. to trad., he was destined to suffer a long period in hell before being reborn. His story is told in the *Cullavagga* of the → *Vinaya-Pitaka;* he is mentioned also in the → *Saddharma-Pundarika,* and in the commentary on the → *Dhammapada.*
Malalasekere, *D.P.P.N.,* vol. I, pp. 1106ff.

Deva-Dūta In B. thought, the 3 *deva-dūtas* or messengers to man from the heavenly beings (→ Deva) are age, disease and death. These remind man of his mortal condition, and serve to encourage him to seek more earnestly the holy life. Acc. to trad. account of life of the Buddha, it was when, as a young man, he saw, on the same day, a very old man, a sick man and a corpse being carried out to the burning ghat, that he was stirred to consider the meaning of human striving (→ Buddha, Gotama).

Devānam-Piyatissa (Lit. 'Tissa, beloved of the gods') The honorific title of the King of Ceylon (247–207 BC), under whose patronage Buddhism was introduced into → Ceylon. The connotation of title would be, perhaps, 'His sacred majesty, Tissa.' He is credited with having had various important B. buildings erected, notably the 'Great Monastery' (Mahā Vihāra) at → Anuradhapura, which was for cents. the home of the orthodox → Theravādins. The events of the D.'s reign, which marked beginning of B. hist. of Ceylon, are described in the Pali → *Mahāvamsa.*

Devil, The (Buddh.) → Māra, the Evil One.

Devotions Acts of devotion constitute import. part of the Buddh. relig. life, both for monks and laymen, as the many popular manuals and books of worship publ. in Asian countries such as Ceylon and Burma testify. Such a manual has recently been published in Eng. for Western Buddhists. B. devotion consists primarily of recollection of greatness and honour of Buddha, his Doctrine (→ Dhamma), and his Order (Sangha), i.e. the 'three jewels' (Tri-Ratna), the praising of them, and commitment of oneself to them. Such an act of devotion, together with affirming of the 5

Devotee, Lay

moral precepts, is the common daily practice of both monks and laymen. This may be performed, in case of laymen, at a small shrine in house or in a public place such as pagoda or temple. Often, and espec. at the pagoda, to such devotions will be added the offering of flowers, lights and incense, together with reciting of verse which connects what is offered with some specific B. intention: thus 'I offer this good light in memory of the Enlightened One; by meritorious action I would dispel the darkness.' The posture for devotion is usually kneeling, with hands placed in front of face, palms together, and at certain points in the devotions there will be complete prostration, with forehead touching ground. Corporate devotions, with chanting of verses, often from scripture or from devotional writings, take place in the monastic assembly hall; in these the monks take part daily, in morning and evening; on B. holy days (full moon and new moon) lay people may join in the special devotions of day. There is no set form for these; the length and order of devotions may be left to senior monk who conducts them. On holy days there will also frequently be a sermon, in which a senior monk explains some aspect of B. teaching or reminds his hearers of moral disciplines of the B. life.

K. Wells, *Thai Buddhism* (1960); Pe Maung Tin, *Buddhist Devotion and Meditation* (1964); Saddhatissa Mahathera, *Handbook of Buddhists* (1956); T. O. Ling, *Buddha, Marx and God* (1966), ch. 6.

Devotee, Lay → Upāsaka.

Dhamma (Pali); **Dharma** (Skt.) Word occurring frequently and in many connections in Buddhism; it has no one gen. applicable meaning. D. is trans. into Eng. variously as religion, truth, doctrine, righteousness, virtue, essence, elemental ultimate constituent or 'atom,' phenomena, nature, law, norm, property, and entity. Some meanings are common usage in Indian relig. gen.; others are peculiar to Buddhism (e.g. 'ultimate constituent'). The Skt. root *dhṛ*, from which it is derived, has sense of 'bearing,' 'upholding,' 'supporting,' 'that which forms a foundation.' → Buddhaghosa, in his commentary on the *D.N.*, distinguishes 4 meanings of D.: (1) having ref. to good conduct (2) moral instruction (3) doc. of Buddha as contained in the scriptures (4) cosmic law (*D.A.,* I, 99). In his comy. on the → *Dhamma-Saṅganī,* he gives another list of four meanings: (1) doctrine (2) condition, or causal antecedent (3) moral quality (4) what is 'phenomenal,' as opp. to what is 'noumenal' or 'substantial.' The primary meanings in B. usage are, therefore, doctrine, righteousness, condition and phenomenon. Of these, most prominent is the first; by this is understood the Dhamma (Dharma) of the Buddha, one of the *three jewels* (Tri-Ratna) of the B. system: the Buddha, the Dhamma, the → Sangha. In this usage, D. means the universal truth proclaimed by Buddha. The D. is itself ontologically anterior even to the Buddha, who is also the expression or historical manifestation of the D. (→ Tri-Kāya). Buddhas appear, at intervals, in course of time; they come and go, but the D., as it were, goes on for ever. In this usage, D. corresponds in some sense to Gk. concept of the *Logos.* It is in the D., in this sense, that the Buddh. 'takes refuge' (→ *Tri-Ratna*). The discourses of Buddha, since they set forth this ultimate reality, or truth, of the D., are referred to collectively as the D., the meaning here being that of 'doctrine' or 'teaching.' A life lived consonantly with the truth, set forth by Buddha, is a life characterised by D. or, in this case, 'righteousness.'

The sense of 'that which is ultimate' underlies also the special usage of *dhamma* (usually repr. by a small initial letter) by the Theravādin school, who signify by this 'an ultimate constituent,' i.e. of human existence. The → Theravādins hold that there is a certain fixed and limited number of such 'atoms' of existence (some being material, but the majority psychological); it is this view-point which is repr. in their → Abhidhamma lit., a view for which they were criticised by the Mahāyāna schools (→ Mādhyamika). *The Pali Text Society's Pali-English Dictionary* (1921), p. 171; W. Geiger, *Pali Dhamma* (1920) (for philology); E. Conze, *Buddhist Thought in India* (1962), pt. I, sect. 7; D. T. Suzuki, *Studies in the Lankavatara Sutra* (1930), pp. 154–6.
Dhammapada An import. and widely known book of the

Dhamma-Cakkappavattana Sutta

Thv. Buddh. Pali canon; it is incl. in the 5th (*Khuddaka*) *Nikaya* of the *Sutta-Pitaka*. It consists of 423 verses, each verse consisting of a proverb or pithy saying concerning the Buddh. life. The verses are arranged in 26 chapters, acc. to types of verses, or subject: e.g. ch. 1, 'The Twin-Verses,' where verses are paired, dealing with opposite aspects of a single statement; 2nd ch. deals with 'Vigilance'; 3rd with 'Thought,' and so on. The whole book is an anthology of sayings; it is the work of a fairly early editor; many verses occur in other canonical texts. The word *dhammapada* means lit. 'a line of the → *Dhamma*' (i.e. the Doctrine), or a portion thereof. The sayings or proverbs, of which book consists, are well known in Buddh. countries, espec. those of → Thv. school of S.E. Asia, being memorised by monks; often by lay people also, who may possess copies of book. Thv. Buddhists regard the D. as brief summary of essent. teaching of Buddha. The Pali text was ed. by Suriyogoda Sumangala, and pub. in Roman script by the PTS in 1914. E.T.'s have been made by Max Müller (*S.B.E.*, vol. X, 1898), by S. Radhakrishnan, 1950 (repr. 1958) and various others.

The D. is also title of a similar collection of Buddh. proverbs in Gandhārī Prakrit, partly recovered in mod. times and ed. by J. Brough; about $\frac{3}{8}$ of orig. text is still missing. Brough has estimated that the Pali and Prakrit versions had a common nucleus of about 330 verses, and considers that both collections had an earlier, common source, which different schools have used, each having 'to a greater or less degree modified, rearranged or expounded a common fund of inherited materials.'

W. Geiger, *Pali Literature and Language* (1956); P. V. Bapat (ed.), *2500 Years of Buddhism* (1956), pp. 156–8; S. Radhakrishnan, *The Dhammapada: Pali Text* (E.T. and Notes) (1950, repr. 1958); John Brough, *The Gandhārī Dharmapada* (1962).

Dhamma-Cakkappavattana Sutta Name of Buddh. Sutta which is trad. regarded as the Buddha's first sermon, viz. 'The Setting in Motion (*pavattana*) of the Wheel (*cakka*) of the Dhamma.' This is said to have been preached in the Deer Park at Isipatana, near Banares, on full moon day of the month of Āsālha. The discourse contains the fundamental teaching of the Buddha, viz., (1) the necessity for avoidance of the two extremes of sensual indulgence and fanatical asceticism (both of these were features of the anc. Indian scene) (2) the → Four Holy Truths and → Eightfold Path; although latter is regarded by some scholars as a formulation of Buddh. scheme of life, developed somewhat later as an elaboration of the earlier three-fold way. The *Sutta* occurs in the Pali canon in the *Samyutta-Nikaya* (V:420) and in the *Vinaya* (I:10f.); the name, *Dhamma-Cakkappavattana*, however, is applied to it as a title only in refs. to it in later Pali literature, e.g. in *Jāt.* I:82; in commentary on the *Dīgha-Nikaya* I:2, etc. Skt. versions of it are found in the → *Lalita-Vistara,* and in the → *Mahāvastu.* The 'setting in motion' or 'turning' of the 'wheel of Dhamma' is regarded as one of the 4 great events of Buddha's life, the other 3 being the birth, enlightenment, and passing into *parinibbāna.*

Dhamma-Saṅganī Pali B. work of the Theravādin school. It forms part of third section of the canonical writings, viz. the → *Abhidhamma-Pitaka,* of which it is the 1st of 7 books. The title means lit. a 'recital of *dhammas.*' It consists of an enumeration of various poss. psychic elements, or → *dhammas,* and brings together into systematic arrangement terms which occur throughout earlier books of the → *Sutta-Pitaka.* The terms are arranged in numerical groups, in twos, threes, and fours; the primary concern is with the ethical significance of these terms. It is said to have been trans. into Sinhalese by King Vijayabahu of Ceylon, but this trans. is now lost. It was trans. by Mrs. Caroline Rhys-Davids into Eng. as 'A Buddhist Manual of Psychological Ethics.' A commentary on the D.-S. was composed by the great Theravādin writer → Buddhaghosa, entitled *Atthasālinī.*

Nyanatiloka, *Guide through the Abhidhamma-Pitaka* (1957), pp. 12–23.

Dharma-kāya In Buddh. thought, one of the 3 aspects of the Buddha-nature (→ Buddha-Kāya).

Dharmapada → Dhammapada.

Dhātu

Dhātu Term widely used in Buddhism, meaning gen. 'an element,' being etymologically closely rel. to → *dhamma.* It is used in various different senses, of which principal ones are: (A) The physical 'elements,' which in pop. B. thought were earth, water, fire and wind, and were regarded as primary forms of matter (B) the 18 D.'s or psycho-physical elements of consciousness, viz: (1) eye (2) ear (3) nose (4) tongue (5) body (6) visible object (7) audible object (8) odorous object (9) gustative object (10) tactile object (11) visual consciousness (12) aural consciousness (13) olfactory consciousness (14) gustatory consciousness (15) touch-consciousness (16) the mind (17) mental object (18) mental consciousness. (C) the 3 'elements' or spheres into which cosmos is divided in B. thought, viz: (1) *Kāma-dhātu,* the sensual sphere (2) *Rūpa-d.,* the fine-material sphere (3) *Arūpa-d.,* the immaterial sphere (→ Cosmology). The word is used also of group of 6 'elements,' viz: solid, liquid, heat, motion, space and consciousness; also of remains of mortal body after cremation. In this latter sense of 'relic,' the word is a component of *dhātu-garbha,* i.e. 'relic-chamber,' which in its shortened form is known as → *dagaba.*

Dhātu-Kathā Name of a book of the Pali canonical scriptures of the Theravāda Buddh. It is one of the 7 books of third section of canon, i.e. of the → *Abhidhamma-Pitaka,* and is usually listed as 5th. The title means 'Discussion of the → *Dhātus* or 'elements,' which in this case means largely the psychological elements occurring in the more spiritually advanced. The book serves as a supplement to the → *Dhamma-Sanganī*; it may have been designed as such. A commentary on the *D.-K.* was composed by → Buddhaghosa.

Dhātuvaṃsa Pali Buddh. work, attr. to writer named Dhamma-kitti. The work, which is in form of poem, tells story of sacred Tooth-relic of the Buddha, said to have been taken to Ceylon from India at begin. of 4th cent. In addition to narrative-material derived from the → *Mahāvaṃsa,* the poem makes use of other local trads. of Ceylon, and was prob. composed in early part of 13th cent. CE. The text was published in Roman script by Rhys-Davids in 1884 in *Journal of the Pali Text Society.*

Dhyāna → *Jhāna.*

Diamond Sūtra Name of a Mahāyāna Buddh. treatise, belonging to type of lit. known as → *Prajnā-Pāramitā Sūtras.*

Digha-Nikāya (Pali), **Dirghāgama** (Skt.) 1st of the 5 major divisions (→ *Nikayas*) of the Buddh. *Sutta-Pitaka,* or Discourse-Collection, which in turn is second of 3 main divisions of canonical scriptures of Thv. (Pali) Buddhism. The *D.N.* consists of 34 basic lit. units known as *suttas,* or 'connected discourses,' i.e. usually of Buddha. The Mhy. collection, the *Dirghagama,* which exists in a Chinese version, consists of 30 sutras; 27 of these are common to both collections. The title *Digha/Dirgha,* meaning 'long,' refs. to fact that the DN/DA contain some of the longest *suttas,* although not all are long compared with *suttas* contained in other *Nikayas;* about 16 of the *suttas* of the DN are 'long.' The 34 *Suttas* of DN are arranged in 3 sections, or *vaggas.* The first *vagga* contains 13 *suttas,* whose titles are as follows: (1) Brahmajāla (2) Samannaphala (3) Ambattha (4) Sonadanda (5) Kutadanta (6) Mahali (7) Jaliya (8) Kassapasihanāda (9) Potthapāda (10) Subha (11) Kevaddha (12) Lohicca (13) Tevijja. The second *vagga* contains 10 *Suttas:* (14) Mahāpadāna (15) Mahānidāna (16) Mahāparinibbāna (17) Mahāsudassana (18) Janavasabha (19) Mahā-Govinda (20) Mahā-samaya (21) Sakkapanha (22) Mahā-Satipatthāna (23) Pāyāsi. The third *vagga* contains 11 *Suttas:* (24) Pātika (25) Udambarika-sīhanāda (26) Cakkavatti-sīhanāda (27) Aggañña (28) Sampasadaniya (29) Pāsādika (30) Lakkhana (31) Sigālovāda (32) Ātānātiya (33) Sangīti (34) Dasuttara. The better known and more import. of these are (1) the Brahmajala, which enumerates both popular superstitions and pastimes of anc. India in early Buddh. period; also different philosophical theories of same period; (2) the Samannaphala, which sets out doctrines of six other non-Buddh. teachers of the time, and the great benefits or fruits (*phala*) of life of the Samanna, or Buddh. monk; (3) (4) and (5) are all concerned with refuting claims of the brahmans of anc. India to be a social and relig. elite; (14), which sets

forth legends of the six Buddhas reputed to have preceded Gotama the Buddha; (15), which provides exposition of Law of Dependent Origination (→ Paticca-Samuppada); and poss. most import. of all (16), which describes in detail events of last few weeks of Buddha's life, his entry into 'final' → nibbāna, or pari-nibbāna, the ceremonial cremation of his body and distribution of remains and building of → Stupas over them; (31) is import., espec. for Buddh. lay people, since it contains what are set out as proper duties to be observed by them in their various roles as parents, children, masters, servants, teachers, pupils, etc. (→→ Mahā-Parinibbāna Sutta; Mahāpadāna Sutta).
Dialogues of the Buddha, 3 vols., trans. and ed. by T. W. and C. A. F. Rhys-Davids (1899–1921, repr. 1965–66); A. A. G. Bennett, *Long Discourses of the Buddha,* I–XVI, n.d.

Dipankara Name of a legendary Buddha, reputed to have lived long ages ago; the first of 24 Buddhas who are held to have preceded Gotama the Buddha (→ Buddhas (other than Gotama)). The details concerning him are all of gigantic kind: he was 80 cubits tall, always attended by 84,000 saints (*arahants*), he lived for 100,000 years; the *stupa* in which his remains were enshrined was 36 yoganas high. He is remembered espec. for fact that, acc. to legend, it was while D. was Buddha that Gotama, who became the Buddha in 6th cent. BC, and was then an ascetic named Sumedha, made his vow to become a Buddha.
Buddhavamsa, II, pp. 107f.; Malalasekere, *D.P.P.N.,* vol. I, p. 1087; *Mahāvastu,* I, pp. 231–9; E. Conze, *Buddhist Scriptures* (1959), pp. 20–4.

Dīpavamsa The oldest of B. Pali hist. chronicles. The title means 'The Island Lineage (or Chronicle),' and indic. contents of work, viz. the hist. of island of → Ceylon; the work tells of intro. of Buddhism to island and continues story up to end of reign of Mahāsena (CE 325–52). It is thought to have been compiled some time after 352 and before *c.* 450. The compiler appears to have used an older work, the → Atthakathā, as main source. The hist. reliability of the D. has been questioned in mod. times (e.g. by R. O. Franke); but Geiger held that its frequent agreements with contemporary trads. of India was sufficient guarantee that it was 'the vehicle of an old hist. tradition.' It is recorded that a 5th cent. King of Ceylon, Dhatusena (460–78), provided endowment for regular recitals of the D.

W. Geiger, *Pali Literature and Language* (2nd edn. 1956), pp. 27f.; G. R. Malalasekere, *D.P.P.N.,* vol. I, p. 1088.

Discipline The disciplinary code which governs life of the Buddh. monastic community, or → Sangha, is contained in the *Pātimokkha* (lit. 'that which is binding'), an anc. text which forms part of the B. → *Vinaya-Pitaka*. The *P. Sutta* is gen. held to be nucleus and oldest part of the Pali *Vinaya-Pitaka*. It is extant also in Skt. versions (*Prātimoksa Sūtra*), which have been discovered in mod. times. It has 2 parts: one set of rules for monks, the *Bhikkhu-patimokkha;* and another for nuns, the *Bhikkhuni-p.* The scheme followed is an enumeration of offences in descending order of seriousness: first, those for which penalty is expulsion from community viz: sexual misconduct, theft, murder, boasting of power to perform miracles; second, those which merit temporary suspension (with poss. of re-admission, if offender was subsequently found worthy), and which incl. offences concerned with improper relations between men and women, independent setting up of a hermitage, making of false accusations, causing dissension and so on. The 3rd section (2 kinds of offences), the 4th (26 offences), the 5th (92 offences), the 6th (4 offences) all require restitution (where applicable) and formal confession of guilt before community as proper method of dealing with offences concerned. The 7th section consists virtually of advice on matters of etiquette—how to eat inoffensively, enter a sick-room, etc. The 8th section sets out seven ways for settling disputes within community. The complete set of these rules is to be recited by monks in full assembly on full-moon and new-moon days every month (→ Monasticism).

S.B.E., vol. XIII, pp. 1–69; P. V. Bapat (ed.), *2500 Years of Buddhism* (1959), pp. 163–5; S. Dutt, *Buddhist Monks and Monasteries of India* (1962).

Chinese and Japanese Buddhism: Except for its ethical

Disease

codes and its teaching concerning need for self-D., → Buddhism imposed no formal D. on the laity. Within the Buddh. order, each monastery took over training and D. of its novices and monks. The large corpus of Vinaya rules was studied, and generally observed, incl. the 250 prohibitions of the Pratimoksa and the 58 prohibitions of the *Sūtra of Brahma's Net*. But many of the D.-rules devised for Indian Buddhism were found impracticable in China and Japan and were tacitly ignored, e.g. rules concerning money, the holding of personal property, the duty of begging, etc. The *Pure Rules of Pai Chang* (*Pai Chang Ch'ing Kuei*) composed by a Ch'an monk of 9th cent. CE (d. 814), revised and re-edited frequently during subsequent cents., exerted great authority in Buddh. monasteries down to present day. In addition, each monastery drew up its own code of rules (*kuei yüeh*). In gen., the D. of → Ch'an (Zen) monasteries was harsher and more exacting than that of → Pure Land monasteries. Certain monasteries became famous for strictness of their D., e.g. Chin Shan and Kao-min-Ssu in China. Punishment for offences took various forms and varied from monastery to monastery. In some, corporal punishment was common. The heaviest penalty was expulsion from the monastery, normally the prerogative of the abbot.

H. Welch, *The Practice of Buddhism in China, 1900–1950* (1967), pp. 105ff.

Disease Acc. to popular B. trad., disease is one of the 'messengers' (*dūta*) from the heavenly beings (*devas*), reminding man of his mortal condition (→ Deva-Dūta).

Disease and Medicine (China–Japan) in the popular religs. of E. Asia, nervous disorders and diseases are usually attr. to supernatural agencies. Consequently, in their cure, though medicines are extensively used, they are supplemented by such practices as faith-healing, exorcism, spiritism and provision by priests of charms, amulets, magical potions and the like.

Yao Shih Fo, or the Buddha Physician (*Baishaj-yaguru*) is worshipped by Buddh. in China, Japan, Tibet and Manchuria. Having received healing powers from Gautama, he dis-

penses spiritual medicine to those who worship him.
The arts of medicine were introduced into Korea and
Japan by Buddh. monks, who took over Chi. medical practice. Until intro. of Western medicine, Chi. theories concerning disease and its cure were gen. accepted throughout Far East. Even today much of influence of modern
Buddh. and Shinto sects in Japan is attributable to reputation of their practitioners for success in faith-healing, exorcism and the like.

Ditthi (Pali); **Dṛsti** (Skt.) Lit. 'a view,' word used in Buddhism
for a speculative opinion; it normally refers to one that is
discountenanced, on ground that it is based not on reason,
but on desire. Most prominent example is belief in the permanent, individual ego, or *atta,* ref. to as *atta-ditthi,* against
which B. teaching was partic. directed. This (wrong or perverted) view takes 2 forms, acc. to B. teaching: either the
'eternity-belief' (*sassata-ditthi*), i.e. that there is an eternal
individual ego which is independent of physical and mental processes and persists eternally; or the 'annihilation-be-
lief' (*uccheda-ditthi*), i.e. that human existence is nothing
other than physical and mental processes, and will, at
death of individual, be annihilated. The 1st *Sutta* in the →
Dīgha-Nikaya of the Pali *Sutta-Pitaka,* entitled *Brahma-jāla
Sutta,* sets out 62 different false speculative 'views' or theories concerning nature of human existence, based on the
initial false premise of existence of a permanent self or
ego.
Nyanatiloka, *Buddhist Dictionary* (1956), pp. 47–8; T. W.
Rhys-Davids, *Dialogues of the Buddha, S.B.B.,* vol. II (1899),
pp. 1–55.

Divyāvadāna Buddh. anthol. of stories of the → *Avadāna*
type; title means 'the heavenly Avadānas.' The collection
incls. very old material derived from → Hīnayāna schools.
The D., as it stands, is confused and disorderly, being work
of a compiler who borrowed *verbatim* from number of earlier sources. One of more import. of these appears to have
been entitled 'The Book of King Asoka,' which is thought
to have orig. in → Mathurā approx. 150–50 BC, and is known
only in Chinese trans. Other materials are taken from lit. of

various periods, the work of compilation having been carried out at some time during 4th cent. CE. One of best known and most import. stories is the strange tale of how → Māra, the Evil One, was 'converted' by a Buddh. monk named Upagupta; this is thought to have been based on a popular 'morality play' or Buddh. drama, well known in the early cents.

M. Winternitz, *Hist. of Indian Literature* (1933), vol. II, pp. 284–90.

Doctrine, Buddh. → Dhamma.

Dōgen (CE 1200–53). Founder of the Sōtō division of the → Zen sect of Japanese Buddhism centred in the Eiheiji temple in the province of Echizen. The greatest figure in Jap. Zen, and venerated by all Japanese Buddhs. as a → bodhisattva. A man of incorruptible integrity, genuine humanity, creative thought and relig. intuition. Of noble parentage, he was orphaned when 7 years of age. Was ordained in CE 1213, and journeyed to China in 1223, where after much searching he achieved enlightenment under the famous → Ch'an master, Ju-ching (1163–1268). Returned to Japan in 1227; under his leadership the first fully independent Zen monastery, the Kōshōhōringji, was built in 1236. Here D. attracted many gifted disciples, including numerous lay people, both men and women. Teaching that the essence of man and all things is the Buddha-nature, which is realised by purification of the ego, the elimination of all selfish desires and complete surrender of self, D. gave precedence above all else to relig. practice. He cultivated the practice of Zazen, or sitting upright with legs crossed in meditation. He saw in Zazen the realisation and fulfilment of the whole law of Buddhism, since the unity of practice and enlightenment is rooted in the one Buddha-nature. Philosophically, his monistic pantheism equated the phenomenal world with the Absolute, leaving no room for transcendence; but, as a great religious leader, he stressed the importance of faith and relig. devotion to the Buddha. D. eliminated the endless stages on the way to salvation by finding in Zen a way of perfect unity. Unlike many Zen masters, D. advocated the diligent reading of the sūtras, the respectful veneration of sacred Buddh. objects, and considered the → kōan as of secondary importance. He condemned the sectarianism of Buddhism, and refused to recognise existence of the Sōtō sect as such. His outstanding literary work is the *Shōbōgenzō,* of which a modern edition was published in Tokyo in 1939–43.

H. Dumoulin, *A Hist. of Zen Buddhism* (1963).

Dōshō (CE 629–700). The most prominent Buddh. leader in Japan in 7th cent., who went to China and studied → Yogacara teachings under the famous → Hsüan Tsang, and introduced the relig. philosophy of → Hossō to Japan. Though he left no writings, D. was a pioneer in Japan of Buddh. philosophy, practised mystical meditation, and spent the last years of his life in actively promoting the building of Buddh. monasteries, almshouses, etc. He was a pioneer in the practice of cremation in Japan.

M. Anesaki, *Hist. of Japanese Relig.* (1930).

Drama, Relig., China In 8th cent. CE the T'ang emperor Ming Huang founded a college known as the Pear Garden for training of singers and dancers of both sexes. Whether these court entertainers were actors is uncertain; but 'youths of the pear garden' became term to designate the dramatic fraternity in China. It was during the T'ang Dynasty that Buddh. monks propagated and popularised the faith by enacted scenes from Buddh. history and legend (similar to Christ. miracle plays), in towns and villages throughout the land.

Japan Drama in Japan was in its beginning closely associated with relig. It grew out of the pantomimic dance, known as *Kagura,* performed from antiquity at Shinto festivals to sound of music. When dance and music were supplemented by spoken dialogue, the result was *Nō* drama, which, dating from about the 14th cent. CE, drew its inspiration from the Buddhism of the Nara period, and from Chinese and Indian influences. At first the Nō plays were purely relig. performances acted at temples and shrines and intended to propitiate Shinto and Buddh. divinities. Later Nō theatres came under the patronage of the shoguns. The librettos of most plays were the work of Buddh.

Dress, Relig.

monks or persons impregnated with the spirit of Buddhism. Embracing within their scope legendary lore, relig. sentiment and classical poetry, their object was to promote piety. The *kyōgen* or satirical farce, though acted on the same stage as the Nō, was different in character and had different actors. Whilst the Nō are permeated with relig. idealism, the *kyōgen* reflect a more secular realism.

Dress, Relig. The primary feature of Buddh. relig. dress is its simplicity. The only distinctive dress used is that of the *bhikkhu* or monk, which in India and Ceylon and S.E. Asia is a saffron coloured cotton robe. This is usually presented to him by relatives or friends at his → Ordination, and renewed by laymen at annual ceremony when robes are presented to the → Sangha: the materials for these robes are usually spun and woven in course of one night by lay women of local village or township; the ceremony is a great social occasion. The robes consist of (1) the *antaravāsaka,* or sarong, which covers lower half of body from the waist (2) the *uttarasanga,* or upper garment, which in Thailand is called also the *cīvara* (elsewhere gen. term for monks' clothing) (3) the *sanghāti,* a long piece of cloth about 8 ft. by 10 ft., folded into 12 folds, somewhat in shape of a stole, and worn over left shoulder, above the *uttarāsanga;* this is worn at relig. ceremonies, and only by fully ordained monks, not by novices.

Dukkha (Pali); **Duhkha** (Skt.) Term used in Buddh. trad. for one of the 3 characteristic marks of existence or → Ti-Lakkhana. Variously trans. into Eng. as 'suffering,' 'ill,' 'evil,' 'unsatisfactoriness,' the term covers all these meanings. The affirmation that all human existence is characterised by D. is the first of the Buddh. → Four Holy Truths.

Dvi-yāna → Yāna.

E

Education, Buddh. → Monasteries.

Ego → Anatta.

Eightfold Path The holy, or noble (*arya*), Eightfold Path (*at-thangika-magga*) is a schematic description of the Buddh. life. It has been noted that this 8-fold exposition of the Buddh. way is not found in some of earliest Buddh. sacred texts, e.g. the → Sutta-Nipāta, and that it may therefore be a later expansion of what in earlier texts is the *three*fold scheme of Buddh. life, viz: (1) initial faith (*saddha*), which ultimately becomes wisdom (*pannā*); (2) morality (*sīla*); (3) concentration, or meditation (*samādhi*). Each of these aspects is subdivided: faith, into right understanding and right thought; morality, into right speech, right bodily action, and right livelihood; meditation, into right (spiritual) effort, right mindfulness and right concentration. At a more advanced stage of Buddh. practice, what was initially an attitude of faith, namely the way of understanding and thinking, accepted on trust from the Buddha, becomes, because of experiential verification, direct perception of what was initially accepted in faith, i.e. wisdom. The diversification of the orig. threefold scheme may be set out as follows:

8-fold path

(i) *faith*
    1. right understanding⎱
    2. right thought   ⎰ = (iv) *wisdom*

(ii) *morality*
    ⎧1. right speech
    ⎨2. right bodily action
    ⎩3. right livelihood

Eightfold Path

(iii) *meditation*

{
1. right effort
2. right mindfulness
3. right concentration

The items of the 8-fold path are not to be understood as steps or stages, each of which must be mastered before one can progress to next. The progression, if there is any, is from the initial, preliminary attitude of faith to moral living as a whole; thence (without passing beyond, or abandoning, moral living) to meditation, which is possible on basis of precedent faith and moral living. Within the groups of items, e.g. *morality,* the separately listed items are to be practised concurrently; thus also with items under *meditation.* The 3-fold structure of the Buddh. way is ref. to in the → *Mahā-Parinibbāna Sutta* (I.12), where the Buddha, during last days, is repr. as discoursing to the monks 'on the nature of *sīla* (morality), *samādhi* (meditation), and *paññā* (wisdom)'—'great is the fruit, great the advantage of *meditation,* when surrounded by *morality;* great the advantage, great the fruit of *wisdom,* when surrounded by *meditation.*' This formula occurs in the *M.-P.Sutta,* as Rhys-Davids comments, 'as if it were a well-known summary' and is constantly repeated in the *Sutta.*

The amplification of these 3 items into the 8-fold scheme may be seen as a natural process of expansion and exposition, for benefit of Buddh. disciples. By *faith* is meant (1) acceptance of the kind of *understanding,* derived from Buddha, viz. understanding the world and human existence in terms of the → 4 Holy Truths, and (2) right mental attitudes, viz, a turning away from attitudes based on sensuous desire, malice, and cruelty. By *morality* is meant (3) right speech, viz., saying nothing that is untrue; (4) right bodily action, viz., abstaining from taking life, from stealing, from unlawful sexual pleasure; (5) right livelihood, viz. avoidance of such occupations as that of butcher, trader in arms, or in intoxicants, or drugs, or any other occupation out of keeping with Buddh. principles. By *meditation* is thus meant: (6) right effort, viz, the effort to avoid evil and unwholesome states of mind, and to develop and

110

maintain wholesome states; (7) right mindfulness, viz, a true awareness of physical body and of feelings (agreeable, disagreeable, or neutral) and of mental impressions; (8) right concentration, viz, the practice of 'one-pointedness' of mind (→ Samādhi). The outcome of practice of this 8-fold way is held to be the attainment of state of *wisdom,* that is state when right understanding and right mental attitudes become direct and immediate, where formerly they were based on *faith.* The 8-fold path is thus a systematic setting out of way that the tiniest germ of right understanding, beginning as an attitude of faith in the Buddha's knowledge, can grow eventually to highest state of enlightenment.

Eisai (Zenchō Kokushi, CE 1141–1215). The founder of Japanese → Zen Buddhism, who became a monk when still a boy, and was trained at the Tendai monastery on Mt. Hiei. Twice visited China (1168 and 1187), where, deeply impressed by the spirit of Ch'an, he became convinced that it could contribute towards a Buddhist awakening in Japan. E. received enlightenment in the Linchi sect, which he transplanted to Japan as Rinzai, building the first Rinzai temple, Shōfukuji, at Hakata in S. island of Kyushu in 1191. Opposed by Tendai monks on Mt. Hiei, he received protection and help from Shogun Minamoto Yoriie, who appointed him head of the Kenninji temple in Kyoto, built in 1202, which harboured Tendai and Shingon as well as Zen. E. intro. the Zen trad. to Kamakura, and became abbot of 3rd Rinzai temple, Jūfukuji. There he combined relig. fervour with national aspiration, expounded Zen meditation, and strove for recognition of Zen as an independent school. He composed a treatise on 'The Spread of Zen for the protection of the country.' Though not the first to introduce tea into Japan, he is regarded as the father of Jap. tea culture.

E. Takeda, 'Eisai,' in *Gendai Zen-Kōza* (2nd edn. 1956), pp. 198–205; H. Dumoulin, *Hist. of Zen Buddhism* (1963).

Eka-Yāna → Yāna.

Elders → Thera.

'Emptiness' → Śūñyata.

Enlightenment

Enlightenment → Bodhi.

Ennin (CE 794–864). Third patriarch of great Buddhist monastery on Mt. Hiei in Japan, he emphasised the occult mysticism of → Shingon. His diaries, containing account of his travels in T'ang Dynasty China, provide an important source for study of Chinese → Buddhism at period of its great expansion in that country.
E. O. Reischauer, *Ennin's Travels in T'ang China* (1955).

Envy Envy (Pali, *issā*) is regarded in Buddh. trad. as a mental factor (*cetasika*), producing unwholesome Karma. It comes 9th in a list of 14 unwholesome mental factors given in the → *Abhidhammattha-Sangaha* (Pt. II, §2, III).

Eschatology Term, *ex.* Grk. *eschata*, 'last things,' used to denote beliefs concerning death, judgment, purgatory, heaven and hell. With variations, this eschatological pattern occurs in all religs. Buddhism has no E. in the strict sense of term, as this is understood in Christianity, since there are no ultimately 'last things' so far as cosmos as whole is concerned (→ Eternity, Buddh.). So far as individual human existence is concerned, acc. to Buddh. thought, the consummation of this is in the 'deathless' state of → Nibbāna. Buddh. → cosmology has its heavens and hells, but no one is condemned to eternal existence in these; eventually the inhabitants of both the Buddh. heavens and hells will return to other levels of existence; in this respect the Buddh. hell is more akin to Christ. Only human beings can achieve *nibbāna,* hence the only strictly 'eschatological' moment for the Buddhist is moment when a man achieves awakening or enlightenment (→ Bodhi). Such E. ideas as the Chinese possess were intro. into China by → Buddhism, and largely taken over and adapted by Taoists. Buddhism, with its concept of rebirth, and cyclical view of time, envisaged great cosmic cycles (*kalpas*) through which the soul proceeds in countless rebirths until its final absorption in → Nirvana. Both Buddhism and Taoism teach that the soul, immediately after death, is led before tribunal of ten judges of the dead, who decide its fate with strict impartiality, after which it is taken to live for a period in one of the heavens or hells of Buddhist or Taoist mythology. Millennialist theories, connected with Chinese Buddhism, grew up with cult of → Maitreya (Mi Lo Fo), intro. into China in 4th cent. CE. Acc. to these theories, 3,000 years after the Buddha, Buddhism will have reached such a state of decline that Maitreya will appear and establish his millennial kingdom, and a new cycle of life with hope of redemption for all living creatures. It is thus that Chi. Buddhism inculcates hope that, at the last hour of a final dispensation (*mo-fa*), a great saviour and renewer will descend from the Tushita heaven to establish on earth a new era, leading to universal salvation.

K. L. Reichelt, *Truth and Tradition in Chinese Buddhism* (1927), pp. 87; 186ff.

Eternity The nearest approach to conception of eternity in Buddh. thought is the *kappa* (Pali) *kalpa* (Skt.), which is an inconceivably long period of time. The k. is divided into 4: period of world-dissolution; period of chaos; period of world-formation; period of world-continuation (*AN.IV.* 156). A simile, used in a discourse of Buddha (*SN.XV.*5), is as follows: 'Suppose, O monks, there was a huge rock of one solid mass, one mile long, one mile wide, one mile high, without split or flaw. And at the end of every 100 years a man should come and rub against it with a silken cloth. Then that huge rock would wear off and disappear quicker than a *Kappa.*' Of such world-periods (*kappas*), acc. to Buddha there have been many hundred thousands. In the Buddh. view of things there is no termination to process of world-dissolution, chaos, world-formation, continuation, nor to the number of Buddhas who will appear in course of this process (→→ Buddhas other than Gotama, Creation).

W. M. McGovern, *Manual of Buddhist Philosophy*, vol. 1, *Cosmology* (1923).

Ethics In Buddh. trad. the principles governing human conduct relate the characteristic *condition* of humanity (suffering, unease, ill (→ Dukkha), caused by the basic evil of → Desire) to the recognised *goal* of Buddh. endeavour, viz. complete enlightenment and → nirvāna. Buddh. ethics thus favours those attitudes and kinds of behaviour which help humanity towards ultimate goal of transcendental enlightenment; as an intermediate criterion, the goal of auspicious and wholesome rebirth is import.: whatever is conducive to this end is to be encouraged; whatever detracts is to be discouraged or renounced. The outworking of the Buddh. ethic is seen at the most elementary level in the 5 basic moral precepts, binding upon all Buddhists, monastic and lay; to these may be added, by lay people, a further 3, and by monks a further 5. It is explicated more fully in the formula called the → Eightfold Path, for both monks and laymen: for the monk it is set out in detail in the monastic rule of life called the *Patimokkha* (Pali)/*Pratimoksa* (Skt.). (→ Discipline, Buddh. Monastic). For lay people the outworking of the ethical principles governing their domestic and social inter-relationships is set forth in the well-known → *Sigālovāda Sutta*.

Evil, in Buddh. Thought There is no term in Buddh. usage which exactly corresponds to the term 'evil' in West. relig. usage; the nearest is → *dukkha* variously trans. 'ill,' 'suffering,' 'unsatisfactoriness,' 'evil.' Buddh. thought on subject of E. does not concern itself with origins; the fact of E. inclinations and attitudes is recognised, the reality of E. is affirmed, and way to overcoming and negating of such E. is proclaimed. In Buddh. thought, E. is most characteristically seen in its three basic roots: *lobha, dosa, moha* (greed, hatred, illusion). The degree to which these factors are present in the human mind, in varying degrees and combinations, determines from moment to moment the 'given' situation in which a human individual acts. The presence of the evil factors, at any given moment, is regarded as result of previous actions and attitudes (just as is also the presence of the opposite, good factors, in varying degrees). The situation is not envisaged, however, as one of mechanistic determinism. At each moment, confronted by a given combination of such factors produced by previous events, or finding himself in a certain given moral state, each individual is free to act; his action may perpetuate the moral state he is in, or change it, for better or worse, so that the immediately succeeding moment, the result of the preceding one, may be characterised by an intensification of the evil condition, or its alleviation. (→ Māra, The Evil One).

Excommunication The only kind of excommunication practised by Buddhists is that which is applied in case of fully ordained monk who is found guilty of one of the offences mentioned in the *Patimokkha* (→ Discipline, Buddh. Monastic), for which prescribed penalty is permanent expulsion from the Order (→ Sangha); sexual misconduct, theft, murder, boasting of supernatural powers. For offences of serious nature, other than these, the offender may be temporarily suspended, with prospect of readmission later, if found worthy. It will be noted that there is no E. on grounds of heretical beliefs; the unity of the Order is regarded as consisting primarily in a common discipline of life and standard of morality, rather than in a confession of belief. The four offences, for which the penalty is expulsion, are known as *pārājikā*, i.e., 'involving defeat': this may mean moral defeat suffered by individual concerned; it may refer also to defeat which has to this extent been suffered by Order as a whole, and threat to its proper nature which has been sustained.

S.B.E., vol. XIII, pp. 1ff.; S. Dutt, *Buddhist Monks and Monasteries of India* (1962), pp. 68f.

Exercises, Spiritual →→ Devotions Meditation

Extinction Where term 'extinction' occurs in Buddh. trad. it refers to E. of feeling and perception in the special state of meditation achieved only by one who attained mastery of the 8 → Jhānas, and is an → Anāgami or an → Arahant. It is incorrectly used in connection with state of *nirvāṇa,* if it is applied to the one who has achieved *n.* The state thus achieved is not one of 'extinction' or 'annihilation' of all existence; what has suffered total extinction, acc. to the Buddh. view, are the passions, greed, hatred, and illusion, which are the roots of all evil and suffering (→ *nibbāna,* i.e. *nirvāṇa*).

F

Fa Hsien Famous Chinese Buddhist monk and pilgrim. Surname—Shih. Born in Shansi, he was trained at Buddhist
centre in Ch'ang-an, the W. capital of China. He left
Ch'ang-an in CE 399 with several companions, to visit India
and Buddhist countries of W., in search of a complete
canon of Buddhist scriptures. After 6 years of adventurous
travel through C. Asia, he finally arrived in India with one
disciple, Tao Chêng. There he spent another 6 years in
travel and sojourn, and collected and copied sacred texts
of various schools. He returned by sea from Ceylon, visiting Sumatra, arriving home in CE 414. He inaugurated a period of intensive trans. work on Buddhist scriptures. He
wrote famous account of his travels, known as the *Fa Hsien
Chuan* ('The narrative of Fa Hsien'), and later as the *Fo Kuo
Chi* ('Record of the Buddhist Countries'), trans. into Eng. by
S. Beal (1869, and 1884), by J. Legge (1886), by H. A. Giles
(1923).
H. A. Giles, *The Travels of Fa Hsien* (1923, 3rd impr. 1959);
E.R.E., XII, pp. 841, 843.

Faith Faith (*saddhā,* Pali/*sraddhā,* Skt.) has an import. place
in the Buddh. scheme, both at the entry upon the Buddh.
way, and in perseverance in the way. F. is said to be a factor assoc. with any karmically wholesome state of consciousness whatsoever, at any stage of the relig. life. In a
more formal analysis, F. is said to be one of the 5 *balas,* or
powers assoc. with the Buddh. life, the other 4 being energy, mindfulness, concentration and wisdom. The initial
adoption of the 2 preliminary Buddh. attitudes, described
in the → Eightfold Path as right understanding and right
thought, is that stage of relig. life only poss. in faith; later,

116

what is accepted in faith is apprehended directly, and experientially confirmed. Primarily F. has the → Buddha, the → Dhamma, and → Sangha as its objects; but always with the eventual confirming of faith by direct apprehension in view. F. never depends on authority alone; experiential verification as the vindicating of F. is always held to be part of the intention of F. Jayatilleke describes this as 'provisional acceptance . . . for the purposes of verification.' The same writer has analysed F., in the Buddh. context, as of 3 kinds: affective, conative, and cognitive. Affective F. is very close to → *bhakti* or devotion, and produces serene pleasure (*pīti*); conative faith produces spiritual energy (*viriya*); cognitive faith, or 'belief,' is the antidote to doubt (*vicikiccha*) and delusion (*moha*), since it is a rational faith.

K. N. Jayatilleke, *Early Buddhist Theory of Knowledge* (1963), pp. 383–401.

The → Mahayana Buddhism of China and Japan, and in particular the → Amida sects, developed a doctrine of salvation by F. A distinction is made between the Buddha's grace and our F., both being recognised as essential. As in Christianity, the question was even raised as to whether F. is not itself the free gift of grace. The centrality of Saving F. is notably developed in the treatise, *Ch'i Hsin Lun* (*Awakening of Faith in the Mahayana*, E. T. D. T. Suzuki, 1900, Y. S. Hakeda, 1967) which has had an immense influence in Chi. and Jap. Buddhism. There it is argued that 'fundamental' F. is joyous recollection of 'Suchness' (*chen ju*). Such 'fundamental F.' is finally attained by (1) F. in the illimitable merits of Buddha, resulting in worshipping and reverencing him, (2) F. in the benefits of → Dharma, leading to practice of charity, morality, patience, energy and tranquillity with insight, and (3) F. in the → Sangha in which one's identity with all the Buddhas and → bodhisattvas is realised.

Family and Social Duties For the Buddh. monk the relig. life means renunciation of home and family life, and membership instead in the 'clan' of the Buddha. For the Buddh. layman, however, the relationships of family life are subject of specific guidance from Buddha. For Buddhists of S.

Family and Social Duties

Asia this is set forth in its best-known form in the *Sigālo-vāda Sutta* (part of → *Digha-Nikaya*). This consists of advice reputedly given by Buddha to the 'young householder' on his duty in various social roles: duty to parents, to teachers, to wife and children, to friends and companions, to servants and to relig. perceptors. In each case, 5 responsibilities are mentioned: (1) towards parents, to support them, perform duties for them, keep trad. of the family, maintain family lineage, and make oneself worthy of them (2) towards children; in showing love for them, he must restrain them from vice, exhort them to virtue, train them for a profession, contract suitable marriages for them and in due time hand over to them their inheritance (3) towards teachers, in order to honour them, he must rise in salutation, attend upon them, show eagerness to learn, offer personal service and pay attention when being taught; (4) concerning pupils, he should pass on to them the learning or training which he has himself received, ensure that they retain what they are taught, make them thoroughly conversant with every art, speak well of them among friends and companions, and provide for their safety. Husbands and wives have reciprocal responsibilities; the husband is to respect his wife, be courteous to her, be faithful, hand over authority to her, and provide her with adornment; the wife is to see that her duties are well performed, offer hospitality to both his and her kin, be faithful, watch over her husband's goods and show skill and industry in business. Similarly, reciprocal responsibilities are laid upon masters and servants: masters are to assign their servants work acc. to their strength, to supply them with food and wages, to care for them in sickness, share any unusual delicacies with them, and grant them leave of absence from time to time; servants, in return, are to rise before their master in the morning, go to rest after he does at night, be content with what they receive, do their work well, and maintain their master's good reputation. Similar reciprocity of generosity, courtesy, benevolence, fairness and keeping of promises is enjoined upon friends and companions. Finally, the reciprocal roles of relig. preceptors and householders are described: the householder is to show affection to his preceptors in act and word and thought, offer them hospitality, and supply their temporal needs; the relig. preceptor is to restrain householder from evil, exhort him to good, be kindly disposed towards him, teach him what he does not know, correct him when he makes mistakes and reveal to him the way to heaven.

The responsibilities of a young wife to her husband are described at length in the *Uggaka Sutta,* found in the → *Anguttara-Nikaya.* A gen. dissertation on social duties is found in the *Mahāmangala Sutta* of the → Sutta–Nipāta. In Mhy. Buddhism the ideal householder is described in the *Vimala-kirti-nirdesa Sūtra;* this ideal has strongly influenced social life of Buddh. China and Japan.

R. Gard, *Buddhism* (1961), ch. VI; T. W. Rhys-Davids, *Dialogues of the Buddha,* vol. III, pp. 180–3; E. M. Hare, *Gradual Sayings,* vol. III (1934, repr. 1952), pp. 29–30; E. M. Hare *Woven Cadences* (2nd edn. 1948), pp. 40–2; Tsunoda R., de Bary and Keene, *Sources of the Japanese Tradition* (1958), pp. 101–6.

Fasting, Fasts Fasting, in a Buddh. context, normally refers to practice, enjoined by monastic regulations, of taking no food between mid-day and following morning. This is the regular daily custom of Buddh. monks; the drinking of water during time of fasting is, however, allowed. This practice is followed also by some lay people as a specially meritorious discipline; is usually undertaken on the Buddh. holy day (at new moon or full moon). One of the ten points of indiscipline of which the Vajjian monks were accused at the 2nd Council at Vesali (→ Councils, Buddh.) was that of taking food when sun was past zenith. In gen. the Buddh. attitude is one which favours restraint in taking of food rather than long periods of complete fasting. Among the 13 practices which are regarded as aids to the holy life, or 'means of purification' (*dhutanga*), and which are to be observed for short or long periods, 3 concern food, viz., eating one meal a day, eating only from alms-bowl, declining 'second-helpings.' The import. of an accompanying good moral intention is emphasized in connection with such habits of restraint; mere external performance is in itself of no value (*Puggala-paññatti* 275–84); they are useful only 'if they are taken up for sake of frugality, contentedness, purity, etc.'

Fatalism (Buddh. Rejection) → Determinism.

Feeling Feeling (*vedanā*) is one of the 5 primary groups of aggregates, or → *khandhas/skandhas,* into which human 'personality' is divided. It is, in Buddh. literature, formally divided into 5 kinds: (1) physically agreeable (2) physically disagreeable (3) mentally agreeable (4) mentally disagreeable (5) neutral or indifferent. There is also a 6-fold classification of feeling in terms of the senses, viz: sight, hearing, smelling, tasting, touch, and mental impression.

Festival(s) Public celebration of relig. occasions is a prominent feature of Buddh. countries. The major occasions are (1) regular annual → Holy Days in Buddh. calendar, together with (2) such others as occur intermittently in course of life of monastery and its neighbourhood, such as ordinations to monkhood, special days of merit-making, the giving of new robes to monks, and other similar occasions. The most universally celebrated is *Vesākha,* which belongs to first category; it is a celebration of birth, enlightenment, and passing into final *nibbāna* of Buddha. This is a monastery-centred festival, of great importance for monks, but an occasion in which entire neighbourhood also participates.

In rural areas of continental S.E. Asia this festival spreads over three days, from 14th to 16th day of sixth month (by Buddh. calendar). The festival is marked by public reading of lessons concerning life of Buddha, hearing of sermons preached by monks, expounding significance of the day, and by public processions in open air, with circumambulation of local Buddh. shrine. In urban areas the festival is limited to one day. In Bangkok a royal procession circumambulates the Royal Chapel, or *Bōd,* of the Emerald Buddha; the king and queen of Thailand take part in this, leading royal family and officials; the procession takes place in evening of full moon; the people carry lighted tapers, and the *Bōd* is decorated with candles and lights and flowers. Similar ceremonies are held in villages, where abbot of monastery leads other monks and lay people 3 times round the *Bōd*. As they go, they chant stanzas of praise to Buddha. When the 3 circumambulations are completed, monks and people usually enter the sanctuary for further devotions and readings, which may go on until late hour of night. Similar ceremonies may be held on *Māgha Pūja*, 3 months earlier, which commemorates Buddha's promulgation of monastic code of discipline, the → Vinaya. An import. festival which comes at end of Buddh. 'Lent' or *Vassa* is that connected with presentation by lay people of new robes to monks. This is called *Kathina* (i.e., 'cloth') ceremony. The gift of robes may be sponsored by a number of villagers, or by one wealthy person, or a local business firm. Since occasion marks end of Lenten period, it is noisiest and gayest of popular festivals. In add. to robes, it is usual for other gifts to be presented to monks (candles, soap, tea, note books, etc.). Various kinds of entertainment for lay people are also provided, and stalls are set up to provide food. (See H. K. Kaufman, *Bangkhuad* (1960), pp. 185–9; Manning Nash, *The Golden Road to Modernity* (1965), pp. 132–7). A further occasion for public festivity is → ordination of a local inhabitant into Buddh. Sangha. This will be preceded by procession, sometimes led by local band of musicians, and followed by outdoor entertainment and feasting. The considerable expense of such festivities is often shared by the guests, who make contributions. In rural areas, therefore, ordinations are often, though not always, held after rice-harvest, when funds are more plentiful. Fund-raising efforts on behalf of local temple are also occasions for celebrations and parades; the relig. significance of event is 'merit-making,' which it entails for all donors (in Thailand, '*tham-bun*'; in Ceylon, a '*pin-kama*').

Various other festivals are observed in Buddh. countries of S. Asia, which vary from country to country, such as New Year's Day, Rice-Pagoda Ritual, First-Fruits Ritual, the celebration connected with → *paritta*, or ceremonial changing of protective formulas on some special occasion:

these enjoy varying prominence and importance, and some are only marginally Buddh. (→ Holy Days).

J. G. Scott, *The Burman: His Life and Notions* (1903, repr. 1963); W. A. Graham, *Siam,* 2 vols. (1924); B. Ryan, *Sinhalese Village* (1958); (for Burma) Manning Nash, *The Golden Road to Modernity* (1965); (for Thailand) H. K. Kaufman, *Bangkhuad: A Community Study in Thailand* (1960); Phra Anuman Rajadhon, *Life and Ritual in Old Siam* (1961); K. E. Wells, *Thai Buddhism* (1959); (general) Manning Nash et al., *Anthropological Studies in Theravāda Buddhism* (1966).

First Sermon, of Buddha → Dhamma-Cakkappavattana Sutta.

Fo Chinese term for → Buddha, but it is a mistake always to equate Fo with the historical Buddha, who is known in China as *Shih-chia-mou-ni Fo* (Sakyamuni). The Chi. equivalent of → Tathāgata is *Ju-lai Fo* (Thus-come Buddha), who is regarded as all-powerful and omniscient; he is usually repres. as gilded image, seated cross-legged upon a lotus blossom, his eyes half-closed in contemplation. The most universally worshipped Fo is → Amitabha (*O-mi-t'o Fo*), whilst → Maitreya (*Mi-lo-Fo*) is regarded as the Buddha who is to come and his image, repres. in nearly all temples, is easily recognised by his laughing and hope-inspiring face. In Chi. → Mahāyāna Buddhism, every intelligent person who has broken through bondage of sense, perception and self, knows unreality of all phenomena and is ready to enter into → Nirvana, is reckoned as a Fo. The term is often used as an honorific for some person who is noted for saintliness or kingly virtue.

E. T. C. Werner, *Dictionary of Chinese Mythology* (1932), pp. 130ff.

Food, Rules The most import. single rule with regard to food, in Buddh. trad., is, espec. for the monk, that of restraint in eating, which covers also obligation not to eat after 12 noon. (→ Fasting). Apart from this, alcohol of any kind is forbidden 'as tending to cloud the mind' (→ Eightfold Path). The vow, incumbent on all Buddhists, monastic and lay, not to take life, causes them to be vegetarian in their food habits, though with varying degrees of strictness. Among Buddhists, emphasis is laid on wrongfulness of kill-ing an animal (since it is a sentient being), rather than on eating its flesh when dead. The onus of bad *karma* comes upon the slayer rather than the eater—a somewhat different attitude from that found among Hindus, who regard eating of meat as equally fraught with bad karmic consequences.

Four Holy Truths The E.T. of the Buddh. *cattarī-ariya-saccāni* (Pali)/*catvari-ārya-satyāni* (Skt.) as 'four holy truths' is somewhat inadequate. These are, in fact, 4 principles concerning human existence, which, when apprehended in *experience,* are said to be recognized by Buddhs. as together constituting ultimate truth or reality. Through realisation of this 4-fold set of principles Buddha gained enlightenment, so it is claimed. It is for this reason that they are called *ariya,* i.e. 'holy' (sometimes trans., inadequately, 'noble'). In form in which they are found in Pali Buddh. scriptures (in the → *Mahā-Parinibbāna Sutta* of the → Dīgha-Nikāya), they are as follows: 'The holy truth concerning ill; the holy truth concerning the cause of ill; the holy truth concerning the cessation of ill; the holy truth concerning the path which leads to that cessation. When these holy truths are apprehended and known, the craving for further rebirth is rooted out, that which leads to renewed becoming is destroyed, and there is no more rebirth' (DN.II.90). The 1st *H.T.* sets forth nature of human existence—that it is characterised by → *dukkha.* This incl. suffering, i.e., physical pain or mental distress, and also the gen. unsatisfactory quality of existence where all joy is fleeting and life is repeated process of descent into death. This principle (that all existence is *dukkha*) may not be immediately apparent to the 'worldling' (*putthujana*); it is proclaimed as part of truth revealed by Buddha. The 2nd *H.T.* offers explanation of how *dukkha* comes to be conditioning factor of all life. Human existence is seen as a continuous causal process (described in terms of 12 related phases in the formula known as → *paticca-samuppāda.* The process repeats continually, and thus forms a cycle; but the phase in cycle which is of partic. importance, since it provides as it were the motive power to keep process

Free Will

going, is *tanhā* (Pali) or *trsnā* (Skt.), i.e. thirst, → craving, or desire. It is this which initiates new *karma,* and continues process, producing resultant states of being which are conditioned by antecedent *tanhā.* Since they are *tanhā*-conditioned, they have no absolute nature, they are impermanent, and the process of decay and re-death is repeated. The 3rd *H.T.* affirms that this *dukkha*-characterised life can be brought to an end; that there is a way out of the apparently endlessly repeated cycle, and that another kind of life is poss., viz., that of → *nibbāna/nirvāna.* The 4th *H.T.* points to means by which this freedom, this new life, can be achieved, viz., the 'way' of the Buddha, the holy → eightfold path. The following of this way incl. in itself full realisation of 1st *H.T.,* understanding of 2nd *H.T.,* and the actualising of what is promised in 3rd *H.T.*

Walpola Rahula, *What the Buddha Taught* (1962); Piyadassi Thera, *The Buddha's Ancient Path* (1964); Th. Stcherbatsky, *The Conception of Buddhist Nirvāna* (1927).

Free Will Determinism (Buddh. Rejection), Predestination.

Funerary Rites The methods of disposing of the dead practised by Buddhists are those inherited from Indian culture. The Buddha was cremated with honours customarily given to a great king, acc. to the → *Mahā-Parinibbāna Sutta.* The cremation was carried out by the Malla tribes-people of Kusinagara, where he died, after they had enquired of → Ananda his personal attendant and disciple, how the remains of a → Tathāgata or Buddha should be dealt with (*S.B.E.,* 11, pp. 125ff.). After 7 days of ceremonial homage, the body was wrapped in 500 layers of new cloth, placed in an iron sarcophagus, filled with oil, and placed on funeral pyre, made of many kinds of fragrant wood. They were unable to ignite the pyre, however, until 500 Buddh. monks led by Mahā Kassapa had arrived and reverenced the Buddha's body. After that, the pyre is said to have burst into flames spontaneously. When the fire had died down, only the bones were left: 'the body of the Blessed One burned itself away . . . neither soot nor ash was seen.' For 7 days the closely guarded bones were honoured 'with dance and song and music, and with garlands and perfumes.' King →

124

Ajātasuttu, hearing of Buddha's death and cremation, proposed to build a → *stupa* over the remains. The Licchavis, the Sakiyas, the Bulis, the Koliyas, and the Mallas and a brahman of Vethadipa also claimed a right to build the *stupa*. The remains were, therefore, divided into 8 parts, and 8 *stupas* were built, by the various claimants in their respective territories. This building of 8 *stupas* is considered by mod. scholars a later embroidery of the narrative, in the interests of providing a justification for the *stupa*-cult, as it had developed by time of *Ashoka* (→ Stupa).

That the Buddha was cremated indicates not that this is universal practice among Buddhists, but rather his status as a great man. At that time in India, as now, not all dead bodies are cremated; those of children, and of holy men, and of very poor are notable exceptions: these are buried, or even left in a charnel field to be devoured by beasts and birds of prey. Bodies thus disposed of, and in various stages of decomposition, are mentioned in Buddh. scriptures as subjects for meditation by monks, espec. those who by their nature are tempted to sensuality. Practice among Buddhists varies nowadays in disposal of dead. In Ceylon, e.g. espec. in villages, burial is more usual: Ryan estimates only 1 case in 25 is dealt with by cremation; this where family is sufficiently wealthy. In S.E. Asia, both burial and cremation are used, but cremation is more usual. This will take place from 3 to 7 days after death, and is occasion more than any other in the human life-cycle when Buddhist monks have an import. relig. role. Various ceremonies take place throughout the 7 days after death, in which groups of monks take part; these ceremonies are partly expressive of non-Buddh. ideas, such as aiding transition of dead man's spirit, and partly occasions for monks to offer solace and comfort to bereaved, and to remind them of Buddh. doctrines. Where, as in Burma and Thailand, the population is predominantly Buddh., the funerary rites provide occasion for communal participation, both financial and devotional, for the villagers; in doing so they are considered to gain merit. Cremation, the more usual method in S.E. Asia, is carried out on unused open ground

Funerary Rights

outside village; in more urban areas, within compound of Buddh. temple.

S.B.E., vol. XI, pp. 122–36; S. Dutt, *Buddha and 5 After Centuries* (1957), pp. 168–71; B. Ryan, *Sinhalese Village* (1958), pp. 103–4; J. E. de Young, *Village Life in Modern Thailand* (1955), pp. 68–74; Manning Nash, *The Golden Road to Modernity: Village Life in Contemporary Burma* (1965), pp. 151–6.

G

Gandhabbas (Pali); **Gandharvas** (Skt.) A class of celestial beings in anc. Indian cosmology, whose existence is taken for granted in early Buddh. world-view reflected in canonical scriptures. They are regarded as lowest class of → *Devas,* and are mentioned in conjunction with → *Asuras.* Rebirth as a G. is regarded as result of observance of the minimum moral precepts only. G. are credited with being musicians of the heavenly realm; they also serve as attendants upon the higher Devas. The *Ātānātiya Sutta* of the → Digha-Nikāya mentions that they are a source of disturbance to monks and nuns engaged in meditation. It is sometimes asserted that they are effective agents in human conception; but this is a misunderstanding of statements on subject of Pali Buddh. scriptures, where it is said that one factor in conception is presence of a karma-complex or 'being,' ready to enter into a new embodiment (e.g. *M.N.,* I, pp. 157; 265f.). It is explained in Pali commentaries that what is meant here by G. is a being who is ready to enter a human womb to be born (→ *Conception in Buddh. thought* (2)).
T. W. and C. A. F. Rhys-Davids, *Dialogues of the Buddha,* vol. II (1910, repr. 1966), pp. 288, 308; vol. III (1921, repr. 1965), pp. 142f., 188f.

Gandhāra (Kandahar) Region to extreme N.W. of India (now southern Afghanistan), notable in connection with develop. of the Buddh. → Mahāyāna and Buddh. art. The region came under Indian control, when the Hellenistic Syrian ruler Seleucid ceded it by treaty to the Mauryan emperor Chandragupta in 4th cent. BC. G. was open to Buddh. influence at least from time of emperor → Ashoka,

Gandhāra

since Ashokan edicts have been discovered there, the latest (in Greek Aramaic) in 1958; the region is mentioned in other Ashokan records as a frontier-region to which Buddh. missions were sent during his reign. G. had also been, and continued to be, subject to Graeco-Roman cultural influence. It was here (and at Mathurā, on the Jumna, S. of Delhi) that use of a statue, image, or ikon to repr. the Buddha developed. It is gen. recognised that the G. type of image, the portrayal of an idealised human form, was to large extent a reflection of kind of anthropomorphic representations of the divine, characteristic of east. part of Roman empire, but with a distinctive Indian contribution (→ Rūpa). Under the Kusāna kings (→ Kanishka), i.e. during approx. the first 3 cents. CE, this area was one of flourishing and vigorous Buddh. culture, with many monastic centres of learning; the most import. was Taksasilā (Taxila). Many of these centres have been uncovered by archaeological research in mod. times. The large number of monasteries indicates substantial lay Buddh. pop. at the time, since monasteries were (and are) built with funds or labour provided by lay supporters; many donors in G. were prob. wealthy merchants, since it was a transit-centre of international trade. During 2nd cent. CE and after, G. was an area which nourished Buddh. missionary expansion N.-wards and then E.-wards into China. The multi-storied pagoda, which emperor Kanishka built at Peshawar, was regarded as one of the wonders of world at that time; it prob. had import. influence on evolution of the Chinese type of pagoda. Among the more famous of learned Buddh.-monks of region were the two Mahāyāna writers and teachers, the brothers → Asanga and → Vasubandhu, whose home was at Purusapura (Peshāwar). Many monasteries of G. were devastated in 5th cent. CE during the Hūna invasions. By 7th cent., when the Chinese pilgrim → Hsüan Tsang visited India, the prosperity and splendour of this Buddh. region was of the distant past: Buddhism was in decline there; most monasteries were 'deserted and in ruins . . . filled with wild shrubs, and solitary to the last degree. . . .'

God, Concept of

S. Dutt, *Buddhist Monks and Monasteries of India* (1962); Dietrick Seckel, *The Art of Buddhism* (1964), pp. 30–7.

Gāya A town in Bihar, N. India, near to the → bodhi-tree which was the scene of the → Buddha's enlightenment. The Chinese pilgrim → Fa Hsien recorded (in 5th cent. CE) that the bodhi-tree was 3½ miles from the town. The place is mentioned as having been visited again on several occasions by Buddha in the course of his ministry. Buddha-Gaya, the scene of the enlightenment, is one of the 4 places of Buddh. pilgrimage (→ Holy Places, Buddh.). An import. monastery, 'The Great Enlightenment Monastery' (*Mahā-bodhi Sanghārāma*), was built at Buddha-Gaya by a king of Ceylon; monks from Ceylon used to stay there. Inscriptions made by Burmese and Chinese pilgrims have also been found, recording repairs and offerings made at the *Mahā bodhi* temple on various occasions. Acc. to the Sinhalese chronicles, the great teacher → Buddhaghosa left Ceylon at end of life to go to Gāya, where he died.

P. V. Bapat (ed.), *2500 Years of Buddhism* (1956, repr. 1959), pp. 308–11.

Genshin (CE 942–1017). Better known in Japan as Eshin-Sōzu, G. was a great exponent of cult of → Amida Buddha. He emphasised idealistic tenets of → Tendai philosophy, and sought to purify Buddhism from abuses of mystic ritualism. His writings and paintings, combining vivid imagination with mystic vision, depicted various resorts of transmigration, states of perdition or spiritual beatitude, and glories of Amida's paradise, and proved to be a great inspiration to Buddhist faith in Japan throughout succeeding cents.

M. Anesaki, *Hist. of Japanese Buddhism* (1930), pp. 151ff.

God, Concept of (Buddh.) → Deva. **(China–Japan)** Fundamental to Chinese and Japanese religs., whether Confucian, Buddh., Taoist or Shinto, is belief that at basis of all created and manifested existence is an underlying unitary, spiritual Reality, the absolute spiritual source of all things. For this Reality it is doubtless incorrect to use the term 'God,' with its Chr., Jewish and Islamic connotations. Philosophically this supreme being is conceived of in impersonal or rather supra-personal terms: In Confucianism as cosmic counterpart of moral principle in man; in Taoism as unnameable and unknowable Tao, the source and sustainer of all that is; in → Mahāyāna Buddhism of China and Japan as the → Adi-Buddha or the → Dharmakāya (Body of righteousness). The Supreme Reality, however conceived, is considered to be beyond reach of finite intelligence, and Far East. philosophies are pervaded by spirit of agnosticism. Yet recognition that the life-principle, permeating whole of nature, is fundamentally one with the Supreme Reality, leads to belief that man, by penetrating to depths of his own nature, may arrive at an intuitive recognition of Supreme Reality. In Confucianism this is achieved through full development of one's own moral nature; in Taoism, by a return to Tao; in Buddhism, by a realisation of one's Buddha-nature.

In practical relig. expression a theistic tendency is observable in all Far East. religs. Popular relig. is incurably polytheistic, and worship is given to a whole hierarchy of spiritual beings—gods, Buddhas and deified men and animals; but at head of this hierarchy is a Supreme Being, worshipped and honoured under different names; the Shang Ti or T'ien of Confucianism; the Yü Huang of relig. Taoism; the → Amitabha Buddha of Buddhism; and Amaterasu in Shintō.

Shang Ti or T'ien in Confucianism was considered to be such an august being that only the emperor, as Son of Heaven, was worthy to render adequate worship and homage to him in an elaborate State Cult. All others offered worship to various deities who, in a spiritual hierarchy, were agents of his supreme will and intermediaries between God and man. Though no worship was offered to him in temples of popular relig., almost every Chi. peasant recognised his supremacy under name Lao T'ien Yeh.

Though it is true to say that Buddhism, including the Mahāyāna of China and Japan, philosophically speaking denies existence of a Creator God who controls destinies of mankind, in practical relig. expression the Dharma-kāya of the Adi-Buddha, manifest supremely in → Amitabha

(Amida), is regarded as supreme Deity, endowed with personality, will, intelligence and love. By millions of Buddhists in China and Japan, Amitabha is regarded as supreme God with attributes of grace, mercy, omniscience and omnipotence. In all the → Pure Land sects he is regarded as supreme object of homage and worship. In relig. Taoism and in Shinto the same theistic tendencies are apparent.

E.R.E., VI, pp. 269ff.; 294–5; D. H. Smith, *Chinese Religion* (1968), pp. 33ff.; 50ff.; 138ff.; 263ff.; D. C. Holtom, *National Faith of Japan* (1938), pp. 123ff.; 171ff.; 292–3; W. G. Aston, *Shinto* (1905) pp. 69ff.; 121ff.; M. Anesaki, *Hist. of Japanese Buddhism* (1930), pp. 170ff.

Good Life, Ideal → Nibbuta.

Gotama (Pali); **Gautama** (Skt.) → Buddha, Gotama.

Grasping Grasping (*upādāna*) or, as sometimes trans., 'clinging' is, acc. to Buddh. thought, an intensified form of *taṇhā* (→ Craving). It is of 4 kinds: (1) sensuous-clinging, i.e., clinging to sensuous desires and pleasures (2) clinging to views (i.e., false or mistaken views) (3) clinging to rules and rituals, with the idea that one may through them gain salvation (4) clinging to notion of individual personality. The → Anāgami is regarded as entirely free from all these manifestations of grasping or clinging.

Greed In Buddh. trad., G. (*lobha*) is one of the 3 morally unwholesome 'roots' of thought and action (the other 2 being hatred and illusion). It is often used as synonym of *taṇhā* (→ desire or thirst).

H

Hakuin (CE 1685–1768). Next to → Dogen, the greatest of Japanese → Zen masters, who by his efforts towards renewal of → Rinzai laid foundations of modern Zen. Though he left home at the age of 15 to become a Buddh. monk, it was not until his 24th year that H. had his first experience of enlightenment, to be followed by a vigorous and painful training under the aged hermit and Zen master, Etan. In CE 1716, H. settled permanently at the Shōinji temple near his birthplace, which under his guidance became strongest Buddh. centre of Tokugawa period. In H. Zen enlightenment and intense ecstatic and mystical experiences were combined with genuine artistic ability. His rich humanity, deep piety, tireless zeal in study, and great gifts as preacher, writer, poet and artist drew to him a multitude of disciples. 'Through his undemanding goodness, his candour and religious enthusiasm H. won the hearts of the common people; he belongs among the greatest relig. reformers of Japanese hist.' (cf. Dumoulin, p. 247). He deprecated the 'easy way' of the → Amida Sects, and emphasised the incomparable power of Zen meditation and the → koan exercises. The core of his doc. of enlightenment, which rested in his own experience, may be summed up in a trio of mystical states: the Great Doubt, the Great Enlightenment and the Great Joy.

H. Dumoulin, *Hist. of Zen Buddhism* (1963), pp. 242–68.

Happiness, Buddh. concept of The word *sukha* used in Buddh. lit. has the general sense of 'agreeable,' 'happy,' 'joyful,' and is the opp. to → *dukkha*, an import. term which in Buddh. usage refers to chief characteristic of mortal existence, viz., its unsatisfactoriness, painfulness, and basic unease. *Sukha,* however, is not given such a fundamental sense; it denotes agreeable bodily or mental feeling. It is import , in Buddh. view, chiefly because it makes successful concentration, or meditation, poss. This is ref. to in a number of passages in the Suttas: 'It is a natural law that the mind of the happy one becomes concentrated' (*A.N.,* X, 2). Apart from this, there is no Buddh. term that approx. to West. abstract notion of 'happiness.'

Hatred, (Dosa) in Buddh. Thought In Buddh. analysis H. is one of the 3 morally unwholesome roots, the other two being → Greed (*lobha*), and Illusion (→ *moha*). The presence of these morally unwholesome qualities, or 'roots,' conditions the mental attitude and volitional state; in other words, produces morally unwholesome → *karma.* H. is said to be present as result of aversion, or unwise contemplation of a repulsive object (*A.N.,* III, 68). Its range covers all degrees of hostile feeling, from annoyance to most violent extreme of wrath. In Buddh. analysis, repres. in → Abhid. lit., it is held that the 3 unwholesome roots are eradicated by deliberate encouragement of their opposites. In case of H. (*dosa*), the opp. is *adosa* or non-hatred, and means attitude of love to all sentient beings. This is held to be achieved by one who cultivates type of meditation which focuses on Universal Love (*mettā bhāvanā*). (→→ Meditation; Mūla).

Heart Sutra The *Hrdaya Sūtra,* name of a → Mahāyāna Buddh. treatise, belonging to type of literature known as → Prajñā-Pāramitā Sūtras.

Heaven → Cosmology.

Hell → Cosmology.

Heresy H. is primarily a West. relig. concept; there is no exact Buddh. equivalent. The nearest approximation is → *ditthi* (Pali) *drsti* (Skt.), literally a view, usually a 'wrong' view, that is due not to reason but to → craving or → desire (*tanhā*). The most serious form of *ditthi,* acc. to Buddh. trad. is to assert the reality and permanence of the individual human ego, i.e., the assertion of *atta* or *ātman.* Since the West. concept of H. implies an orthodoxy capable of denouncing H. and willing to do so, the approx. of Buddh.

ditthi to West. H. here comes to an end, since Buddhism has no authoritative hierarchy, and no sacramental sanctions. Even the most serious form of *ditthi*, assertion of reality of a permanent individual human 'self,' was maintained by certain Buddh. known as → Pudgala-Vādins. They were regarded by all other Buddh. schools of thought as weaker brethren, and in error; but they maintained their existence and monastic institutions; as late as 7th cent. ᴄᴇ, Pudgala-Vādin monks amounted to about quarter of total number of Buddh. monks in India. On the whole, the attitude of other schools seems to have been that more prolonged meditation would eventually cause them to see error involved in their view, and its abandonment.

E. Conze, *Buddhist Thought in India* (1962), pp. 122–31.

(China and Japan) The degeneracy and disintegration of great Buddh. centres led to rise of schismatics and heretics, who organised themselves within churches and formed secret societies. With the 17th cent. Buddh. doctrines were systematized and respective Buddh. sects formulated their orthodox dogmas. Ecclesiastical authorities attempted to enforce orthodox teachings of Buddh. Church, and this was accompanied by a vigorous fight against H. With 18th cent. revival of Shinto, diversion from nationalist ideas of State Shinto were considered heretical and political measures were taken to suppress all who refused to conform with the orthodox state doctrine.

M. Anesaki, *Hist. of Japanese Buddhism* (1930), pp. 191ff., 229ff., 305.

Hetu Buddh. term for a 'root-condition,' viz. a morally wholesome or unwholesome primary mental state which conditions thought and action. Thus H. is not the *cause* of thought or action but the *conditioner* of the thought or action when it arises, given a cause. The 6 kinds of H. distinguished in Buddh. psychology are: (morally unwholesome), greed (*lobha*), hatred (*dosa*), and illusion (*moha*); (morally wholesome), generosity (*alobha*), non-hatred (*adosa*), and absence of illusion (*amoha*).

S. Z. Aung (tr.), *Compendium of Philosophy* (*Abhidhammattha-Sangaha*) (1910, repr. 1956), pp. 279–81.

Hīnayāna Buddh. term, used in anc. India, for one among several 'means' or methods of attaining enlightenment. H. was method of limited appeal, compared with the → Mahāyāna, held to be of universal appeal. *Yāna* means, method (→→ Yana; Theravāda).

Holy, The It has been observed by West. scholars that while Buddhism has no place for an omnipotent personal deity of kind affirmed in theistic religions, it has a concept of the holy, and this constitutes focal point of its relig. ideas and teachings. (Cf., e.g. E. Durkheim, *Les Formes Élémentaires de la Vie Religieuse,* 1912.) The concept of the holy manifests itself at one level in the → Four Holy Truths, and the → Eightfold Path; at another level, in popular devotional Buddh. practices, espec. veneration of the → *stupa* or → pagoda, as symbolising Buddha, and in notion of the → 'holy places,' to which it is desirable that → pilgrimage should be made.

Holy Days These are of 2 kinds: those occurring monthly, and those annually. Of former, the more import. are the day of full moon, and day of new moon. On these the ceremony of reciting the → *Patimokkha,* or disciplinary code, is carried out by → Sangha in each local monastery. These two, together with the two intervening days of first quarter and last quarter of moon, together make up the four Uposattha days in every month. These days are trad. times for special relig. observances by Buddh. lay people; in theory these are days for attending the monastery and taking part in devotions led by monks (in forenoon), or hearing sermon (dhammadesina) by a monk (usually in evening). In mod. S. Asia such attendance is frequently left to women, the elderly and very young. In Ceylon these days are known as 'poya' days, and are observed as public holidays, corresponding to the Christ. Sunday; but since their incidence is determined by phases of moon they do not always fall on same day of week. In Burma and Thailand they are not public holidays, the international Sunday being observed instead. In Thailand there is trend towards using Sunday, as day free from work, for devotional services at the monastery attended by lay people or for preaching of sermons,

Holy Days

giving of public lectures on Buddh. doc., and holding of Sunday-schools for children; lunar holy days, however, are also observed, and are still ref. to by their trad. name in Thai: 'Wan Phra' (lit. 'holy day'). The Uposattha days are trad. also the occasion for more devout lay people to take the eight moral precepts (three extra to universal five) ref. to as *attha-sīlā* (morality); in add. to fasting, they spend day at monastery in meditation; in all Buddh. countries of S. Asia, however, only a small minority of people, usually the elderly, actually do this. The eve of the Uposattha day is occasion for monks to reshave the hair of head. Nowadays Uposattha days are occasion for special radio broadcasts on relig. subjects; these have large audiences, even though only a minority attends the monastery. In rural areas, however, esp. in Thailand, a higher proportion of lay people attend Uposattha services in monastery than is case in urban areas. Of annual holy days the most import. is Vesak, or *Vesākha-pūjā* (Pali)/*Vaiśākha-pūjā* (Skt.), which falls on full-moon day of May. On this day are commemorated jointly the Buddha's birth, his attaining enlightenment, and passing into parinibbāna. This also is observed as public holiday in Buddh. countries of S.E. Asia; it is marked by publication of special collections of articles dealing with various aspects of Buddh. relig., as well as by special ceremonies, and popular festival activities. Three months before this, on full-moon day of February occurs Māgha Pūjā, on which promulgation by Buddha of the monastic disciplinary code, or → Vinaya, is commemorated. Another period of special relig. significance in Buddh. year is that of Vassa, sometimes referred to as the Buddh. Lent. This is season of monsoon rains in India and S.E. Asia, and is observed by Sangha as period of retreat, when monks may not travel about country as at other times of year, but must remain in own monastery. For Buddhs. it begins on first day of waning moon in eighth month (by the Roman calendar this is usually in July); it lasts until full moon of eleventh month (in Roman calendar, October). It is time specially devoted to relig. study by monks, and instruction of lay people. More people than usual are likely to attend

monasteries to hear sermons. There is a considerable increase in number of monks in Sangha during Vassa, as it is
customary for some to take ordination for this period even
although they may return to laymen's life when Vassa is
ended. A monk's seniority is measured by number of Vas-
sas he has spent in Sangha, rather than by complete calendar years. It used to be trad. for theatrical performances
and public amusements to be suspended during Vassa period; but this is no longer strictly observed, at least in the
urban areas (→ Festivals).

Holy Places Every → stupa or → pagoda is regarded as a place
to be venerated, symbolising as it does the Buddha and his
→ Dhamma; but the holy places *par excellence* are the 4
sites in N.E. India connected with events of the life of the
Buddha. These are (1) → Lumbini, his birth-place; (2) →
Buddha-Gaya, scene of his Enlightenment; (3) → Isipitana
(Sārnāth), where his First Sermon was preached, and thus
place of 'setting in motion' of the 'wheel of Dhamma'; (4)
→ Kushinagara, or (by its anc. name) Kusinārā, the place of
his entry into *parinibbāna*. Without being identified by
name, these 4 places are mentioned in the → *Māha-Pari-
nibbāna Sutta* of the Pali canon: (1) 'The place at which the
believing man can say "Here the → Tathāgata was born!";
(2) the place at which (he) can say, "Here the T. attained to
the supreme and perfect enlightenment!"; (3) the place at
which (he) can say "Here was the wheel of the Dhamma
set in motion by the T.!"; (4) the place at which (he) can
say, "Here the T. passed finally away in that utter passing
away which leaves nothing whatever to remain behind!" '
Each of these four places, it is said, the believer 'should
visit with feelings of reverence' (*D.N.,* II, pp. 140–1).
T. W. and C. A. F. Rhys-Davids, *The Dialogues of the Buddha* (part II), (*Sacred Books of the Buddhists,* vol. II), 1910
(repr. 1966), pp. 153f.

Holy Truths → Four Holy Truths.

Honen (Also called Genku: CE 1133–1212). Founder of → Jodo
sect of Jap. Buddhism in 1175. As a boy he entered the
Tendai monastery on Mt. Hiei, but later withdrew to give
himself up to seclusion and study. His fundamental tenet

Hossō

was belief in power and grace of the saviour → Amida, lord of Sukhāvati (the Western paradise). He advocated repeated invocation of Amida's name, by which anyone, ignorant or wise, high or low, could be saved. His teaching was based on that of → Hui Yüan (Jap., Zendō), the Chi. founder of the → Pure Land sect. His greatest disciple was → Shinran, who developed Pure Land doctrines further and founded Jodo Shin-shu or True Pure Land. Saintly, pious and of sincere conviction, H. exerted great influence, until the jealousy of his Tendai rivals led to his exile.
H. H. Coates and R. Ishizuka (trs.), *Hōnen, the Buddhist Saint* (Kyoto, 1925); M. Anesaki, *Hist. of Japanese Religion* (1930), pp. 170ff.

Hossō (Skt.: *dharma-lakshana,* the 'criteria of Laws and Truths') A school of Jap. Buddhism, introduced from China by → Dōshō (CE 629–700), who studied → Yogacara doctrines under the famous → Hsüan Tsang. H. philos. was highly analytical, and a peculiar combination of Idealism and Realism. It taught that ultimate reality is to be found in the mind, in the *Ālayā* or 'store-consciousness' of each individual. The store-consciousness has within it an inexhaustible store of 'seeds' (*bīja*), which manifest themselves in innumerable varieties of existences. Phenomena (*dharmas*) exist by virtue of these 'seeds,' and whole cosmos is made up of various combinations of their qualities. Thus, the infinite varieties of existence all participate in the prime nature of *Ālayā* (cf. the 'unconscious' in modern psych.), and are pervaded by universal foundation (*dharmatā*) of existence. The school elaborated ten stages in mystical contemplation, which finally led to immediate realisation of innermost nature of all being. Thus the aim of an elaborate Buddh. training and discipline was to discover the ultimate entity of cosmic existence in contemplation, through investigation into the specific characteristics of all existence and realisation of fundamental nature of soul in mystic illumination, attained only by a select few.
E.R.E., IX, p. 870b; M. Anesaki, *Hist. of Japanese Religion* (1930), pp. 94–6.

Hsüan Tsang (Tsang) (Hsüan Chuang) CE 596–664. Jap.— Genjo. The greatest Chinese pilgrim to India, and one of most import. figures in Chi. → Buddhism. Ordained at age of 13, he left for India in 629 by the C. Asian route, and arrived in 633, to spend ten years there in travel and study. He arrived back in China in 645, with 657 Buddh. texts, and was received at capital, Ch'ang-an, in triumph. The rest of his life was spent in trans. work under imperial patronage, and he completed some 75 trans., mostly → Yogācāra works. He introduced into China the teachings of → Vasubandhu (*c.* CE 420–500) and → Dharmapāda (439–507). His most famous philos. work is the *Ch'êng Wei-shih lun* ('On the establishment of the doctrine of Consciousness-only'). The *Hsi Yu Chi* (an account of the journey to the W.) is based on diaries of his travels. It is one of greatest Chi. literary treasures, and indispensable for study of Indian Buddhism. It was trans. into Eng. by S. Beal in 1884 under the title *Si-yu-ki, Buddhist Records of the W. World trans. from the Chinese of Hsien-tsiang.* 2 vols., London.
W. T. Chan, *Source Book in Chinese Philos.* (1963), ch. 23; Fung Yu-lan, *Hist. of Chinese Philos.,* vol. 2 (1953), pp. 299ff.

Hua Yen Import. school of Chi. → Buddhism, of which the highly metaphysical doctrines repres. highest development of Chi. Buddh. thought. The school based its principal teachings on the *Hua-yen Ching* or the *Mahāvaipulya Sūtra* (The expanded Sūtra of the adornments of the Buddha). This was accepted as first discourse of Buddha on his enlightenment, preached to → bodhisattvas, and beyond comprehension of mortals, to whom he proceeded to preach a simpler doctrine. Tu-shun (CE 557–640) is reputed to be its first Chi. master, followed by Chih-yen (601–68) and Fa-tsang (643–712). Fa-tsang, who had been disciple of → Hsüan Tsang, was greatest exponent of Hua Yen philosophy. Whilst other Buddh. schools (e.g. → Ch'an) taught that Being and Non-Being are alike illusion and negated in the Void, Hua Yen taught a permanently immutable 'mind,' which is universal in scope and basis of all phenomenal manifestations. It was thus more adaptable to indigenous Chi. thought.

Fung Yu-lan, *Hist. of Chinese Philos.*, vol. 2 (1953), pp. 339ff.; W. T. Chan, *A Source Book in Chinese Philos.* (1963), pp. 406–8; C. B. Day, *The Philosophers of China* (1962), pp. 172–5.

Hui Nêng (CE 628–713). Known in S. China as Wei Lang and in Japan as Eno, he was sixth and last patriarch of → Ch'an Buddhism in China (the first being → Bodhidharma, or in Chinese—Ta Mo). As leader of S. branch of Ch'an school, he taught doc. of Spontaneous Realisation or Sudden Enlightenment, through meditation in which thought, objectivity and all attachment are eliminated. He wrote the only sacred Chi. Buddh. writing which has been honoured with the title → Ching or Sūtra, the famous *Platform Sūtra of Hui Nêng.*

C. B. Day, *The Philosophers of China* (1962), pp. 139ff.; E. Wood, *Zen Dict.* (1962).

Hui Yüan (CE 334–417). Surname Chia. A native of Lou-fan, in Yen-mên, Shansi, his early years were spent in study of Confucianism and Taoism. In his 21st year, was converted to → Buddhism and became most brilliant disciple of Tao-an (312–85). His fame as a Buddh. master and expositor of Buddh. teachings spread far and wide. He founded the Tung-lin monastery on Lu Shan in C. China, to which he retired, and this became most famous centre of Buddhism in S. China. He drew his inspiration largely from the Greater and Lesser *Sukhāvatī-Vyūha Sūtras,* with their vivid descriptions of the → 'Pure Land' and infinite compassion of → Amitabha Buddha. In CE 402 he founded the White Lotus Society (*Pai Lien Chiao*), when he assembled monks and laymen of his community before an image of Amitabha, stressing importance of worship, the use of icons in meditation and devotion to Amitabha. In later times, this event was taken to mark beginning of Pure Land Sect, of which H.Y. is reckoned first patriarch. He carried on extensive correspondence with great Buddh. translator → Kumārajīva. These letters give insight into nature and scope of his doc. He combined Buddh. devotion and secular scholarship.

E. Zürcher, *Buddhist Conquest of China* (1959), pp. 204–59.

I

Iddhi Buddh. term for 'psychic power,' said to be one of the 'higher powers' which result from → *abhiññā*, and were held to incl. power to assume many outward forms of various kinds, to make oneself impervious to bodily harm, walk on water, etc. These powers are described in → *Visuddhimagga*, XII. The power of mind to remain imperturbable amid distractions is described as *ariyā-*(or holy) *iddhi* in the *Sampasādaniya Sutta* (*D.N.*, iii, 112f.), where it is said that the monk, by means of this power, can 'remain unconscious of disgust amid what is disgusting; or conscious of disgust amid what is not disgusting; or unconscious of disgust amid what is both d. and not-d; or remain indifferent to them both as such, mindful and understanding' (*Dialogue of the Buddha*, pt. III, 1921 [trans. T. W. Rhys-Davies], p. 107). The display, before lay people, of any supernatural power which is the monk's as result of his special insight, is strictly forbidden by the Buddha (*Vinaya* II., 112). In the *Kevaddha Sutta*, Buddha is repr. as saying, 'It is because I perceive danger in the practice of mystic wonders [i.e., 'psychic powers'] that I loathe, and abhor, and am ashamed thereof' (*D.N.*, i, 213). (See *Dialogues of the Buddha*, pt. I, pp. 276ff.).

Ignorance → *Avidya*.

Image(s) → *Rūpa*.

Immolation → Self-immolation.

Immortality In Buddh. thought I. or the death-less state is nirvāna (→ Nibbāna). One of the adjectives applied to nirvāna from earliest days is *amata*, i.e. deathless (e.g. *Sutta Nipāta* 960). The deathless realm is considered to be gained not at end of one human individual's span of existence, but as result of spiritual refinement which may be continued throughout many generations; it is held to be outcome of process of moral and spiritual refinement initiated and pursued by free choice of the human will, when once possibility of such a goal has been heard of, through the Buddha-Dhamma.

A modification of this view occurs in the → Pure Land Buddhism of China and Japan, where an intermediate goal is introduced, attainable without long preparation through many existences necessary for nirvāna. This short-term relig. goal is rebirth in heaven of the → Bodhisattva, known as the Pure Land or Paradise. Such rebirth is made poss. by compassion, grace and spiritual power of the Bodhisattva and faith of believer. Strictly, however, this is not I., in that even such blissful rebirth must be followed by further rebirth, as human, before the ultimate goal, i.e., the absolute deathlessness of nirvāna, is reached.

Belief in I. was greatly reinforced by intro. of → Buddhism into China, and popular Chi. interpretation of Buddh. theory of rebirth. The Chi. Buddh. belief in a soul, which does not perish at death, is actually a distortion of true Buddh. view, which denies existence of an enduring entity or soul. The vast mythological structures of Buddhism and relig. as they developed in China with their numerous heavens and hells, are based firmly on belief in personal survival and immortality of soul.

Incense The burning of aromatic substances in worship is a widespread custom of great antiquity. It seems to have two motives: that pleasant odours were naturally pleasing to gods, and that rising smoke naturally suggested ascent to heaven.

(China) I. is extensively used in both public and private cults. It is burned before the ancestral tablets and the household gods, in the daily worship offered in temples, in almost all festivals and processions. In Buddh. monasteries periods of meditation are marked by burning down of incense sticks. I. plays import. part in ceremonies connected with birth and death.

India, Buddhism in

E.R.E., VII, pp. 204–5; K. L. Reichelt, *Truth and Tradition* . . . (1927), pp. 279ff., 294–5.

(Japan) There is no evidence in early Shinto records of use of I., but after intro. of → Buddhism, I. came to be commonly used at Buddh. and Shinto ceremonies. The elaborate ceremony known as 'incense-sniffing' was from about CE 1500 enthusiastically taken up by the aristocracy, but seems to have had only aesthetic and not relig. significance.

B. H. Chamberlain. *Things Japanese,* 5th edn. (1905), p. 245.

India, Buddhism in → Buddhism: general survey.

Indian Religions Buddhism has largely disappeared in Indian subcontinent, save the Himalayas and to some extent in Maharashtra.

Indo-China Continental S.E. Asia, the peninsula formerly known as Indo-China, has a predominantly Buddh. culture, and majority of population of countries of region are Buddh. There were two underlying foreign cultural influences (prior to that of West), viz. of India, in west. part of peninsula; of China in east. part. The area of Indian cultural influence is repr. by the mod. states of →→ Burma, Thailand, Cambodia and Laos. The area of Chinese cultural influence is thus considerably smaller, and is confined to → Vietnam. With these two cultural sub-divisions goes differentiation in the types of Buddhism; in W. part the predom. trad. is that of → Theravāda, while in Vietnam it is that of → Mahāyāna, which came into country from China. The Mhy. form existed formerly in other areas of Indo-China; having been intro. there prob. from E. India; from about begin. of 11th cent. CE has been replaced by the Theravāda form.

Indonesia Bhm. had been intro. into Java some time in 1st half of 5th cent. CE. Acc. to Chinese pilgrim → Fa Hsien, who visited island in 418, at that time 'it hardly deserves mentioning'; but, later in same century, it had made much progress as result of work of Buddh. monk from India. In island of Sumatra, Bhm. became import. from latter half of 7th cent., when kings of Srivijaya became its patrons, and Srivijaya became an import. centre of learning in S. Asia, a fact which is testified by Chinese traveller → I-Tsing, who visited Sumatra about 671 CE. The form of Bhm. which flourished there appears, from archaeological evidence, to have been → Mahāyāna, although I-Tsing mentions the → Hīnayāna form; this latter could have been of the → Sarvāstivāda school, a form of Hīnayāna not too dissimilar from Mhy. By end of 8th cent. the → Tantric form of Bhm. had spread to these islands from E. India. From the archipelago Mhy. Bhm. spread to Malay peninsula. It enjoyed period of great prosperity from late 8th cent. onwards under the Sailendra Dynasty, rulers of a kingdom which incl. the Malay peninsula as well as much of archipelago. There were strong connections between the Sailendra kings and those of E. India; Indian Buddh. scholars appear to have moved back and forth between great centres of learning such as → Nalanda and Vikramasila in India and those of 'Suvarnadvipa,' as part of Indonesia was then called. The great symbolic stone structure known as Borobudur in Java is evidence of the importance of Bhm. in island at that period. Gradually, however, the Tantric form of Bhm. was merged in Brahmanic and Saivite relig., and with coming of Islam, finally disappeared, from Sumatra by end of 14th cent., and from Java early in 15th.

D. G. E. Hall, *A History of South-East Asia* (1955); G. Coedès, *Les États Hindouisés d'Indochine et d'Indonésie*, 3rd edn. (1964); Sir Charles Eliot, *Hinduism and Buddhism* (1921, repr. 1957), vol. III, ch. XL.

Indriya Term of considerable importance in Buddh. psychology and ethics. Derived from 'Indra,' name of anc. Indian god who was the 'mighty one,' 'the ruler,' the term denotes 'controlling principle,' 'directive force' or 'dominant.' There are many such I.'s, and various classifications and groupings are given, the most usually accepted being that found in the → Abhidhamma book, the *Vibhanga*, which gives a list of 22. First there are the sense-perception 'dominants', eye, ear, nose, tongue, and body; then the mind; femininity and masculinity; vitality; the feelings, bodily pleasure, bodily pain, gladness, sadness, and indifference; after these come the five 'spiritual' dominants, faith, en-

Influxes

ergy, mindfulness, concentration and wisdom (these 5 are also called → *bala*); finally come the 3 'supermundane dominants,' viz., (20) the assurance: 'I shall know what I do not know,' which comes to the → *sotapanna* or one newly entered on Buddh. path; (21) the dominant called 'higher knowledge,' which belongs to one who has passed through Sotapanna stage; finally (22), the dominant which characterises one who has attained → Arahantship.

Influxes → *Asava*.

Ingen (CE 1592–1673). Jap. name for the Chi. → Zen master, Yin Yüan, who founded the → Obaku sect in Japan. When over 60 years of age, in response to repeated invitations, I. left China for Japan with 20 disciples. He stayed first in the Kōfukuji temple at Nagasaki but moved in following year to Kyoto, where he established chief temple of Obaku sect.

H. Dumoulin, *Hist. of Zen Buddhism* (1963), p. 229.

Initiation → *Ordination*. Initiation into the Buddh. Order in China follows usual Buddh. practice. After a long novitiate under guidance of a 'Master,' the candidate usually presents himself for ordination to priesthood at one of the great monasteries, where elaborate ordination ceremonies are conducted. Formerly novices had to be 20 years old before they could be ordained, and a considerable time had to elapse between the three stages of ordination; for practical reasons these rules are no longer adhered to, and boys of 15, 16 or 17 are frequently ordained. For a good account of I. ceremonies into Buddh. order see K. L. Reichelt, *op. cit.* Rites of I. into Taoist priesthood were in large measure copied from Buddh.

J. Legge (tr.) *Li Chi, S.B.E.,* vol. 28 (1885, repr. 1966), ch. 40; K. L. Reichelt, *Truth and Tradition in Chinese Buddhism* (1927), ch. 8; J. D. Ball, *Things Chinese,* 5th edn. (1925), pp. 605ff.; B. Favre, *Les Sociétés Secretes en Chine* (1933), *passim*.

Insight →→ *Abhinna; Vipassanā.*

Ippen (CE 1239–89). Known in Japan as the itinerant sage, because of his method of propagating Buddhism. An outstanding preacher and missionary of the faith in → Amida

Buddha, his missionary journeys covered nearly the whole of Japan. I. combined relief work with his preaching; he propagated practice of repeating the Buddha name, with which he linked idea that the believer is thus prepared for death at any moment. His followers formed a separate sect, called Jishū (Time doctrine), which inculcated pious thoughts at every moment, and a relig. service six times a day.

M. Anesaki, *Hist. of Japanese Relig.* (1930), pp. 186–7.

Isipatana Name of open space near Banares, where the Buddha is reputed to have preached the famous 'First Sermon,' later described as the 'Setting in motion of the Wheel of the Dhamma' (→ Dhamma-Cakkappavattana Sutta). The open space known as I., trad. location of this sermon, was also noted for its deer-park, or *Migadāya,* where deer were allowed to roam in safety. The Buddha is also said to have spent the first rainy season, after enlightenment, at I. It is a place of Buddh. pilgrimage; one of the → 4 Holy Places. The location is now known as Sārnāth, 6 miles from Banares. A rock-pillar, erected by → Ashoka, stands on site, on which is inscribed the emperor's *'Sanghabhedaka'* edict, i.e., 'concerning dissension in the → *Sangha.'* The remains of monasteries cover a considerable area, some of which are of great antiquity. At time of Chinese Buddh. pilgrim → Hsüang Tsang's visit in 637 CE there was a flourishing monastic community at Sarnath. There are known to have been two → *stupas* of unknown age, one of which was destroyed in 1794 by an Indian prospecting for building materials. A *vihāra* has been built at S. in mod. times by the →Mahabodhi Society.

S. Dutt, *Buddhist Monks and Monasteries of India* (1962), pp. 215–7; P. V. Bapat (ed.), *2500 Years of Buddhism* (1956), pp. 311–3; Malalasekere, *D.P.P.N.,* vol. 1, pp. 323–6.

I Tsing (I Ch'ing, 634–713 CE). A famous Chinese Buddh. pilgrim to India, Sumatra and Java, who spent 25 years abroad, collecting and copying Skt. Buddh. texts. He was partic. concerned to observe and record in minute detail the → Vinaya rules and practices of Indian monks, espec. of the → Sarvāstivāda school. He spent 10 years studying at

I Tsing

celebrated Buddh. centre at → Nalanda. Whilst sojourning at Palembang, Sumatra, he sent home to China *A Record of the Buddhist Relig. in India and the Malay Archipelago,* published in Chinese in 690 and trans. into Eng. by J. Takakusu in 1896. A further record, giving biographical notices of 56 Chinese monks who journeyed to India, and describing his own experiences, was trans. into French by E. Chavannes in 1894. On his return to China in CE 695, I.T. engaged in an influential trans. work under imperial patronage until his death.

J. Takakusu, *Record* (as above) (1896); E. Chavannes (tr.), *Voyage des pélerins bouddhistes, mémoire composé à l'époque de la grande dynastie T'ang sur les religieux éminents . . . dans les pays d'occident,* par I Tsing (1894); *E.R.E.,* XII, pp. 842f.

J

Japanese Religion Japan is the meeting place of four religs.: Shinto, Buddhism, Confucianism and Christianity. Of these Shinto alone is native to Japan. About middle of 6th cent. ce, Buddh., Taoist and Confucian influences came into Japan from China along with Chi. culture, literature and art. The Japanese accepted the Confucian morality with its emphasis on filial piety; but it was Buddh. monks who made the greatest impact, and for 1,000 years Shinto was in large measure absorbed into the Buddh. system. Christianity came to Japan about middle of 16th cent.; after initial success it was practically obliterated until Chr. missions began again in middle of 19th cent.

It was → Buddhism, intro. in 6th cent. ce from China, which became main relig. force in life of Jap. people. It provided a satisfying cosmology and eschatology, elaborate systems of spiritual disciplines and training, and well-organised eccles. organisations. It stimulated creative philosophical speculation, and production of magnificent works of art and literature. It provided great seats of learning, and brought to flower the relig. and aesthetic sentiments of the people. As a popular relig. of the masses, Buddhism provided, on one hand, a satisfying ritual for repose of dead; on the other hand, magical and supernatural assistance for production of mundane benefits. The great → Jodo and Shin sects taught absolute faith and trust in → Amida Buddha. → Zen Buddhism offered discipline and guidance for those who sought enlightenment through self-reliance.

Buddhism, with its numerous sects and entrenched in

149

Jātaka

traditionalism, is still a living relig. in Japan, but has lost much of its early vigour.

M. Anesaki, *Hist. of Japanese Religion* (1930); W. K. Bunce, *Religs. in Japan* (1955); J. M. Kitagawa, *Relig. in Japanese Hist.* (1966); J. Herbert, *Shinto* (1967); J. Boxer, *The Christian Century in Japan*, 1549–1650 (1968).

Jātaka Type of Buddh. lit., viz. a 'birth-story.' By this is meant a story of the Buddha, or of some prominent character among early Buddh., in some previous existence, or 'birth.' The principal character may appear as a man, a *deva*, a demon, or more usually, an animal. The present characteristics or situation of person concerned are supposed to be at least partly explainable in terms of his conduct in previous existence of which the J. tells. The → Pali canon contains collection of 547 such stories, which forms part of the → *Khuddaka-Nikaya*. Many stories are anc. folk tales of Indian pre-Buddh. origin, which have been taken over and adapted for Buddh. use by add. of an explanatory prologue giving the *mis-en-scène,* often in connection with travels and preaching of → Gotama the Buddha, and with epilogue added, in which the characters in the anc. story are identified with prominent persons of time of Buddha. The most import. element in these J.'s are the verses, which sometimes express the moral of story, sometimes form part of narrative and dialogue. Strictly it is the verses alone which are regarded as canonical; the narrator was allowed certain liberty of expression in prose passages. Besides the Pali canonical collection of 547, there are several Chinese collections, based on Skt. or Prakrit originals; variant collections are known to exist in Buddh. countries of S.E. Asia, some of which have recently become known to West. scholars. From early times Buddh., e.g. → *Ajantā* have delighted in providing pictorial or *bas-relief* versions of J.'s for embellishment of pagodas and monasteries and for edification of the Buddh. populace, who thus from an early age have become familiar with the virtues regarded as admirable in Buddh. trad. Beside their familiarity with these pictorial versions of the J.'s, the Buddh. lay people of S.E.

Asia are usually familiar also with at least the major J.'s in their lit. or recited forms.

Jātaka Stories, trans. by various hands under editorship of E. B. Cowell, repr. in 3 vols. (1956); T. W. Rhys-Davids, *Buddhist India,* 8th edn. (1959), ch. XI.

Java → *Indonesia.*

Jhāna (Pali); **Dhyāna** (Skt.) Buddh. technical term for progression through certain mental states, the climax of which is a special experience of enhanced psychic vitality. The use of term may have been pre-Buddh. Usually 4 stages are distinguished: concentration of mind on single subject; mental and physical joy and ease; then a sense of ease only; finally, sense of perfect clarity and equanimity. In the → Abhidhamma lit. 5 stages are distinguished, the 1st of the 4 subdivided into two; these divisions are arbitrary and schematic only; the order of progression could be divided up into yet other stages. The 4 Jh.'s are described in a number of passages in the Pali canon, e.g. in the *Samaññaphala Sutta* (*D.N.,* i, 73ff.), (*Dialogues of the Buddha,* Pt. I, pp. 84–6). The experience thus achieved is regarded as means to further spiritual progress and not as an end in itself; from a relig. or spiritual point of view the Jh.'s as such are of neutral value. The view that achievement of the Jh.'s was equivalent to attaining spiritual state of → nirvāna is repudiated in the *Brahma-Jala Sutta* of the → Digha-Nikaya (*D.N.,* i, 37ff.) (*Dialogues of the Buddha,* pt. I, pp. 50–2).

The hist. of word *jhāna/dhyāna* is noteworthy. In its Skt. form, the term passed into Chinese Buddh. usage as → Ch'an, and hence into Japanese as → Zen. A somewhat different arrangement of *dhyāna* under 4 heads is characteristic of → Mahayana, and espec. of the → Yogācāras; it is dealt with by D. T. Suzuki in his *Essays in Zen Buddhism,* Series I, pp. 81f., and *Studies in the Lankavatara Sutra* (1930). The Yogācāras laid special emphasis on experience of withdrawal from world by means of *dhyāna.*

Jinjō (d. 742 CE). Korean monk who introduced the → Kegon school of Buddhism into Japan.

Jodo Jap. name for Chi. Ching T'u or → Pure Land school of

Jojitsu

Buddhism. The great → Amida school of Jap. Buddhism, which proclaimed the Buddha of Infinite Light and Great Compassion, won adherence of the masses and became most popular form of Buddhism in Japan. Founded by → Honen in CE 1175, it was developed into Jodo-Shinshu by → Shinran (CE 1173–1263). It proclaimed the doc. of *Tāriki* ('other-effort'), or salvation by faith and grace. It encouraged practice of → *nembutsu*, the constant repetition of Amida's name by which birth in the West. Paradise was effected. Devotees were taught childlike trust in compassion and infinite merit of Amida and → Kwan-On. The result was a pietistic form of relig., regarded as an easy way to salvation. There are four sects of Jodo in Japan, with minor differences: Jodo proper with about 4 m. adherents; → Shinshu with about 13 m., and Yuzunembutsu and Ji, each with a much smaller following. The principal scriptures of school are the smaller and large *Sukhāvatīvyūha Sūtras* and the *Amatāyur-dhyāna Sūtra*.
M. Anesaki, *Hist. of Japanese Relig.* (1930), pp. 170ff.; E. Steinilber-Oberlin, *The Buddhist Sects of Japan* (1938), chs. 9, 10; *E.R.E.,* VII, pp. 483–4.

Jojitsu School of Jap. Buddhism intro. from Paikche (S. Korea) by Korean monks Kwanroku and Ekwan about 625 CE. Its nihilistic teachings drew their inspiration from the Hindu patriarchs Nagarjuna and Deva, and teachings of Chinese monk → Hsüan Tsang. A school of analytical study devoted to cosmological and psychological problems, its teachings were freely studied during Nara period, but school soon merged with Sanron. It taught that both the 'ego' and all *dharmas* are equally illusions; the past and future non-existent and the present vanishing as soon as born.
E. Steinilber-Oberlin, *The Buddhist Sects of Japan* (1938), ch. 2.

K

Kalpa (Skt.); **Kappa** (Pali) In Buddh. usage: (1) a measure, rule or practice (2) a certain period of time—in common with all Indian thought, the Buddh. K.'s are held to be of incredibly long duration: 'an age'; 'an eternity' (→ *Creation*).

Kāma Term used in Buddhism as in Hinduism for 'pleasure,' 'sense-enjoyment,' 'sensuality.' K. is used to characterise existence in all but the higher or more refined planes or 'realms'; it occurs in combination with *loka* (world) or *vacara* (sphere of existence), to designate the world in which majority of inhabitants of universe are found, i.e. *kāma-loka,* or *Kāma-vacara* (→ Cosmology). K. is always regarded in Buddh. thought as first and chief obstacle to spiritual progress; it is frequently assoc. with passion (*rāga*), impulse (*chanda*) and greed (*gedha*).

Kamma (Pali); **Karma** (Skt.) In Buddh., as in Indian thought gen., K. is the universal law of act and consequence. The primary meaning is that of *action* or *deed;* from this follows the applied meaning of deed as expressive of the doer's will, and thus the causal factor in doer's subsequent state or condition. K. thus comes to be 'a law, the working of which cannot be escaped' (PTS Pali-Eng. Dict.). Every being thus 'inherits' his own K., and also continues to produce further K., the consequences of which will be felt at some later time. In the Buddh. analysis of the human situation, however, K. does not constitute a doc. of determinism, since one is free to act for better or for worse within situation which his K. has produced; his K. does not determine his *response to* situation, it only presents him with the datum of situation itself. Moreover, it is the volition, rather than the action alone, which, in the Buddh. view, is

153

Kanishka

of greatest importance in producing fresh K. The consequences of K. may be experienced during life-time of the
doer, or in next birth, or in some successive birth (A.N., VI,
63). In gen. the Buddh. view is that volition characterised
by greed, hatred and delusion produces unwholesome K.,
while volition characterised by opposite qualities produces
wholesome K.

It is sometimes assumed that belief in → rebirth was accepted by Buddha without question from earlier Indian
relig. This is a controversial question, discussed at length
by K. N. Jayatilleke, who argues that there is no evidence
that such a belief was 'universal or even widespread prior
to advent of Buddhism,' or for assumption that Buddh.
took such a notion for granted in sense of accepting it un-
critically from prevalent trad. It is poss. that early Buddh.
thought may in fact have contributed towards formulation
belief. Buddh. saw difficulty of reconciling belief in K. and
transmigration with doc. of → *anatta,* yet regarded belief
in *K* as essential to their position, and asserted it over
against contemporary materialist thinkers and others who
did not hold such a belief.

K. N. Jayatilleke, *Early Buddhist Theory of Knowledge,* 1963,
ch. VIII.

Kanishka Buddh. ruler of Kushan empire, which lay to N.W.
of India. His accession is dated variously as 78, 128 and 144
CE, the 2 latter now being regarded as more probable. A
Buddh. council, reckoned by Mhy. Buddh. as the 4th (→
Councils, Buddh.) was held in his reign, at Jālandhar acc. to
one trad. in Kashmir; acc. to another. K. is repr. in trad. as
desirous of settling disputes among various schools of
Buddh. thought, and has a place in estimation of Mhy.
Buddh. similar to that given to → Ashoka by Teravādins.
H. Winternitz, *History of Indian Literature,* vol. 2, ch. 5.

Kapilavatthu (Pali); **Kapilāvastu** (Skt.) Paternal home of →
Gautama the Buddha; a town in Himalayan foothills in
what is now Nepal, it was in Buddha's time the capital of
the → Sakya tribe. The Buddha was born at → Lumbini,
near K., and spent his childhood and early manhood in K.
Acc. to Pali texts (*Jat.,* I, 87ff.; *Vin.,* I, 82), the Buddha visited

K. again in year after his enlightenment. He preached his doc. to the people of K., and his father → Suddhodana became a → *sotapanna*. The Buddha's son → Rāhula, who was at this time still a child, became a → *samanera*, or novice-candidate for the → Sangha. A large number of Sakyans also entered the Sangha. The Buddha visited K. on a number of other occasions; various discourses and → Jātaka stories contained in the Pali canon are said to have been preached by him at K. Towards end of Buddha's life the town was attacked and destroyed and the Sakya people massacred by Viḍūḍabha, a Kosalan prince, in revenge for insult he received there. Nevertheless, at Buddha's death, the people of K. are said to have claimed a share of his ashes after cremation, and to have erected a shrine over them in town (D.N., II, 167). At time of the Chinese pilgrim Fa Hsien, who visited India early in 5th cent. CE, however, there were only ruins to be seen at K.; the site of town is now unidentified.

Malalasekere, *D.P.P.N.,* vol. I, pp. 516–20.

Karma Karma, sometimes transliterated *karman,* lit. means 'deed' or 'act,' but more partic. is used to ref. to law governing deeds, whereby they have more and material effects in this life and future lives. It is thus closely connected with belief in reincarnation or → rebirth, and is related to analogous conceptions in Jainism and Buddhism.

Karunā In Buddh. thought *karunā,* or compassion, holds import. place as one of the 4 'spiritual abodes,' i.e., → *brahma-vihāras.* In partic., this is the unmotivated graciousness of attitude shown by → Buddhas and → Bodhisattvas towards mortal beings. The Buddh. life is understood as consisting of cultivation of both wisdom (*prajñā*) and compassion; it is held that, without former, the emotion of compassion may be erroneously directed, i.e., it may be engaged in for unwise motives. The older, → Hīnayāna, form of Buddhism tended to lay principal emphasis on need for wisdom; the → Mahāyāna emphasised both as equally important, over against earlier emphasis on wisdom predominantly, which could, acc. to the Mhy., result in an isolated intellectualism. Eventually this emphasis on

K. became the more predominant, and in later forms of Mhy. developed into concept of the 'saving grace' of the Buddha → Amitabha, which he offers to those who call upon him in faith.

Kathā-Vathu One of 7 books of the Pali → Abhidhamma-Pitaka of the Theravāda school; considered by some authorities to be historically the most import. of the seven. Acc. to the trad. (*Mahāvamsa*, V, 278; *Dipavamsa*, VII, 41:56–8), *K.-V.* is said to have been recited by the Elder named Moggaliputta Tissa at 3rd Buddh. Council (→ Councils), held at Patna in reign of emperor → Ashoka. The work, in 23 chapters, consists of discussion (*kathā*), and refutation of 219 different erroneous teachings then being propounded by schismatic groups of monks. Some mod. scholars are inclined to doubt that work, as it now exists, was compiled by Moggaliputta Tissa, as some heretical views confuted are those of schools which arose some cents. later than Council of Patna.

S. Z. Aung-C. A. F. Rhys-Davids, *Points of Controversy* (1915, repr. 1960); Nyanatiloka Mahathera, *Guide through the Abhidhamma-Pitaka* (1957), ch. 5.

Kāya (Buddh.) → Buddha-Kāya.

Kegon School (→ Hua Yen). This school, intro. into Japan by Korean monk, → Jinjo (d. 742) played import. role in Buddhism of Nara period. Based on the *Avatāmsaka Sūtras,* with their doc. of the Buddhahood of all sentient beings, the identity of → nirvāna and → samsara, and wisdom and compassion of the → bodhisattvas who guide errant beings to Buddhahood, the school had considerable influence on development of → Zen. Its teaching that aim of relig. is to dispel illusion of the separate ego may be described as cosmotheism. Though its philosophical appeal was considerable, it did not exert much practical influence. H. Dumoulin, *Hist. of Zen Buddhism* (1963), pp. 38ff.; M. Anesaki, *Hist. of Japanese Relig.* (1930), pp. 93ff.

Khandha (Pali); **Skandha** (Skt.) Buddh. term meaning 'group' or 'aggregate' of factors. What is commonly regarded as a human 'individual' may, in Buddh. terms, be analysed into 5 K.s. The 1st group of factors is *rūpa* (form) = the physical or corporeal; 2nd: *vedanā* = sensation or feeling; 3rd: *sannā* (Pali)/*samjnā* (Skt.) = perception; 4th: *sankhāra* (Pali)/*samskāra* (Skt.) = formative principle or volition; 5th: *viññāna* (Pali)/*vijñāna* (Skt.) = consciousness. Each of these is a group, aggregate or 'bundle' of elements of that type which are continually in flux; thus the physical nature of individual is at any moment a process or flux of physical elements; similarly with sensations, perceptions, volitions and consciousness. The whole process constituted by the 5 groups is the human individual at any given moment of his life-history; at different stages in that hist. he exhibits different appearances and characteristics. This process of continual change is evident, even to the eye of 'common-sense,' in the difference between the individual as a baby, a youth, a mature man, and old man. Physically the process of change is continuous; similarly, it is held, at the level of sensation-volition; and of the state or condition of consciousness. The 5 K.'s are sometimes given in a 3-fold scheme: (1) physical, viz., *rūpa;* (2) sense-perception and reaction, viz., *vedanā, saññā,* and *sankhāra;* (3) consciousness, or *viññāna.* In this case the 3 groups are called *rūpa, cetasikā* (concomitants or conditioning factors of consciousness) and *citta* (state of consciousness). This is scheme used in the → Abhidhamma; e.g. in → *Dhamma-Sanganī* of the Theravādin Abh.-Pitaka. More simply the 5 K.'s may be arranged in 2 groups: (1) *rūpa* (2) *nāma* (viz. the other 4 K.'s. There is thus nothing ultimate or absolute about the 5 K.'s; they are simply abstract classifications used in Buddh. analysis of human existence, useful as analytical categories, but themselves only concepts, just as the 'individual' is only a concept, having no abiding reality. In the Theravādin view, the ultimate elements of psycho-physical existence are the → *dhammas:* these are the 'atoms' of which the K.'s are groups or aggregates. The *dhammas* are of momentary existence only; before they arise they have no reality, when they have passed they have no reality; they are thus as it were 'flashes' of reality. The → Mādhyamika school of → Mahāyāna criticised the Theravādin for not applying relentlessly analytical method

Khuddaka-Nikāya

by which it was perceived that K.'s are only relative categories to the *dhammas* also, but instead, arbitrarily, stopping at *dhammas* as the 'atoms.'

Khuddaka-Nikāya Collection of Buddh. canonical books, forming 5th section of the → Sutta-Pitaka of Pali canon. The name *khuddaka* designates this Nikāya as one of 'short pieces.' These are 15 in number, as follows: (1) *Khuddaka-pātha*, a miscellaneous collection of lists of moral rules, catechism questions, Buddh. formulae incl., e.g. that of taking refuge in the Buddha, Dhamma, and Sangha (→ Tri-Ratna) widely used in Buddh. devotions; (2) → *Dhamma-pada*; (3) → *Udāna*; (4) *Itivuttaka*, collection of miscellaneous verses dealing largely with morality, and intro. in most cases by formula *'iti vuccati'*—'thus it is said'; (5) → *Sutta-Nipāta*; (6) *Vimāna-vatthu*, collection of 83 stories, arranged in 7 groups, concerning lives of → devas (heavenly beings) in their celestial palaces, where they enjoy rewards for some previous good acts; this, and (7) → *Petavatthu*, describing sad fate of those who in spirit-realm are now expiating some past misdeed, are gen. held to be later in origin than other parts of canon, largely on linguistic grounds; (8) → *Theragāthā*, and (9) → *Therīgāthā* are, respectively, collections of 'songs of the Theras' (elder monks) and of the Therī (elder nuns); (10) → *Jātaka* stories; (11) *Niddesa*, a commentary on part (the *Atthakavagga*) of the → Sutta-Nipāta, (which testifies to early date of latter, that it should have a canonical commentary); (12) *Patisam-bhida-magga*, an analytical treatise in style of the → Abhidhamma works; (13) *Apadāna*, collection of stories in verse of previous existences of certain monks and nuns; (14) → *Buddha-Vamsa*; and (15) *Cariyāpitaka*, selection of *Jātakas* arranged specially to illustrate certain Buddh. moral virtues, regarded by Geiger, following Winternitz, as work of a monk 'who manufactured edifying stories for the elucidation of the doctrine on the basis of the existing Jātakas.' The K.N. thus incl. a variety of types of Buddh. texts, both in contents and date of composition, embracing as it does what is undoubtedly one of the earliest Buddh. documents, the *Sutta-Nipāta,* as well as some of the latest of canonical lit., such as (11), (12), (13) and (15) listed above. (→→ *Tipitaka; Sutta-Pitaka*).

Kilesa (Pali); **Kleśa** (Skt.) Term used in Buddhism for 'defilements,' i.e. 'morally defiling passions.' In the → Theravadin sch., these are ten in number: (1) greed (*lobha*) (2) hatred (*dosa*) (3) delusion (*moha*) (4) conceit (*māna*) (5) speculative views (*ditthi*) (6) doubt (*vicikiccha*) (7) mental sloth (*thina*) (8) restlessness (*uddhacca*) (9) shamelessness (*ahirika*) (10) moral carelessness (*anottappa*). This list of 10 occurs first in the Thv. scriptures in the → *Abh.-Pitaka*, in the *Dhamma-Sangani;* it is thus a feature of the reflective systematic stage in hist. of B. thought. The → Sarvāstivādin school affirmed first six of these as fundamental K.'s, (acc. to the → *Abh.-Kosa*), and to them added list of 10 subsidiary K.'s, viz. anger, hypocrisy, selfishness, envy, gloom, shamefulness, enmity, deceit, dishonesty and arrogance. The Mhy. school of → Yogācāra also affirmed first 6 as fundamental K.'s and added list of 20 subsidiary K.'s (acc. to the *Vidhyāmātra Siddhi* of Dharmapāla). These 20 are virtually the 10 given in the Sarvāstivādin list with add. of: shamelessness, impudence, torpor, recklessness, lack of faith, idleness, carelessness, forgetfulness, confusion and wrong judgment. Some Yogācāra lists give 24 subsidiary K.'s. In the Yogācāra view, K. is regarded as something foreign to basic consciousness or *Ālaya-vijñāna;* a kind of 'dust' or impurity, 'spoiling the immaculate Alaya' (Suzuki), or the 'guest who is uninvited'—a somewhat different doc. of man from that reflected in Thv. phenomenology.
Nyanamoli, *The Path of Purification* (1964); W. M. McGovern, *Manual of Buddhist Philosophy,* vol. I (1923); D. T. Suzuki, *Studies in the Lankavatara Sutra* (1930).

Kings (Buddh.) → Buddhism, Political Power.

Kōan (Jap.) From Chinese *kung-an*—an official record, a public notice. A technical term used in → Zen Buddhism for an exercise given by a Zen master to his disciple and designed to break through intellectual limitations and lead to a flash of sudden intuition for attainment of → satori. The Kōan are often couched as problems insoluble by, and nonsensical to, the intellect. In almost all of them the striking ele-

Kōbō Daishi

ment is the illogical or absurd act or word. Collections of kōan were made in China in the Sung Dynasty, notably the *Pi-yen-lu* and the *Wu-mên-kuan,* and they provided an effective method for systematic guidance towards enlightenment in Zen monasteries both in China and Japan. Those in actual use by Zen masters are numerous and varied, some 1700 in all. Attempts have been made to classify them into five or more groups.

H. Dumoulin, *Hist. of Zen Buddhism* (1963), pp. 126ff.; D. T. Suzuki, *Essays in Zen Buddhism* (2), 1933, pp. 83ff. *Studies in Zen* (1955), pp. 24ff.

Kōbō Daishi (CE 774–835). Posthumous name of Kūkai, Jap. Buddh. saint and founder of → Shingon sect of Buddhism. Having studied in China, he intro. into Japan, and brought to its final systematization, the pantheistic mysticism of the Tantric (Chên Yen or True Word) sect. Acc. to K.D.'s philosophy, the universe is the exterialised form of Maha-Vairochana Buddha. It is his real body (*dharma-kāya*), divided into two complementary constituents, the mental and the material. K.D. classified various forms of the relig. life, incl. Hinduism, Confucianism, Taoism, and other Buddh. sects, into ten grades of development, culminating in the mystic pantheism of Shingon, in which full blessedness of Buddhahood is realised. He taught an all-embracing syncretism of a highly mystical nature, and thus paved the way for → Ryōbu Shinto. K.D. had a far-reaching influence both in court circles and among the common people. He built a monastery on Mt. Kōya, which became headquarters of Shingon sect. His body is believed never to have decayed, but awaits resurrection at advent of → Maitreya Buddha. (→ Dharma-Kāya).

Korea The religs. of K. are Animism, Confucianism and Buddhism, with some 3 m. Christians in the S. Buddhism, intro. from China from about 4th cent. CE, was a powerful influence in court circles and grad. permeated down through all strata of population, providing in its temples and monasteries great centres of culture, and stimulating works of art, literature, philosophy and relig. But by 14th cent. CE, it was largely moribund.

Kumārajīva

Kosa → *Abhidharma-Kosa.*

Koyasan A famous Jap. monastery of → Shingon sect, S.E. of Osaka, where lies tomb of → Kōbō Daishi, where he sleeps until awakened at coming of next Buddha, Miroku. The monastery is place of pilgrimage, and the cremated remains of devout Buddh. are often sent to be deposited there.

Kuan Yin (Jap. Kwan-On, Kwannon). Chinese name for famous → bodhisattva, → Avalokitesvara, next to → Amitābha, the most popular deity of → Pure Land Sects of Mahāyāna Buddhism throughout the Far East. The Chi. name, Kuan Yin ('the One who hears the cry'), seems to have arisen through a confusion between the Skt. words *īśvara,* 'lord' and *svara,* 'sound, noise.' The cult of K.Y. was intro. into China about 5th cent. CE. The bodhisattva is repres. in early iconography in male form, sometimes with a thousand eyes and arms, sometimes with eleven heads, or with a horse's head, etc. But it was as a great female divinity, the Goddess of Mercy, that K.Y. gained a supreme place in Chi. popular relig. as the protectress of women and children, the bestower of children and the all-compassionate Mother-Goddess. Numerous legends and stories have arisen in China regarding her origin, life and saving activities. Temples in her honour are to be found all over China, and it is practically impossible to distinguish her from the Taoist-inspired T'ien Hou (Empress of Heaven), T'ien Shang Shêng Mu (The Holy Mother) and the Pi-hsia-Yüan-Chün (Princess of the Variegated Clouds).
H. Maspero, 'Mythology of Modern China,' in J. Hackin (ed.), *Asiatic Mythology* (1932, 1963), pp. 352ff.; H. Doré, *Chinese Superstitions* (E.T. 1914), vol. 6; K. L. Reichelt, *Truth and Tradition in Chinese Buddhism* (1927), pp. 179ff.; J. H. Chamberlayne, 'The Development of Kuan Yin,' in *Numen,* vol. 9 (1962).

Kumārajīva (CE 344–413). Buddh. monk and eminent translator, also import. agent in spread to China of Indian → Mādhyamika school of Buddh. philosophy. Before 20 yrs of age, K. studied → Sarvāstivādin Abhidharma literature in Kashgar; but, on meeting a Mahāyānist named Suryasama,

Kusha School

was converted to the → Mādhyamika views. Ordained monk at age of 20 at Kuchā, he spent some years there studying Mahāyāna literature. When about 40, K. was captured by a Chinese raiding force and taken to China, where he remained for rest of life. He learnt Chinese and trans. into this language many → Mahāyāna texts, mostly of Mādhyamika school.

Richard H. Robinson, *Early Mādhyamika in India and China*, 1967, ch. 3. (K. in Chi. context).

(Chinese—Fa Hu) CE 344–413. One of greatest of early translators of Buddh. scriptures from Skt. into Chinese, K. headed famous school of translators in capital city, Ch'ang-an. Born in Kuchā of Brahmin father and Kuchean princess, he studied Buddhism in Kashmir, after which he returned to Kuchā to be ordained. There for 20 yrs. he studied the Mahāyāna. Taken as a prisoner to China, he arrived in Ch'ang-an in CE 401, where he was venerated by members of ruling family and drew disciples from all quarters of empire. Through his efforts the great philosophical treatises of Mahāyāna were made comprehensible to the Chinese; in partic. works of →→ Nagarguna, Aryadeva, Vasubandhu and Asanga. He engaged in extensive correspondence with → Hui Yüan. Largely through his efforts, Buddh. philosophy came to be regarded on an equal footing with indigenous thought; to his success in trans. may be attributed much of progress of Buddhism among the gentry.

E. Zürcher, *The Buddhist Conquest of China* (1959), *passim*; D. H. Smith, *Chinese Religions* (1968), pp. 115f. 127f.

Kusha School School of Jap. Buddhism, long extinct, was intro. into Japan from China by two Japanese monks Chitsu and Chitatsu in CE 658. Its highly metaphysical teachings are based on the Abhidharma-Kosa, attr. to celebrated Indian Buddh. sage Vasubandhu (*c*. 5th cent.).

Kushinagara One of the 4 Buddh. → *holy places,* location of the → Buddha's decease. The events leading up to and following the decease are recounted in detail in the → *Mahā-Parinabbāna Sutta* of the Digha-Nikaya; here Kushinagara, with its anc. name Kusināra, is described as an insignificant 'wattle and daub' township of the Malla tribe, 'set in the midst of jungles.' After death of Buddha, his body was taken through town, from north gate to the east, and cremated outside at a shrine of the Mallas. The trad. is that, after cremation, some of the relics were deposited in a → *stūpa* at K., known as the Mukutabandhana. A large monastic settlement (*vihāra*) appears to have been built there, but was already in ruins by time the Chinese pilgrim → Hsüan Tsang visited site in 7th cent. CE. Before this, it had been place of sacred pilgrimage; the reason why it fell into ruins is unknown. The remains of *stupa*, built by the Mallas over their share of the relics, is thought to be repr. by the large ruined mound called locally 'Ramabhar.' The village, which stands on the anc. site, at junction of river Rapti and the Gondak, is known as Kasia, in the east of the Gorakhpur district, in Uttar Pradesh, to the south of the Nepal border.

Malalasekere, *D.P.P.N.,* vol. I, pp. 653–5; S. Dutt, *Buddhist Monks and Monasteries of India* (1962), pp. 217f.; P. V. Bapat (ed.), *2500 Years of Buddhism* (1956), p. 314.

Kwan-On (or Kwannon) (→ Kuan Yin). Jap. name for great Buddh. *bosatsu* or → bodhisattva, most revered in Japan, to whom many great temples are consecrated. The cult of K. goes back to intro. of → Buddhism into Japan; Prince Shotoku (CE 572–621) was a fervent worshipper. K., together with Daiseishi-bosatsu, was regarded as a companion (or, acc. to → Shingon sect, as a manifestation) of → Amida. He is repres. in many forms (i.e. with six arms, or eleven heads, or with a horse's head), to indicate his infinite power, compassion, and virtue, and his purpose of salvation for all sentient beings, incl. men and animals. He is the all-compassionate Lord of Mercy, represented as healer and saviour, leading souls in whom he has awakened piety to the paradise of Amida. Sometimes, as in China, K. is represented as a female deity.

E.R.E., VII, pp. 763–4; Serge Eliseev, 'The Mythology of Japan,' in J. Hackin (ed.), *Asiatic Mythology* (1932), pp. 438–41.

L

Lalita-Vistara One of most import. texts of → Mahāyāna Buddhism, although it emanated from the → Sarvāstivādin school. The title implies the viewpoint: the Buddha's life and work is seen as 'play' or 'sport' (*lalita*) of a supernatural being, of which the book is a narration (*vistara*). While narrative begins in style of early Pali suttas, 'Thus have I heard,' it soon becomes markedly different in tone and character in its extravagantly miraculous setting. Those portions of work, which are held to be older than main narrative, viz. the *Gāthas,* or stanzas, are in fairly close agreement with early Pali accounts of events of Buddha's life, such as that of the *Mahāvagga* of the → Vināya-Pitaka. It has, therefore, been concluded that the L. is revised form of an older narrative, poss. of Sarvāstivādin school; the revision having taken form of enlarging and embellishing details in accord. with ideas and spirit of the Mahāyāna, as, e.g., in its tendency towards Buddha-bhakti, or adoration of Buddha. When it was cast in present form is unknown; it may poss. have been in period when the art-forms of → Gandhāra were developing, as there are certain agreements and similarities between conception of the Buddha in them and in L. Since, however, it evidently contains anc. material, the L. has been regarded as import. source of evidence of anc. Buddhism.

M. Winternitz, *Hist. of Indian Literature* (1933), vol. 2, pp. 248–56.

Lankā Anc. name for → Ceylon.

Lankāvatāra Sūtra One of the nine principal texts of Mhy. Buddhism (→ Sanskrit Literature). Acc. to full title, '*Ārya-saddharma-lankāvatāronāma-mahāyāna-sutram,*' it contains the 'noble orthodox teaching [i.e., of Buddhism], given [i.e., by the Buddha] (on occasion of) entering into Ceylon.' It consists of conversations Buddha had with both Ravanna, the mythical lord of → Ceylon, who is here repr. as a good Buddh. layman; and also, at more profound level with a Bodhisattva named Mahāmati (or → Mañjuśrī). The Sutra embodies critique of Hindu philosophy, and also essays explanation of resemblance between Mhy. Buddh. and Hindu philosophy which had come to be recognised by time of composition of this work. An early form of sūtra existed in CE 420, when it was trans. into Chinese. Three subsequent trsls. into Chinese were made, the last of these in CE 704; the earlier Skt. text, on which 1st trans. was based, appears to have received some elaboration by 8th cent. The sūtra is import. source so far as Chi. and Jap. Bhm. is concerned, esp. for notions of → *alaya-vijñāna* and docs. of → Yogācara school → Ch'an (Zen) school. It has no recognisable systematic structure; it is, acc. to Suzuki, 'a collection of notes unsystematically strung together.' For summary of contents cf. E. J. Thomas, *Hist. of Buddhist Thought*, 2nd edn. (1951), pp. 230–6; see also D. T. Suzuki, *Studies in the Lankāvatāra Sūtra* (1930), *Essays in Zen Buddhism* vol. I (1927).

Laos, Buddhism in → Cambodia.

Literature (Sacred) → Sanskrit.

Lobha Buddh. term for 'greed,' which is regarded as one of the 3 'roots' of the evil condition of human existence, the others being Dosa and → Moha. Buddh. discipline, moral/meditational, aims at bringing about eradication of L., principally by cultivation of its opposite, viz. generosity (→ Dāna), which can take practical form, as in giving of one's possessions or money or other resources to others for their welfare; it can also be cultivated in its mental form of thinking generously of others.

Lohan (Chinese term, derived from Skt. *arhan, arhat;* Jap. and Korean—*rahan, rahat*). Signifies one who has attained Buddh. enlightenment and perfection. The L. are personal disciples and worthies of Buddha. Originally 16 in number, from 10th cent. CE 18 have been gen. recognised in China;

Lotus Sūtra

their images were intro. into halls of Buddh. temples, where they are regarded as patrons and guardians of Buddhism throughout world.

For detailed description, E. T. C. Werner, *Dict. of Chinese Mythology* (1932).

Lotus Sūtra → Saddharma-Pundarīka.

(Chinese—*Miao Fa Lien Hua Ching*) The L.-S., or the Lotus of the True Doctrine (*Saddharma-Pundarīka Sūtra*) was first trans. into Chinese by Dharmaraksa (Fa Hu), who flourished *c.* CE 266–308. With its doc. of the one Buddha-vehicle, which opens way to Buddhahood for all believers, its stress on the eternal and omniscient Buddha, and its wealth of images and parables, it soon became venerated as a fundamental scripture of Chi. Buddhism. Trans. again by → Kumārajīva early in 5th cent. CE, it came to be regarded by the → T'ien T'ai school as highest fulfilment of Buddha's teaching and complete exposition of Truth. It was treasured by most sects of the → Mahāyāna; it is of paramount importance for develop. of a rich Buddh. mythology in China, in which the eternal Buddha-principle, repr. in innumerable forms, is shown as working out purpose of salvation for all suffering humanity. To quote W. E. Soothill, the L.-S. is 'unique in the world's relig. literature. A magnificent apocalypse, it presents a spiritual drama of the highest order, with the universe as its stage, eternity as its period, and Buddhas, gods, men, devils as its *dramatis personae*. From the most distant worlds and from past aeons, the eternal Buddhas throng the stage to hear the mighty Buddha proclaim his ancient and eternal Truth. . . . On earth he has assumed human form with all its limitations. Now he reveals himself *sub specie aeternitatis* as the Eternal, Omniscient, Omnipotent, Omnipresent Buddha, creator-destroyer, recreator of all worlds.'

W. E. Soothill, *The Lotus of the Wonderful Law* (1930), p. 13; E. Zürcher, *The Buddhist Conquest of China* (1959), *passim*; D. H. Smith, *Chinese Religions* (1968), pp. 114f., 132f.; K. L. Reichelt, *Truth and Tradition in Chinese Buddhism* (1927), *passim*.

Love → Metta.

Lumbini Buddh. place of pilgrimage, and one of the 4 → Holy Places, since, acc. to Buddh. trad., it was place of the Buddha's birth (*Jātaka*, I, 52, 54). The place is described in Buddh. lit. as a park situated in Sakyan tribal territory between Kapilavastu and Devadaha. L. was visited by Buddha during course of his travels; he there delivered to the monks a discourse known now as the *Devadaha Sutta*. The emperor → Ashoka made a pilgrimage there, *c.* 249 BC, a fact that has been confirmed in mod. times by discovery of a commemorative pillar erected by Ashoka and bearing five-line inscription in a dialect of E. India. This was deciphered in 1898, and found to consist of 3 sentences: 'When King Devānampiya Piyyadesi had been anointed twenty years, he came himself and worshipped [this spot] because the Buddha Sakyamuni was born here. [He] both caused to be made a stone bearing a horse [?] and caused a stone-pillar to be set up [in order to show] that the Blessed One [Bhagavan] was born here. [He] made the village of Lumbini free of taxes and paying [only] an eighth share [of the produce].' The Chinese Buddh. pilgrim, → Fa Hsien, who visited India at begin. of 5th cent. CE, mentions L., but does not appear to have located it nor to have visited it; only the ruins of town of Kapilavastu were then to be seen. Similarly another pilgrim → Hsüang Tsang (*c.* CE 636), visiting Kapilāvastu, heard only accounts of a stone pillar in the outlying forest, but was not able to visit spot. The pillar bearing Ashoka's inscription has now been restored; it is located 2 m. N. of Bhagavanpura, within territory of Nepal; the place is known as Rumindei (→ Kapilavatthu).
S. Dutt, *The Buddha and Five After-Centuries* (1957), ch. 2.

Lü Tsung An import. school of Chi. Buddhism founded by Tao Hsüan (CE 595–667). It is based on the Hinayanist → Vinaya, and more concerned with organisation and gov. of monasteries than with subtleties of doc. The founder believed that morality and discipline lie at basis of the relig. life. The chief monastery of sect is at Pao-hua-shan in Kiangsi province, where only two meals a day are permitted and no drink but tea.
S. Couling, *Encycl. Sinica* (Shanghai, 1917; 1965), p. 318.

M

Mādhyamika School of Buddh. philosophy founded by Nagarjuna (c. CE 150), the central doc. of which is the negation (śūñyatā) of all empirical concepts, such as → dhammas, or ultimate constituents of existence, affirmed in the → Abhidhamma of the Theravādins. The notion of sunyata was already to be found in the Prajna-Paramita literature; it was this which Nagarjuna formulated and expounded in such a way as to make it the basis of a new school of Buddh. philosophy. The criticism levelled by this → Mahāyāna school against the Theravāda was that latter's Abhidhamma method of analysis, while it was true to teaching of Buddha in rejecting notion of a real, eternally-existing self, and in analysing the human individual into → khandhas, and the khandhas into dhammas, failed to carry this method of analysis of concepts to its logical end; the Theravāda stopped short at the dhammas, and affirmed reality of these. Acc. to M., this was an arbitrary halting of method of analysis: dhammas were also concepts which must be seen as only temporary resting places in the analytical process. Acc. to M., dhammas also had no reality; for the real was devoid (śūñya) of all conceptual constructions. M. was thus a doc. of an Absolute which is to be realised only through Prajñā, i.e. Wisdom, or Intuition; Prajnā is itself the Absolute. The dhammas have no nature of their own as the Theravāda affirmed; only the Absolute has this. The M. school held that this was a view which steered between the ātma, or self-affirming doc., and the nairyātma, or self-rejecting doc. of Theravāda; hence the name 'Middle View' (Madhyamaka Darśana), by which this school came to be known; this designation does not, however, seem to have

Magadha

been used by Nargarjuna or his contemporary and associate → Aryadeva.

There were, acc. to Murti, 3 subsequent stages in develop. of the M. school, after formulation of its central principle by Nagarjuna and Aryadeva. These were: the splitting of M. into 2 schools, the Prāsangika, repr. by Buddhapālita, and the Svātantrika, repr. by Bhāvaviveka; then, in early 7th cent. CE, the re-affirming by Candrakirti of the more vigorous Prāsangika or *reductio ad absurdum* method as the norm for M.; finally a syncretism of M. with the → Yogācara sch., carried out by Śāntaraksita and Kamalaśīla; it was this form of M. which became dominant philosophy of Buddhism of → Tibet. Because of its affirmation (*vāda*) of principle of *śūnya,* the M. school is known also as the *Śūñyavāda.*

T. R. V. Murti, *The Central Philosophy of Buddhism* (1955); E. Conze, *Buddhist Thought in India* (1962), part III, 2; Richard H. Robinson, *Early Madhyamika in India and China* (1967).

Magadha Kingdom of N. India at time of the Buddha, notable in Buddh. hist. as region in which Buddhism had its birth. M. was one of four major kingdoms of India in 5th cent. BC (the others being Avanti, Kosala, and kingdom of Vamsas), and consisted of area south of the Ganges River, now known as Bihar. During early Buddh. period, M., like the other kingdoms, was growing at expense of confederations of tribal societies such as that of the → Vajjis. One of results of growth of monarchy of Magadhan pattern was thus the disruption of tribal life and breakdown of old trads. and *mores.* Part of success of early Buddhism may be attributed to its ability to make available a new corporate life to take place of tribal society, and provide a democratic refuge from increasing autocracy of new kingdoms. Something of basic opposition between the two forms of society, the Buddh. → Sangha and the Magadhan kingdom, may be reflected in hostility of Magadha's king → Ajātasattu towards Buddha, although his father, King → Bimbisāra is repres. as supporter of Buddha. The capital of M. was, in earlier Buddh. period, at Rajagaha; later the royal

Magic

centre shifted to Pātaliputta (modern Patna). It was from M. that Buddhism spread into other regions of India after third → Buddh. Council at Pātaliputta. By this time, in reign of → Ashoka, M. had become an extensive empire, with considerable natural resources, mineral and agricultural, and an import. international trade. The connection between language spoken in Magadha at time of Buddha, and the → Pali in which discourses of Buddha have been preserved has been a matter of controversy. The Buddh. trad. of → Ceylon affirms that Pali is in fact the language of M. (known as Magadhī or *Māgadhika-bhāsā*) and that, therefore, the Pali version of the discourses preserves the orig. words of Buddha. But modern critical and linguistic studies have suggested that there were notable differences between Māgadhī and Pali; by some scholars it is suggested that the latter was more prob. a dialect of Ujjayinī, a region somewhat to west of M.

Malalasekere, *D.P.P.N.*, vol. 2, pp. 402–4; Sukumar Dutt, *The Buddha and Five After-Centuries;* D. D. Kosambi, *Culture and Civilisation of Ancient India* (1965); E. Lamotte, *Histoire du Bouddhisme Indien* (1958).

Magic (Chinese) Spec. assoc. with Taoism; but Buddhism and Confucianism admit M. theory and a certain amount of practice. The functions of the early magicians (*wu*) were largely taken over by Taoist and Buddh. priests. Popular temples of both faiths became, and have remained, centres at which almost every conceivable form of M. is performed: to regulate rainfall, to ensure good harvests, to expel disease and misfortune, to attract good luck, to ensure progeny, etc. M. underlies many observances still carried out at popular festivals, and many acts which the family performs for well-being of its members.

(Japanese) After intro. of Buddhism into Japan, these were combined with and elaborated by Buddh. occultism. There grew up a belief that Buddhism offered superior ceremonial M. for calling down favourable supernatural aid, as witnessed by an almost fanatical devotion to reading of luck-bringing *sūtras*. In particular the → Shingon sect made use of ritual utterances, sacred texts, mystic formulae, symbols, postures, movements etc., to invoke aid of powerful deities. As Buddhism, in popular form, became debased, partic. during 14th and 15th cents., the practice of M., sorcery, exorcism and divination swept over whole of society. Confucian teaching in Japan has had restraining influence on practice of M., and W. and Chr. influence is far from negligible; but in mod. Shinto sects there is still great reliance on exorcism, divination and use of M. in healing of diseases.

E.R.E., VIII, pp. 296ff.; D. C. Holtom, *The National Faith of Japan* (1938), pp. 183–4; W. G. Aston, *Shinto* (1905), pp. 327ff.; M. Anesaki, *Hist. of Japanese Religion* (1930), pp. 46, 234.

Mahābodhi Society Buddh. society founded in → Ceylon in 1891 by Ceylonese monk, the Venerable Anagarika Dharmapala. The primary aims of M.S. were, first, restoration of the Mahā Bhodi temple at Buddha-Gāya, in N. India (scene of the Buddha's enlightenment); second, the revival of the Buddha-Sāsana in land of its birth. At that time → Buddha-Gāya (or Bodh-Gāya) was in province of Bengal, then part of British-ruled India. The temple was part of the property of a Shaivite (Hindu) landowner, and was in seriously neglected condition. The M.S. called conference at Bodh-Gāya in Oct. 1891 to enlist support of Buddhists of various other countries; in following year began publication of journal *The Maha Bodhi and the United Buddhist World,* which from then on played a not unimport. part in winning sympathy and support from Eng.-speaking people in India and elsewhere, but partic. from Indian intelligentsia. Opposition from both Hindu landowners and British authorities, however, was such that a lengthy process of legal action became necessary, which ended only with India's independence from British rule and the passing by new Government of Bihar of Buddha-Gāya Temple Act in 1949, under terms of which a temple management committee, consisting of 4 Buddh. and 4 Hindu members, was entrusted with care and control of temple. By this time the M.S. had gained considerable support, in India and elsewhere; besides its headquarters in Calcutta, it had estab.

other centres at Madras, Kushinagara, Sarnath, Bombay and at → Anuradhapura in Ceylon. The first president of Society, Sir Ashutosh Mookerjee, succeeded in 1908 in intro. study of → Pali at University of Calcutta, thus bringing about revival of study in India of canonical scriptures of → Theravāda Buddhism. Other Indian universities also have, since then, joined in revival of Pali studies. The M.S. has branches at Gaya, Sarnath, New Delhi, Lucknow, Bombay, Madras, Nautanwa and Ajmer; it publ. journal in English, *The Maha Bodhi,* which circulates not only in Asian but also in a number of West. countries.

D. Valisinha, 'The Revival of Buddhism: The Maha Bodhi Society, in P. V. Bapat (ed.), *2,500 Years of Buddhism* (1956, repr. 1959).

Mahābodhi-Vamsa Pali Buddh. work, 'the Great Bodhi-tree Chronicle,' which tells story of sacred bodhi-tree under which the Buddha gained enlightenment. The intro. carries story back to time of a former Buddha Dipankara (→ Buddhas, other than Gotama), and continues narrative to incl. the transplanting of a cutting from the Indian tree at Anuradhapura in Ceylon. The work, which is in prose, is attr. to Upatissa, who composed it from older sources prob. during 1st half of 11th cent. The text was edited by S. A. Strong, and published by the Pali Text Society of London in 1891.

Mahākassapa Thera One of most prominent of disciples of the Buddha, concerning whom there are many refs. in the canonical scriptures. He was highly esteemed by Buddha for his equanimity and ability as teacher and preacher. He is said to have lived to a great age.

Mahāpadāna Sutta A *sutta* found in the *D.N.* of the Pali canon, which gives details of the 7 Buddhas up to and incl. Gautama (→ Buddhas other than Gotama). In this *Sutta* a conventional scheme is adopted, whereby details of each of these Buddhas are given under eleven headings: the *Kappa,* or period of world-history in which born; social rank; family or clan; length of life; tree under which Enlightenment was attained; two chief disciples; numbers of → *arahants* present at assemblies held by the Buddha in question; name of personal attendant; name of father; name of mother; birthplace.

Sacred Books of the Buddhists, vol. 2, T. W. and C. A. F. Rhys-Davids (trs.), *Dialogues of the Buddha,* part 2, 5th edn. (1966), pp. 1–41.

Mahā-Parinibbāna Sutta Book of Buddh. Pali canon which relates events of last year of the Buddha's life, his death, cremation and distribution of his relics. It is found in the → *Dīgha-Nikaya* of the → Sutta-Pitaka, and is one of longest of suttas. Much material contained in this sutta occurs elsewhere in Pali canon with only slight differences; acc. to Rhys-Davids as much as two-thirds of *Sutta* can be so identified. The parallel passages are in gen. in books which are the oldest in canon.

T. W. Rhys-Davids, *Buddhist India* (1903), ch. 10.

Mahāsanghikas One of the major divisions of early Buddhism, dating from 4th cent. BC (→→ Councils, Buddh.; Buddh. Schools of Thought).

Mahāsatipatthāna Sutta An import. constituent of Buddh. Pali canon of scripture. The *Sutta* consists of discourse said to have been addressed by the Buddha to monks of Kammāssadamma on subject of the bases of Mindfulness (*Satipatthāna*), by means of which → nibbāna was to be gained, and on the → 4 Holy Truths. It is gen. considered one of most import. suttas, has been much trans., and the subject of numerous commentaries. The recital of it is held to be partic. auspicious; espec. at time of death, whether it is recited by the dying or heard by him. It is found in the → *Dīgha-Nikāya;* also in two separate parts, as the *Satipatthāna Sutta* and *Saccavibhanga Sutta* (the latter dealing with the 4 Holy Truths) in the → *Majjhima-Nikāya.*

Mahāvaṃsa One of Pali chronicles (*vaṃsa*), the Great (*Mahā*) Chronicle sets out hist. of Buddhism in India to time of its intro. into → Ceylon, and subsequent hist. in Ceylon to time of King Mahāsena (poss. 4th cent. CE). The author of M. is gen. held to be Mahānāma, writer of 6th cent. CE. The M. covers much the same grounds as the → Dīpavamsa, and is prob. based on same earlier source; the M. differs from the Dīpavamsa in that it adds certain amount of new

Mahāvastu

material and is in form of epic poem. It has been described as a 'coherent, refined and enlarged version' of Dīpavamsa. The → Culavamsa forms a supplement and continuation of the M. Like the Dīpavamsa, the M. is valuable source of evidence for hist. of early Buddhism in India and Ceylon. It has been trans. into Eng. by W. Geiger, as *The Mahavamsa, or The Great Chronicle of Ceylon* (1912, repr. 1964).

Mahāvastu Title of import. Buddh. work in Skt. (lit. 'The Great Subject' or 'Great Event'). The work forms part of the → Vinaya-Pitaka of the Lokuttaravādin school of the → Mahāsanghikas. The M. consists principally of a biography of the Buddha, told acc. to view of the Lokuttaravādins that Buddhas are 'exalted above the world' (*lokuttara*) and that they only, conventionally and outwardly, conform to this-worldly existence. This is a view which repr. a transitional stage towards that of fully developed → Mahāyāna. The narrative of the M. is interspersed with much material of the → *Jātaka/Avadāna* type, amounting to half the total work; it is thus, acc. to Winternitz, 'especially valuable as a treasure trove of Jātakas.' The date of orig. composition of the M. is difficult to determine; the trend towards Mahāyāna ideas may suggest the very early Christ. period; there are also refs. to the Huns and to Chinese language which suggest date about 4th cent. CE for its final form, although nucleus is prob. older, perhaps as early as 2nd cent. BC.

M. Winternitz, *Hist. of Indian Literature* (1933), vol. 2, pp. 239–47; J. J. Jones (tr.), *Mahavastu,* vol. 1 (1949), vol. 2 (1952), vol. 3 (1956).

Mahāyāna One of main distinctive trads. or schools of Buddhism; lit. means 'great' (*mahā*), 'means of salvation' (*yāna*). Various other yānas were distinguished, such as the Śravaka-yana, the →→ Vajrayāna or Mantrayāna; but the school from which the M. was primarily distinguished was the whole of the older, more conservative wing, consisting of at least 18 separate sects, such as the → Theravādins, the → Sarvāstivādins, etc., which collectively was described by adherents of the newer way as → 'Hīnayāna' or 'small' means of salvation. What was meant by the comparison was that Hīnayāna schools set forth a way of reaching salvation that had only limited appeal; it was not universalist in intention or scope, as the M. claimed to be. The date of emergence of M. is difficult to determine, but was somewhere within period 1st cent. BC–1st cent. CE. Its universalist emphasis was reflected in greater place given to virtue of compassion than had been the case in the Hīnayāna school, which was characterised by its emphasis on wisdom. The M. emphasised both equally. Another characteristic feature of M. was much greater place it gave to the → *Bodhisattva,* as the ideal or goal of human life, towards which all men could and should strive. In acc. with more open, universalist character of M., there was from beginning a readiness to engage wholeheartedly in intellectual debates of the time and to use the *lingua franca* of contemporary Indian intellectual class (mainly Brāhmans), viz. → Sanskrit. This took form, however, of a Sanskritised version of language used by Buddhists (Prākrit) (→ *Pali*), a version that has come to be known by mod. linguists as 'hybrid Sanskrit' or 'Buddh. Sanskrit' (although it is not exclusively Buddh., but a stage in evolution of Indian language). The universalist intention had also effect of rendering M. more flexible, and more ready to incorporate new features of belief and practice, some of which were derived from popular indigenous relig.; others may have reflected the strongly Graeco-Roman influence in N.W. India, where M. developed, such, e.g. as concept of Divine Wisdom or Transcendental Wisdom, *Prajñā-Pāramitā,* thought of as a feminine principle, and given popular currency in notion of Prajñā-Pāramitā as 'mother' of Buddha, i.e., the eternal Buddha. The M. developed also, as its central philosophy, the doc. of *Śūñyatā,* or 'voidness.' The philosophical school in which this doc. was developed notably by → Nagarjuna (2nd cent. CE) was known as → *Mādhyamika.* In course of develop. of Buddh. thought, this was followed by → Yogācāra school, founded by → Asanga and → Vasubandhu (4th cent. CE). The Yogācāra docs. and practices paved way for a yet greater assimilation of M. to popular Indian relig.; this was last phase of the M. and is usually known as Mantra-yāna or → Vajra-yāna, a form which

Mahinda

appears from 8th cent. CE onwards; in a sense this was a new 'yāna,' but it is also the ultimate Buddh. product of the M. school. Known also as Tantric Bhm., it had a counterpart in Tantric Hinduism, into which the Buddh. form eventually, c. 12th CE, disappeared. M. however, by reason of its universalist outlook and missionary spirit, had by this time spread into China, Korea and Japan, there developing yet further new forms in the 'Pure Land' or Amida Buddhism, and in Ch'an or Zen (→ Buddhism in China).
E. Conze, *Buddhist Thought in India* (1962); T. R. V. Murti, *The Central Philosophy of Buddhism* (1955); W. M. McGovern *An Introduction to Mahāyāna Buddhism* (1922).

Mahinda Buddh. monk of 3rd cent. BC, gen. held to be son of emperor → Ashoka, and leader of Buddh. expedition to → Ceylon which resulted in conversion to Buddh. faith of island's king, Devānampiya Tissa, and many of people of Ceylon. M. ordained many monks and lived to see the → Sangha firmly estab. in Ceylon. He died at age of 60; at cremation of his body the highest honours were paid to it. A *cetiya* was erected over his remains. His name is still highly esteemed in Ceylon.
W. Geiger (ed.), *Mahavamsa* (1908, repr. 1958) chs. 12–20, trsl. *Great Chronicle of Ceylon* (1912, repr. 1964).

Maitreya → Metteyya.

Maitreya-Natha → *Asanga.*

Majjhima-Nikāya The *nikāya* (collection, or assembly) of Buddh. Suttas of middle-length (*majjhima*); one of the five *Nikāyas* of the → Sutta-Pitaka of Pali Buddh. canonical scriptures, or → Tipitaka. The M.N. comprises 152 suttas in all, arranged in 3 gps. of approx. 50 each. Acc. to Pali trad., the transmission of the M.N. suttas was entrusted to an Elder named → Sariputta at 1st Buddh. Council, held immed. after the death of Buddha (→ Councils). The commentary by → Buddhaghosa on the M.N. is entitled Pa-pañca-Sūdanī. The M.N. has been trans. into Eng. by J. B. Horner as *Middle Length Sayings,* 3 vols. (1954–9).

Makkhalī-Gosāla Relig. teacher of anc. India contemporary with the Buddha, and mentioned in Buddh. scriptures (D.N., i, 53). He denied that men had moral responsibility for their actions, and affirmed that men's lives were determined by fate and by their social position and psychological make-up. He is mentioned as one of six teachers of what were, acc. to the Buddha, false doctrines; of these M.'s views are regarded as the most dangerous. His followers were known as the Ājivakas.

Man →→ Anatta; Khandha.

(Chinese view) On the whole, → Buddhism in China was dominated by concept of the Buddha-nature which is univ. and primordially inherent in all living beings, including man.

(Jap. view) Jap. concepts of the N. of M. were greatly influenced by Confucian and Buddh. teachings, which derived from China.

Mañjuśrī One of the two most prominent → Bodhisattvas in Mhy. Buddh. belief, the other being → Avalokitesvara, who personifies compassion; M. personifies *prajñā*, wisdom. He is not mentioned in Pali canon, nor in earliest Skt. works; he appears prominently in the → *Lankāvatāra Sūtra,* as one of the two main questioners of the Buddha. He is regarded as principal Bodhisattva in the → *Lotus Sūtra,* where the Bodhisattva → Maitreya is repr. as seeking instruction from him. Buddh. iconography repr. him as having in his hands the sword of knowledge and a book, symbolising his wisdom. He became an import. figure in the Bhm. of China, Japan, Tibet, Nepal and Java. Just as the Dalai Lama is regarded in → Tibet as an incarnation of Avalokitesvara, so outstandingly wise rulers have been regarded as incarnations of M.

Mantrayāna A later form of Mahāyāna Buddhism, characterised by use of *mantras,* or chants, as a method (*yāna*) of gaining enlightenment. (→ Vajrayāna).

Māra Māra, the Evil One, is ref. to many times in Buddh. scriptures. (For comprehensive account of refs. in → Pali canon, cf. T. O. Ling, *Buddhism and the Mythology of Evil* (1962), pp. 96–163). Like the Devil in W. relig. thought, M. is regarded as a demonic being who is arch-enemy of all who seek to live the holy life. Acc. to Buddh. trad., he sought to deflect the Buddha from attaining of enlightenment: the contest between M. and Buddha is ref. to only briefly in Pali texts, but is described in elaborate detail in the Skt. → *Lalita Vistara*. Here, as in subseq. encounters, M. is shown as entirely powerless to influence Buddha in any way; he retires discomforted and dejected (*Sutta-Nipāta* 425–49). M. makes appearance again from time to time in course of Buddha's ministry, sometimes assuming human or animal forms as disguise; but always with same complete inability to effect any evil purpose against Buddha, who always sees through the disguise and recognises his adversary. M. is repr. as seeking espec. to disturb Buddha and Buddh. monks and nuns when they are engaged in meditation. A collection of stories about M., found in Pali canon, is the *Māra-Samyutta* of → *Samyutta-Nikaya*. Another notable appearance of M. occurs in the → *Mahā-Parinibbāna Sutta,* where he seeks to persuade Buddha that it is time for him to leave this mortal existence and enter *pari-nibbāna,* on ground that he had promised to do so once his preaching of the → Dharma had been successful and his relig. estab. among men, and that these conditions had now been fulfilled. Buddha on this occasion, agrees with M., and declares that in 3 months he will indeed pass into *pari-nibbāna.*

In Indian relig. this concept of an Evil One is peculiar to Buddhism. The figure of M. has features which link it with popular beliefs in demons; but M. is also a being whose nature combines those forces which militate against the holy life, espec. the morally unwholesome qualities of greed, hatred and delusion. The name M. means lit. 'the killer' or 'the death-agent'; it indic. by its negative form that the Buddh. emphasis is by contrast a positive one, viz., attainment of life, at a level which Māra cannot reach. In Buddh. → cosmology M. is regarded as dominating lowest of the 3 planes of existence, i.e. the → *kāma* or sensual world. At a more advanced and sophisticated stage of understanding the figure of M. is seen to be but a name for everything that is impermanent (→ *anicca*), evil (→ *dukkha*), and impersonal (→ *anatta*). The role of belief in M. in Buddh. hist. appears to have been to provide transition from popular notions of discarnate evil demons, to the more abstract analysis of the human situation in moral-psychological terms, and a helpful way of understanding resistance to the holy life which a man might experience, but which he is assured can be overcome by following the Buddh. way.

E. Windisch, *Māra und Buddha* (1895); J. Masson, *La Religion Populaire dans le Canon Bouddhique-Pali* (1942); T. O. Ling (*op. cit.*).

Marks, 32, of a Great Man A feature of Buddh. trad. is that there are certain marks, 32 in number, which characterise a great man; or, more properly, a 'superman,' and, hence, a Buddha, although the trad. is pre-Buddh. in origin. These 32 marks are listed in the *Lakkhana Sutta* ('Discourse Concerning Marks') of the → *Dīgha-Nikāya* (in E.T. by T. W. and C. A. F. Rhys-Davids in *Dialogues of the Buddha,* part III, pp. 132–67). The possessor of these marks is to be recognised, acc. to brahmin trad., as either a great king or founder of a relig. movement. Rhys-Davids comments that 'most of the marks are so absurd, considered as marks of any human, that they are prob. mythological in origin, and three or four seem to be solar.' He points out what appears to be the irony implicit in the Lakkhana Sutta in the contrast it makes between the marks and the noble ethical qualities they are supposed to represent. The 32 marks of the superman are as follows: (1) He has feet with level tread. (2) On soles of his feet appear perfectly shaped wheels, thousand-spoked. (3) He has projecting heels. (4) He has long fingers and toes. (5) His feet are soft and tender. (6) He has hands and feet like a net. (7) His ankles are like rounded shells. (8) His legs are like an antelope's. (9) Standing without bending he can touch his knees with his hands. (10) His male organs are concealed in a sheath. (11) His complexion is the colour of gold. (12) His skin is so delicate that no dust cleaves to his body. (13) The down on his skin grows in single hairs, one to each pore. (14) The down on his body turns upward, every hair of it, in little rings curling to the right, blue-black in colour. (15) He has a frame divinely straight. (16) He has the seven convex surfaces. (17) The front half of his body is like a lion's. (18) There is no furrow between his shoulders. (19) His proportions have the symmetry of the banyan tree. (20) His bust is equally rounded. (21) His taste is supremely acute. (22) His jaws are as a lion's. (23) He has forty teeth. (24) He has regular teeth. (25) He has continuous teeth. (26) His eyeteeth are very lustrous. (27) His tongue is long. (28) He has a divine voice, like the karavika bird's. (29) His eyes are intensely blue. (30) He has eyelashes like a cow's. (31) Between the eyebrows appears a hairy mole, white and soft like cottondown. (32) His head is like a royal turban. All these marks of the superman are said in the Lakkhana Sutta to be result of meritorious actions in former existences.

Mathurā Important centre of Buddhism in India from time of emperor → Aśoka. In early Buddh. period, the town was situated about 5 m. to S.W. of modern town of Mathurā or Muttra which is on W. bank of the Jumna River about 100 m. S. of Delhi. There are refs. to M. in the Pali canon; the Buddha is said to have visited town and to have commented unfavourably upon place, to effect that the ground there was rough, that there was much dust, that it was beset with fierce dogs and demons, and that alms were to be had only with difficulty. But even in his lifetime there were apparently followers of the Buddha to be found there. After Buddha's death, a monk named Mahā Kaccana stayed there, and was visited by the king, Avantiputta, to whom the monk is said to have delivered a discourse on subject of caste, now known as the Mathurā (or Madhurā) Sutta (*M.N.*, II, 83–90), after which king became a Buddh. Poss. Mahā Kaccana may have been import. agent in the spread of Bhm. in M. By time of Aśoka, M. had become a prominent centre of Bhm. and after 3rd → Council, held at Patna, the → Sarvāstivādins, moving westwards, made it their stronghold. It was in M. that use of the → *rupa,* or Buddha-image developed; whether it originated here or in area of Greek influence in → Gandhāra being a matter of controversy. The → Milinda-Pañhā, composed in early years of Christ. era, speaks of M. as one of chief cities of India. The Chinese pilgrim → Fa Hsien testifies to strength of Bhm. in the M. region when he visited India in 5th cent. CE, as did Hsüan Tsang in 7th cent. (S. Beal, *Buddhist Records of the Western World* (1884), vol. I, pp. 179ff.); acc. to latter, both → Hīnayāna and → Mahāyāna flourished there. M. was plundered by the Muslim invasion under Mahmud of Ghazni (977–1030). The town is sometimes ref. to as Uttara-Mathurā, to distinguish it from the M. in S. India (Madura).

Māyā Mother of the Buddha, and wife of → Suddhodana. Acc. to Buddh. trad., M. possessed moral qualities that fitted her to be the mother of Buddha, and had lived a pure life from day of her birth. On day the Buddha-to-be was conceived M. had dream, that she was carried by heavenly beings to the Himalayan mountains, where she was bathed by wives of the gods and dressed in robes of a goddess; then she was taken to a golden palace, where, as she lay on a couch, the Buddha-to-be, in form of a white elephant, entered the right side of her body. This dream is a familiar feature of popular Buddh. legend, and is frequently depicted in murals which decorate temples and pagodas in S.E. Asia.

Towards end of her pregnancy, when birth of the child was imminent, M. set out to visit her own people in neighbouring Devadaha. The child was born while she was on her journey, in the sāla grove of → Lumbini, as M. stood beside a sala tree, holding a branch of it. She died seven days later, and, acc. to trad. was reborn in the Tusita heaven, where, after his enlightenment, Buddha went to preach to her the Dhamma. It is a feature of Buddh. belief (found in commentarial literature), that the mother of a Buddha dies soon after birth of Buddha-to-be, since it would not be fitting that she who had given birth to a Buddha-to-be should bear any other child.

Meditation M. is one of the 3 major components of the Buddh. way, the other 2 being morality, which precedes and must always accompany activity of meditation, and wisdom, which is reached as result of meditation (→ Eightfold Path). The West. reader is liable to misunderstand what the Buddh. means by M., and to imagine that it im-

Meekness

plies a 'relaxed' or 'inactive' state. But in the Buddh. view M. is an activity in which one is engaged in subduing discursive thought, destroying or discouraging unwholesome mental states, and initiating or nourishing wholesome mental states. It is a discipline, i.e., it has to be learned by a disciple from a master; without such personal supervision it cannot properly be undertaken. Herein is one of principal reasons for existence of the Buddh. monastery; it is a school of meditation, where younger monk learns from older or more advanced monk. M. is a highly developed and complicated discipline; of the methods used it is sufficient to say that they have to be learnt personally. Classical texts dealing with M. do exist, notably the → Visuddhimagga of → Buddhaghosa. An intro. to *theory* of subject has been made available to Eng. readers by E. Conze in his *Buddhist Meditation* (1960) (→→ Jhāna; Samādhi).
(School of) → Zen.

Meekness Buddhism had great influence in inculcating virtues of meekness, patience under provocation, the nonrequiting of injury, gentleness, forbearance, on grounds that such an attitude led to accumulation of one's store of merit. 'The humble reap advantage; the haughty meet with misfortune.'

Merit The Pali term for merit is → *Puñña,* popular corruptions of which are used in S.E. Asian Buddh. countries: in → Ceylon, *pin*; in Thailand *boon*; in Burma the notion of merit is more usually ref. to by the word *kutho,* which is the Burmese form of the Pali term *kusala,* meaning good in sense of meritorious.

(China and Far East) Buddhism, with its doctrine of *karma,* intro. into China and Far East the idea that cumulative credit of one's own good deeds would lead to a better rebirth. The idea was taken up by Taoism, and in popular relig. to become a chief incentive to virtue. The ordinary layman's desire to acquire M. towards some specific personal end led to wide variety of practice. M. could be acquired by charity, by contracting for recitation of Buddha's name, by release of living creatures (*fang shêng*), by devotion to the → Sangha, abstinence, giving up something desirable, making long → pilgrimages, etc. Numerous popular tracts assessed merit or demerit of partic. actions. The transfer of M. was an import. feature of Far Eastern Buddhism. A good reserve of M. was deemed not only to affect an individual's future, but to promote well-being of one's deceased ancestors, family, clan and descendants. The recitation of Buddh. formulae in monasteries produced M., which could be transferred to benefit others, or accrue to one's own account in the W. Paradise. Buddh. rites for the dead were dominated by idea of M., transferred to soul of deceased so as to ensure an early and better rebirth. The boundless stores of M. accumulated by Buddhas and → bodhisattvas were available to assist the faithful. The desire for accumulation of M. provides a strong incentive to benevolence and compassion.

C. H. Plopper, *Chinese Relig. Seen Through the Proverb* (1926), pp. 224ff.; H. Welch, *The Practice of Chinese Buddhism* (1967), *passim.*

Metempsychosis *Ex.* Grk. 'transferring of soul (*psychē*) from one body to another': other designations are: 'transmigration of soul'; 'rebirth'; 'reincarnation'. The idea of life as a cyclical process, i.e., of passage of soul through successive bodies, is a natural deduction made by many primitive peoples from phenomena of birth and death and reproduction of family features in children. As a relig.-philosoph. doctrine it appeared in India *c.* 600 BC (→ Samsāra), and adopted into Buddhism, which ensured its diffusion throughout Asia.

(China, Japan, Korea) When Buddhism came to China, Korea and Japan, the doc. of *karma* and belief in rebirth, linked to → Mahāyāna ideal of universal fellowship and idea that meritorious actions could be dedicated to assist souls in inferior resorts of M. to progress to better resorts and finally to Buddahood, came to exert an almost irresistible appeal. So long as soul is bound within the karmic process, and not entirely freed from hatred, greed and stupidity, it must inevitably be subject to rebirth in one of resorts of M.

Various modifications of concept of M. were developed

in Buddhism, → Tibet; but essential idea is same. Great mural paintings in popular temples repr. the wheel of M., or wheel of birth and life, whilst idea of M. is disseminated in numerous popular works such as the *Yü Li* or *Precious Records,* which depicts in gruesome detail the underworld of Buddhism and Taoism, where all souls go at death for judgement. The souls of exceptionally virtuous men are re-born as gods; those who have lived a good life return to earth as men or women; some for their sins are reborn as animals, hungry ghosts or denizens of hell.

The wheel of M. represents six modes of existence: gods, demi-gods or *asuras,* human beings, animals, hungry ghosts and demons. These six primary resorts of M. are again sub-divided. All sentient beings are considered to be fettered to wheel of M., until they attain release from karmic proc-ess by entering on Buddahood and → Nirvana.

J. Hackin (ed.), *Asiatic Mythology* (1932), pp. 363ff.; C. A. S. Williams, *Outlines of Chinese Symbolism* (1931), pp. 392ff.; M. Anesaki, *Hist. of Japanese Relig.* (1930), pp. 67–8; *E.R.E.,* XII, pp. 429ff.

Metta Buddh. term for lovingkindness or goodwill; acc. to Buddh. thought, one of the 4 → *Brahma-Vihāras,* or 'spiritual abodes.'

Metteyya (Pali); **Maitreya** (Skt.) Name of the Buddha who is yet to come. This is in acc. with the Buddh. theory that there had been a series of 'Awakened' or 'Enlightened' Ones (Buddhas) prior to → Gotama, who lived in 6th cent. BC, and that there will be others after him. The details of M.'s life story are foretold in many Buddh. works, such as the *Cakkavatti-Sihanāda Sutta* of the → *Digha-Nikaya,* the *Anagatavamsa* and *Maitreyavyakarana;* the details agree closely with those of life of Gotama, but with substitution of other personal names, locations, etc. This future Buddha is regarded by Buddhists as living at present a supernatural existence in a Tusita heaven, in world of the devas (→ Cos-mology). His personal name is held to be Ajita, Metteyya being his *gotra* or clan name, and having ref. to a root which indic. friendship or love. The eschatological hopes inspired by doc. of this future Buddha's coming occasionally lead to forms of Messianism in Buddh. countries, e.g., parts of C. Asia and Burma. The inscription 'Come Maitreya, come!' is found carved on rocks in mountains of Tibet and Mongolia.

T. W. and C. A. I. Rhys-Davids, *Dialogues of the Buddha,* part 3 (1921, repr. 1965), pp. 73f.; E. Conze, *Buddhist Scriptures,* 1959, pp. 237–42.

Middle Way The *Majjhimā-patipadā* (Pali), or *Madhyamā-pratipad* (Skt.), the 'middle way' or 'path' between materialism and sensual indulgence, and rationalism and asceticism, is name used for Buddhism in early period. By avoiding the two extremes, claimed the Buddha, he had 'gained knowledge of that middle path which gives vision, which gives knowledge, which causes calm, special knowledge, enlightenment, nibbāna.' (*Dhamma-Cakkappavattana Sutta*).

Mi Lei Chi. Name for → Maitreya, the most powerful → bodhisattva after → Kuan Yin in the Chinese pantheon. He waits in the Tushiti heaven until his advent as the future Buddha, 5,000 years after → Sakyamuni's entrance into → Nirvana. His image, found near entrance to Buddh. temples, is fat and smiling, so that he became known to Westerners as the Laughing Buddha.

K. L. Reichelt, *Truth and Tradition in Chinese Buddhism* (1927), pp. 186–7; S. Couling, *Encycl. Sinica* (1917, 1965), pp. 322–3.

Milinda King whose discussions with the Buddh. monk Nāgasena are related in the Pali work → *Milinda-Panha,* i.e. 'The Questions of Milinda.' By his Greek name of Menander he was known to classical Gk. historians; by modern authorities, M. is regarded as having ruled in middle of 2nd cent. BC over territory to N.W. of India, which incl. Kabul and → Gandhāra, the Swat valley and poss. part of the west. Punjab. Whether or not he became a Buddh. is unknown.

A. K. Narain, *The Indo-Greeks* (1957).

Milinda-Panha A noncanonical Pali Buddh. work, composed in style of the canonical Suttas, having form of dialogue between Buddh. monk Nāgasena and King → Milinda. The dialogue contains quotations from Pali canonical scriptures and repr. point of view of → Theravāda school. The work has 8 main divisions; in each some 10 or 12 questions are dealt with. These are kind of problems that might present themselves to anyone acquainted with major Buddh. ideas and practices, but who has become aware of what appear to be inconsistencies or uncertainties. The first dilemma, e.g., is why the Buddha, who is regarded as having attained → nibbāna, should accept homage from others: if he had fully attained, would he not be indifferent to homage, and, if he received homage (as he did), then could he be regarded as having attained nibbāna? I. B. Horner, who has recently made a new trans. of the M. into Eng., comments that 'the multitude of topics discussed or touched on makes it difficult to think of any Buddh. theme it ignores entirely.' The Buddh. scholar → Buddhaghosa quotes frequently from the M.: it was evidently well known by his time. The work was composed prob. in India or Kashmir sometime after Milinda's own time, poss. at about begin. of Christ. era. The M. was trans. into Sinhalese in 18th cent CE by a monk named Sumangala. The Pali text, ed. by V. Trenckner, was published in Roman script in 1880 (pts. repr. 1963); it was trans. into Eng. by T. W. Rhys-Davids and publ. as vols. XXXV and XXXVI of S.B.E. in 1890. A new Eng. trans. by I. B. Horner, making use of more recent advances in Pali studies, was publ. in 2 vols. in 1963–4.

Mission (the Propagation of Religion) In Buddhism, the M. motive was implicit from first, in the Buddha's gathering of a company of disciples. His discovery and teaching of the → Dhamma, and his own refusal to enter immediately into → Nibbāna, preferring rather to communicate his discovery to those who would listen, provides starting point of Buddh. M.; the Dhamma has always been taken to have relevance for whole of mankind. The truth is one; mankind is one. The instrument of M. has normally been the → sangha, or monastic community. The proclamation of the Dhamma may thus take place irrespective of local conditions. After an initial period of expansion (→ Buddhism, Gen. Survey), the M. of Buddhism stagnated; it has only

Moha

been taken up again in 20th cent., partly in response to West. and Christ. challenges. The world M. of Buddhism is today acknowledged by virtually all Buddh. groups.

Moggallāna Mahā Moggallāna Thera (i.e., 'the Great,' 'the Elder') was a chief disciple of the Buddha, and close friend from childhood of → Sariputta, another principal disciple. The two were converted to the Buddh. way on same occasion, when they heard Buddha preach. They were ordained together, and are regarded in trad. as the ideal disciples. M. was warmly praised by Buddha for his ability as expounder of the Buddh. way to other monks (S.N. iv, 183ff.). He was charged with welfare of the other monks. Several verses among the → *Theragāthā* are attrib. to M., in which he exhorts his fellow monks to holy living. He is mentioned frequently in Suttas of the Pali canon. He died earlier than Buddha as result of a violent attack on him by brigands; these had been hired by heretics, whose followers had diminished as a result of M.'s preaching.

G. P. Malalasekere, *D.P.P.N.*, vol. 2, pp. 541–7.

Moggaliputta-Tissa A Buddh. Thera, or elder monk, said to have acted as president of 3rd Buddh. Council at Patna in reign of emperor → Ashoka (→ Councils), and to have composed the Pali treatise known as *Kathāvatthu* (Points of Controversy), which now forms fifth of the 7 books of the → Abhidhamma-Pitaka of the → Theravāda school. Acc. to trad., it was M. who, in 6th year of Ashoka's reign, had ordained the emperor's son Mahinda into the → Sangha; after the 3rd Council, M. organised Buddh. missions into various regions adjacent to India by monks from Magadha, incl. the sending of Mahinda to Ceylon. M. is said to have been 80 years of age at death, which occurred in 26th year of Ashoka's reign; he had been a member of the Sangha for 68 years.

Malasekere, *D.P.P.N.*, vol. 2, pp. 664–6; H. Oldenberg (ed. and tr.), *The Dipavamsa* (1879); W. Geiger and M. H. Bode (eds. and trans.), *Mahavamsa; or Great Chronicle of Ceylon* (1912, repr. 1964).

Moha Buddh. term meaning 'illusion,' or erroneous view of things characteristic of the man whose nature is 'unen-

187

Monasteries

lightened'. M. is regarded as one of the 3 'roots' of evil (the others being Dosa and → Lobha). *Avijja* (Pali), → *Avidyā* (Skt.) = ignorance, is a synonym for M.

Monasteries Buddh. monasteries of China, Korea and Japan, of Ceylon, and continental S.E. Asia, differ among themselves in varying degrees, but all repr. continuation of a trad. reaching back to early period of Buddhism in the pre-Christ. era. At time of the Buddha and during cent. after his death, members of the Order (→ *Sangha*), were wandering homeless, almsmen (*bhikkhus*), although even in Buddha's day they had use of *ārāmas,* or private gardens given to them by wealthy laymen. Before 2 cents. had passed from Buddha's death, the practice of living together in shelters known as *āvāsas* had developed. These *āvāsas* were orig. places of shelter to which bhikkhus would resort during monsoon season, when travel was difficult or impossible. The *āvāsas* grad. developed into permanent settlements, called *lenas,* each inhabited by its own regular monk-residents, whereas the earlier *āvāsas* had been centres or, as it were, hostels with no regular, fixed body of residents. In the → Vinaya-Pitaka, which governs common life of Buddh. Order, 5 different kinds of dwelling are mentioned under collective term *lena.* Of these the 2 most import. are the *vihāra* (house for monks) and the *guhā* (a cave). It was in these 2 forms that the earliest settled monasteries were found. On the plains of N. India it was the brick, or brick and stone free-standing *vihāra* which became the monastic institution; in India south of Vindhya mountains it was the *guhā* or cave-dwelling which became more usual place of habitation for monks. These caves were at first fairly simple; it is not always certain whether they were lived in, or were used merely as secluded places for purpose of meditation. But later they were large and elaborate monastic dwellings, consisting of large complexes of rooms, halls, shrines, etc. Since they were less exposed to weather and invading armies than free standing *vihāras* of the plains, many have survived, esp. in the Western Ghats of India. The total number of cave-monasteries which have thus survived is in region of one thousand; the clearing and exploration of these has been a notable feature of archeological work in India since the 1840s. Some of the more import. complexes which have been discovered are → Ajantā, Elephanta, Ellorā, Kanheri, and Karle; there are altogether 44 such centres known at present, scattered throughout S. and W. India. Since some sites are known to have been inhabited for a thousand years, they provide valuable evidence of the develop. of Buddh. art through the cents. A transition from cave, i.e., rock-hewn monasteries, to free-standing, stone-built structures, which succeeded them, can be seen in some places; before Buddhism finally disappeared from India it was the *vihāra* type of monastery which had become normal.

Another change which monasteries underwent in India from about 8th cent. CE onwards was from numerous, small 'parish' monasteries, each of which served as centre of Buddh. teaching and devotion for a village or group of villages, to large, imposing places of learning which more nearly resembled colleges or even universities. Such large monastic centres, → Nālanda, Odantapura (in Bihar), Vikramasilā (in W. Bengal) Amarāvatī, and Nāgārjunakonda (in Andhra Pradesh) were monuments to piety and generosity of kings and rich merchants. The concentration of Buddh. education and learning in such centres was, however, assoc. with decline of smaller, parish-type of monastery, whose life had been oriented much more towards learning 'for faith' rather than 'for knowledge.' By time the Chinese travellers →→ Hsüan Tsang and I Tsing visited India in 7th cent. CE, many smaller monasteries had already been deserted and were in ruins, soon to be lost in encroaching jungle. The large monastic institutions of N. India were rich, and easy targets for Turkish Muslim invaders of 11th and 12th cents.; by that time few of the older, smaller monasteries were left and by 13th cent. Buddh. monasticism had almost entirely disappeared from India. By this time, however, the monastic institution had become a feature of Ceylon, S.E. Asia, China, Korea, Japan

and Tibet. It is even poss. that it may have had some formative influence upon ascetic communities of E. Mediterranean, as there was considerable cultural traffic between
India and Mediterranean world in early Christ. cents.

From India those Buddh. monks who were deprived of
monasteries by Muslim invasion travelled north and east,
esp. to Tibet. The monasteries of Tibet continued to flour-
ish, and provide dominant feature of Tibetan society down
to mod. times (→ *Tibetan Buddhism*). A continuous trad.
of monastic life from 3rd cent. BC to present can be traced
in → Ceylon, and in continental S.E. Asia from about 5th
cent. CE. There were monasteries in S.E. Asian archipelago
from 7th cent. CE (→ *Indonesia, Buddhism in*); but most of
these have not survived to present. Apart from monasteries
of Buddh. → China, Korea and Japan, where Buddhism and
the monastic trad. underwent developments peculiar to E.
Asia, it is in Ceylon and continental countries of S.E. Asia
(Burma, Thailand, Cambodia and Laos) that Buddh. monasticism survives in something like early form.

In S.E. Asia today the Buddh. monastery is still, throughout most of region, the local centre of popular relig., and
bearer and preserver of → Theravāda form of Buddhism,
which places great importance on the Sangha as a community of men dedicated to the holy life. The typical monastery is a group of buildings within compound, enclosed by
wall; the surrounding wall ensures necessary degree of seclusion but in no sense isolates M. from surrounding society. It used to be monks who provided entire education of
lay people; now this is increasingly undertaken by various
national states; but the school will still very often be located within monastic compound, esp. in Thailand.

Within complex of buildings, etc., which together make
up the Buddh. M. of S.E. Asia, the most import. items are:
(1) shrine room or sanctuary, where there is usually a large
→ *Buddha-rupa,* and where → *uposattha* devotional services are held, where ordinations take place, and where the
→ *Patimokkha* is recited by monks; (2) an assembly hall,
usually open on all four sides, where other *Buddha-rupas*
are housed and where in evening of Buddh. sabbath lay

people come to hear sermons by monks, although in some cases, esp. in city monasteries, these may be preached in sanctuary instead; (3) the huts or cubicles in which monks (or guests) are housed, are usually simple wooden rooms with little furniture apart from rolled-sleeping mat, a small shrine and poss. a picture or two; (4) in many monasteries of S.E. Asia, a school-building for the children of the village; (5) one or more → *stupas,* or pagodas, in grounds, usually near sanctuary. The exact number of component features, and size and elaborateness of each item varies from monastery to monastery, and from urban to rural areas. So also does name by which whole complex is known. In Ceylon it is a *vihāra* or *sanghārāma* (see *ārāma,* (above)); in Burma, a *phongyi-chaung,* i.e. a house for monks (*phongyi* ('great glory'), being the popular word in Burma for a monk); in Thailand, it is a *Wat,* a word possibly derived from primitive name of the M., i.e. *āvāsa* (above); in Cambodia and Laos also it is a 'Wat.'

Sukumar Dutt, *Buddhist Monks and Monasteries of India* (1962); R. Gard, *Buddhism* (1961), ch. V; H. K. Kaufman, *Bangkhuad: A Community Study in Thailand* (1960), ch. VI, 'The Wat: its Structure, Economy and Function'; E. Lamotte, *Histoire du Bouddhisme Indien,* 1958, ch. IV; W. Rahula, *Hist. of Buddhism in Ceylon* (1956); J. G. Scott (Shway Yoe), *The Burman: His Life and Notions,* 3rd edn. (1909, repr. 1963), chs. 4, 13.

Monasticism The urge to abandon ordinary domestic life, to concentrate on worship, meditation and sacred study, has found expression in various religs. It has taken form of living solitary life as hermit (e.g. in Hinduism; Taoism; Christianity); but where guidance and instruction are needed, communities have been founded where members live under a common rule. The earliest example of M. is the Buddh. → Sangha.

S. Dutt, *Buddhist Monks and Monasteries of India* (1962); H. Dumoulin, *Hist. of Zen Buddhism* (E.T. 1963); *E.R.E.,* VIII, pp. 781–805; *R.G.G.,* IV, pp. 1070–81, I, pp. 1430–2.

Mongols Mongolia itself was only superficially influenced by Buddhism till late 16th cent., when the M. were converted

Monks

to the 'Lama' form of Mahāyāna Buddhism of → Tibet. From that time onwards, Mongolia was governed by a politico-eccles. authority, the Buddh. monasteries wielding great power. In the 1920s Mongolia became a Peoples' Republic within the Soviet sphere. An intense and bitter campaign against relig. was followed by persuasion and provision of alternative occupations for priests. The number of *lamas* (priests) was reduced from about 100,000 to about 200, and most ex-priests are now married. Several monasteries were brought under State control, and influence of Buddhism has rapidly declined.

Guy Wint (ed.), *Asia: A Handbook,* 1965, pp. 117ff.; Arts in *E.R.E.,* VIII and *Encycl. Brit.,* vol. 15; E. D. Phillips, *The Mongols* (1969), *C.H.I.,* V, ch. 7.

Monks → *Sangha.*

Mūla Buddh. term, meaning lit. 'a root,' used in analysis of the human moral condition. Acc. to Buddh. thought, there are 6 M.'s, or moral conditioners: 3 unwholesome, viz. greed, hatred and illusion, or → *lobha, dosa,* and → *moha;* and 3 wholesome, viz. generosity, love and absence of illusion, or *alobha, adosa* and *amoha.* These M.'s condition the quality of consciousness and volition, and thus the quality of *karma.* Syn. for *alobha* is → *dāna;* for *adosa metta;* and for *amoha* → *paññā.*

N

Nāgārjuna Indian Buddh. philosopher of 2nd cent. CE, founder of → *Mādhyamika* sch. of → Mhy. Buddhism. This N. is to be distinguished from N., the alchemist and exponent of Tantra, who lived poss. as late as 8th cent. CE, and is known as author of a work on *suvarnatantra* ('gold-magic'), entitled *Rasaratnākara*. The two N.'s are regarded in Tibetan trad. as one and same person. N., the Mādhyamika philosopher, is gen. held to have been of Brahman family, and from S. India. He spent most of life in S. India, at Srī Parvata or Srī Śailam, a great centre of Mhy. Buddhism from his day onwards. He was close friend of the Satavahana king, Yajnaśri Gautamiputra (CE 166–96). There is reliable evidence connecting him with the great centre of learning in S.E. India (Andhra) which bore his name, viz. Nāgārjunikonda; also with similar centre in Bihar at → Nālanda. His great work was the *Mādhyamika-kārikā* or *Mādhyamika-śāstra*. Herein was laid the groundwork of school of Buddh. philosophy of which he was founder, and which had many exponents from his time until disappearance of Buddhism from India in 12th cent. CE. The *M.-kārikā* has been described as epitome of the Mahāyāna *sūtras*. The school of thought founded by N. was characterised pre-eminently by its use of term *śūñyatā*, for a method of expounding the 'voidness' of any concepts, and even of the ultimate 'elements' or *dhammas* believed in by the → Theravādins.
T. R. V. Murti, *The Central Philosophy of Buddhism* (1955), pp. 87–91; Richard H. Robinson, *Early Mādhyamika in India and China* (1967), pp. 21–70.

Nāgasena A learned Buddh. monk, whose discussion of controversial points of belief and practice with the Greek king

Nālanda

Milinda (Menander) are recorded in the Pali work → *Milinda-pañhā*, composed in 1st cent. CE. Acc. to text of this work, N. was born in a village in Himalaya; he was of a Brahman family, but entered Buddh. → Sangha in early manhood, and studied the Buddha-Dhamma at various places, incl. Pātaliputta (Patna), where he is said to have become an → Arahant. Thence he moved to Sāgala (Sialkot), where he met King Milinda. However, the Chinese version of text mentions Kashmir as his place of birth. Although text of Milinda-Pañha claims also that N. was a man of such incredible ability that he mastered whole of the → *Abhidhamma-Pitaka* after hearing it once, no other mention of him occurs in contemporary lit., a fact that has led some modern scholars to doubt his historical existence.

I. B. Horner, *Milinda's Questions,* vol. I (1963), translator's Introduction.

Nālanda A centre of Buddh. learning in N. India, founded by a Gupta king prob. in 5th cent. CE or just after. N. is often mentioned in the Pali canon, esp. in the → Dīgha-Nikāya as place visited by the Buddha and his disciples; it was there, e.g., that → Sariputta is said to have uttered his confession of absolute faith in the Buddha, sometimes ref. to as his 'lion's roar,' an incident recorded in the Mahā-Parinibbāna Sutta (*D.N.,* II, 81ff.). N. had not, however, achieved any great prominence when it was selected by the Gupta king as location for a new monastery; the site was selected as auspicious by an augurer. Some time in 6th cent. CE N., which had by then become monastic seminary for training of monks, was developed into centre of secular as well as relig. learning; from this time onwards it is properly ref. to as a monastic university. As such it acquired international fame. In this respect N. was one of a small number of such centres of higher learning (others being, e.g. Nagarjunikonda, Virkramasila, and Odantapura) which by 8th cent. CE had begun to monopolise the monastic scene; the smaller local monasteries as centres of piety were in many places then in decline. So far as Buddh. learning was concerned, N. became a great centre of →

Mahāyāna philosophy. Acc. to the Chinese pilgrims →→ Hsüan Tsang and I Tsing, who visited place during period of its maximum grandeur and prosperity, it housed some 3,000 or more monk-scholars, was of great extent and impressive, even of spectacular appearance; its learned scholars and alumni enjoyed high prestige in Indian society. There was close assoc. between N. and Tibet; such was the continuing prestige of the Indian monastic establishment that a centre of learning was estab. in Tibet in 1351 bearing same name. Acc. to Buddh. historian Tāranātha, the Muslim Turks, who invaded N. India in 12th/13th cents. CE, 'conquered the whole of Magadha and destroyed many monasteries; at N. they did much damage and the monks fled abroad.' Some life was salvaged from the ruins; a few monks maintained a much reduced activity until at some date not exactly known, N. as a monastic centre fell into ruins, some of which still remain. A new monastic centre of learning has in the mod. period been re-estab. at N. The site of anc. N. has been identified with a village 7 miles north of mod. Rajgir (Rajagaha of anc. times) (→ *Monasteries*).

Sukumar Dutt, *Buddhist Monks and Monasteries of India* (1962); S. Beal, *Buddhist Records of the Western World,* 2 vols. (1884).

Nats Term used in Burma for hostile spirit-beings, of whom there are said to be 37 chiefs, or lords. The N. must be propitiated in various ways; they are held to be of destructive nature, and must be continually guarded against. The attitude of peoples of Burma (hill tribes as well as plain-dwelling Burmese speakers) are sometimes described in terms of 'worship,' but this is not entirely accurate; offerings are made to the N., but largely in order to placate them. Their characteristics are similar to those of the → *Yakkhas* of Pali canon; hence popular Burmese Buddh. attitude towards N. is largely same as that of the canon towards Yakkhas. The N. are regarded as having a king, Tha-gya-min, identified in Burma with → Sakka of Pali canon, king of the spirit-beings.

Nembutsu

ShwayZoe (Sir J. G. Scott), *The Burman: His Life and Notions,* 3rd edn. (1909, repr. 1963); Maung Htin Aung, *Folk Elements in Burmese Buddhism* (1962).

Nembutsu (*Namu-Amida-Butsu*), 'Calling the Name.' The practice, fostered by the → Pure Land Sects, of daily repeating name of → Amida Buddha, accompanied by belief that all, through trust in Amida, will be born in the Buddha's paradise.

Nibbāna (Pali)/**Nirvāna** (Skt.) Buddh. term well known, but frequently misunderstood in the West. In its Pali form N. occurs in the most anc. Buddh. texts, such as the → *Sutta-Nipāta;* in its Skt. form, N. continued to have import. place in → Mahāyāna, although what it signified varied to some extent between the schools. In its orig. sense and usage, N. was connected with the verb *nibbati,* 'to cool by blowing'; assoc. is the term *nibbuta,* found in the *Sutta-Nipāta* more often than N., which is a past participle used in adjectival sense to describe the early Buddh. ideal man, 'he who is cooled.' The 'cooling' here ref. to a state of being cooled from 'fever' of greed, hatred and delusion, the 3 principal forms of evil in Buddh. thought. In this sense it was apparently used in anc. India as everyday word for being well, or healthy (i.e. not in state of fever). In Buddh. usage N. thus refers to new level of being of man who is *nibbuta;* a level of being into which Buddha, and other early Buddh. who gained enlightenment, were considered to have entered, when they had become free from the defilements, or → *kilesas,* but still continued to live out what remained of mortal life. This 'nibbana-in-principle' was thus known as *kilesa-nibbāna.* When the physical components of this mortal life had reached moment of dissolution, i.e., when the death of body occurred, *nibbāna* was then complete (*pari*) and this was known as *pari-nibbāna.* The events immediately preceding this in case of → Gotama, and the event itself, are described in the → *Mahā-Parinibbāna Sutta.* N. is described in Pali texts as tranquil, pure and deathless. It has sometimes mistakenly been supposed by West. observers of Buddhism to be tantamount to 'extinction' or 'annihilation'; this is due to misunderstanding of idea of *nibbati* (see above), and the notion that it is life, rather than evil passions, which is 'blown out.' The 'annihilationist' view is explicitly rejected by Buddha (→ Uccheda-Vāda).

With develop. of the philosophical schools of Mahāyāna, the term *nirvāna* (the Skt. form) was related to concepts of an Absolute which these schools developed; thus N. was equated with → *Śūñyatā,* with the essence of the Buddha → *Dharma-kāya,* and with 'ultimate reality,' or *Dharma-dhātu.* In the → Yogācāra school espec., in acc. with view that the illusory world of objects is dependent on real world of consciousness, → Samsāra (empirical existence) was held to be but an illusory aspect of N.

Nibbuta Buddh. term for the man who is 'cooled', i.e., from the fever of greed, hatred and illusion which is common to all humanity, and is thus 'healthy,' or has attained salvation. The state into which such a man has entered is that of → Nibbana.

Nichiren (CE 1222–82). An outstanding figure in relig. hist. of Japan. A prophet, missionary and reformer, who (1253) founded Buddh. sect called after his name. His early life was spent in search for true doc. of Buddhism. Disgusted by corruption of Buddh. hierarchy, the divisions between Buddh. sects, and the calamitous state of country, at age of 30, N. came to conviction that true Buddhism is enshrined in the Lotus Scripture (*Saddharma-Pundarīka Sūtra*). He denounced → Honen and → Jodo Buddhism, and later attacked other sects; the conservative formalism of disciplinary school of Ritsu and newly intro. meditation school of → Zen. He called on government to suppress false teaching, and be converted to unique truth of the Lotus. With fervent zeal, he preached in temple and marketplace. Persecuted, attacked by mobs, exiled, suffering cold and hunger, he was sustained by his sense of mission. He attracted a large following; his sect continues to the present day.

Three things stand out in his teaching: (1) Utterance of name of Lotus Scripture (*Namu-Myoho-renge-kyō*—'Adoration to the Lotus of Perfect Truth') has mantic power. In a degenerate age, meditation on the formula and its simple repetition are sufficient for attainment of enlightenment.

Nikāya

(2) The graphic and symbolical repr. of Supreme Being, who is Buddha in his metaphysical entity, inherent in every being, the oneness of the Buddha-nature and its inexhaustible manifestations. (3) Need to estab. a Holy Centre, a central seat of univ. Buddhism, which is to rule world throughout ensuing ages.

N.'s teaching, which was meant to unify Buddhism, gave rise to most intolerant of Jap. Buddh. sects.

M. Anesaki, *N. the Buddhist Prophet* (1916); *Hist. of Japanese Buddhism* (1930), pp. 191ff.; E. Steinilber-Oberlin, *The Buddhist Sects of Japan* (1938), pp. 238ff.

Nikāya Buddh. term for a 'body' of things, or a collection: thus, (1) a collection of Suttas, or Discourses (usually of the Buddha). Five such *Nikāyas* together make up the → Sutta-Pitaka, second of the three constituent parts of Pali canon of scripture, viz. the *Dīgha-N., Majjhima-N., Anguttara-N., Samyutta-N.,* and *Khuddaka-N.;* (2) a body of monks; the term N. is used in this sense in → Ceylon to distinguish sects or schools of the → Sangha.

Nirvāna → Nibbāna.

Nuns The *therī,* or female parallel to the Buddh. institution of monkhood → *thera,* was recognised in Buddhism from time of Buddha himself, who gave permission for → ordination of women into such an Order, albeit reluctantly, acc. to account given in the → *Vinaya-Pitaka* (II, pp. 253ff.), and largely because he was persuaded so to do by disciple → Ananda. Some of the *therī* in early period achieved great progress in the Buddh. life, acc. to the Pali canon; a collection of verses (*gātha*) expressive of their relig. zeal and attainments forms part of canon, viz. → the *Therīgāthā.* The Order exists now only as a tiny and somewhat insignificant institution in some Asian countries: in Thailand female lay devotees (*upāsikā*), who have not received ordination as *therī,* and who wear white robes, live in permanent quarters attached to certain monasteries where their life is very similar to that of a regular Order of nuns; they are mostly elderly women and are supported by generosity of other Buddh. lay people.

(Chinese) Buddh. nunneries were estab. in China under

imperial patronage about mid. of 4th cent. CE, and nuns exerted considerable influence upon court and government. Fo T'u-têng (d. 349) is regarded as having taken initiative in estab. an order of nuns on Chi. soil. The nunneries were small, governed by old and experienced prioresses, usually situated near and under authority of a large monastery, in which the nuns were ordained. Nuns do a great work from a relig. and financial point of view, mainly among devout Buddh. women. It is estimated that, before Communist regime, there were some 225,000 nuns in China.

E. Zürcher, *The Buddhist Conquest of China* (1959), *passim;* K. L. Reichelt, *Truth and Tradition in Chinese Buddhism* (1927), p. 265; H. Welch, *The Practice of Chinese Buddhism* (1967), pp. 412–6.

O

Obaku One of three sects of Jap. → Zen (→→ Rinzai and Soto) introduced by → Ingen. The name Obaku is Jap. for Huang Po, a famous Chi. → Ch'an master (d. ᴄᴇ 850). O. spread rapidly in 17th cent. In its ascetic practice, it differs but little from Rinzai. It taught that, though sudden enlightenment is for highly gifted, a more grad. way is open for those with less talent. → Zazen and practice of the → kōan are most useful means for sudden attainment of → satori. The grad. way of enlightenment makes use of calling on name of Buddha, i.e. → nembutsu. → Amida is regarded as the Buddha-spirit in every sentient being, having no existence outside one's own mind. Chi. influence is particularly noticeable in O., reflected in architecture of its temples and relig. ceremonies of sect. Today the sect claims more than 550 temples.

Dumoulin, *Hist. of Zen Buddhism* (1963), pp. 228ff.

Ordination Ordination, in Buddh. context, is initiation into the Buddh. Order (→ Sangha) in presence of witnesses (i.e., members of Sangha), and self-dedication to monastic life. It is not a conferring of priestly rights or powers; it is not necessarily life long or unrepeatable. There are two kinds of Buddh. O.: the lower (*pabbajjā*), by which a man becomes a *sāmanera* or novice; the higher (*upasampadā*), by which novice becomes monk (*bhikkhu*). The ceremony for O. to *sāmanera* varies from country to country, and acc. to whether novice has intention to remain in Order for several months or years, or whether he is entering for few days only, e.g. for period of 3 to 7 days on occasion of a relative's cremation (practice followed in Thailand). In latter case the candidate has his head shaved, brings two robes (the lower robe, or sarong, or *antaravāsaka*; the upper robe, or *uttarāsangha*; → Dress, Relig.; but not the *sanghāti* or stole, since this is worn only by monks (*bhikkhus*). He also brings incense and candles, and formally asks abbot for permission to join monastery. After reminding him of privilege of being a novice, and merit it will entail for himself and family, the abbot admits him. The more formal ceremony for admission of novice who intends subsequently to become monk consists of candidate's being brought before a chapter of at least 10 monks, headed by abbot or senior monk of at least ten years standing, and taking part in set form for ordaining of novices and monks. This is held in the sanctuary (*vihāra*). The candidate kneels, and asks for admission as novice, handing to abbot 2 yellow robes in which he is to be ordained. The abbot then formally presents to him these robes, reminding him of frailty and impermanence of human body which they are to cover. The candidate receives them, and retires to put them on; as he does so he recites a formula reminding himself that his robes are worn as protection against cold, and heat, against flies and insects, wind and sun and attacks of snakes, and to cover nakedness, and that he wears them in all humility, for use, and not for ornament. He then returns, makes obeisance, and asks to have administered to him the 3 → Refuges, and 10 precepts. Having received them from abbot, repeating them sentence by sentence, he makes obeisance, seeks forgiveness by his brethren of all faults and declares his wish to share with his brethren any merit he has gained. The *samanera* spends his time in monastery learning life of the Sangha, helping with daily chores, and accompanying a *bhikkhu* on his alms round, etc. He does not attend recitation, twice monthly, of the → *Patimokkha*; this is attended only by *bhikkhus*.

When a novice subsequently seeks higher ordination (*upasampadā*) as monk, he first goes through form for the ordering of a novice again; this is then followed by further and longer ceremony of O. in course of which candidate must be able to answer satisfactorily a list of questions concerning his status and condition (whether he is free

Ordination

from disease, debt, military service, is 20 years of age, etc.). He is presented by one of his two tutors. On this occasion the three robes, incl. stole, are presented, together with candidate's new alms-bowl, which he will use as a *bhikkhu* for receiving food from lay people each day. These are then ceremonially returned to him by abbot. An address is then given by abbot, or president, in which new *bhikkhu* is reminded of glory of life of a *bhikkhu,* and of high moral standards which are now his, and the chaste, honest, peaceable and humble life he must live.

O.'s are held at any time of year except the 3 months of → Vassa; the actual date is agreed upon in consultation with abbot of monastery where the O. is to be carried out, which is usually in man's home village, and with astrologers in order to settle upon an auspicious day for man concerned. A favourite time is just before Vassa, since it is Vassa period alone which is reckoned in counting years of service as a monk. Those who are entering for a few months only (a custom followed in Thailand esp.) will therefore do so at beginning of Vassa, i.e. in May or early June. In continental S.E. Asia another favourite time is a few months earlier, after end of rice-harvest, when funds are more plentiful, since O. is usually accompanied by considerable festivity, which sometimes lasts for more than one day (→ Festivals, Buddh.).

R. Gard, *Buddhism* (1961), pp. 157–66; H. K. Kaufman, *Bangkhuad: A Community Study in Thailand* (1960), pp. 123–31; Manning Nash, *The Golden Road to Modernity* (1965) (for Burmese Buddhism), pp. 124–31; K. E. Wells, *Thai Buddhism: Its Rites and Activities* (1959), *passim.*

P

Pabbajaka (Pali); **Parivrājaka** (Skt.) A 'homeless one,' 'one who has gone forth,' (sc., from home) hence, a name in early Buddhism for member of the Buddhist Order (→ Sangha).

Pacceka-Buddha (Pali); **Pratyeka-Buddha** (Skt.) An 'Isolated' Buddha is one who does not proclaim the transcendental knowledge he has gained by his Enlightenment (*bodhi*). Whereas disciples gain Enlightenment by hearing the truth (*Dhamma*) proclaimed by the Buddha (i.e., by a 'universal,' or *sammā-sambuddha*), the P.-B. attains to transcendental knowledge of the truth independently. Since he does not possess the faculty to proclaim it, he does not rank as a universal Buddha; the term 'P.-B.' is sometimes trans. as 'silent Buddha.' In the *Khaggavisāna Sutta* (part of → *Sutta-Nipāta*), the → Buddha (Gotama) is asked by → Ānanda, his disciple, concerning the way the P.-B. attains Enlightenment. The Buddha, after explaining, gives examples of (private) utterances or soliloquies of former P.-B.'s, each of which ends with the refrain 'fare solitary as a rhinoceros.' → Buddhaghosa, in his commentary on *Sutta-Nipāta*, gives life-stories of the P.-B.'s named in *Sutta*. The Skt. work, the → *Mahāvastu* mentions 500 P.-B.'s said to be living near Banares just before appearance of the Buddha Gautama; on hearing of imminent coming of a universal Buddha, they disappeared.

Sutta Nipāta, P.T.S. (1948), tr. by E. M. Hare as *Woven Cadences of Early Buddhists* (1945); trans. of the *Mahāvastu* by J. J. Jones, 3 vols. (1949–56).

Pagoda A Buddh. sacred shrine or memorial building. The Eng. word is derived from Portuguese *pagode* or *pagoth*, which in turn appears to have been derived by the Portuguese from an Asian word; opinions vary as to what the Asian original was. It was evidently a word encountered by the Portuguese in India and Ceylon; hence the Skt. *bhāgavatha* and the Sinhalese *dāgaba* have both been suggested. Whether derivation from latter is true or not, the word P. usually refers to the kind of Buddh. shrine which in Ceylon is called a *dāgaba,* and which is a develpt. of the anc. Indian → Stupa, which may or may not have contained sacred relics. In Burma this is called a *Hpaya* (object of veneration) or *Zedi* (fr. Pali *cetiya,* a shrine). In Thailand the same kind of structure is called a *Phrayachedi.*

S. Dutt, *The Buddha and Five After-Centuries* (1957), ch. 12; J. G. Scott, *The Burman* (1882); Manning Nash, *The Golden Road to Modernity* (1965), pp. 116–24; Kenneth E. Wells, *Thai Buddhism: its rites and activities* (1960).

Pali Language of canonical texts of → Theravāda Buddhism, which was preserved in → Ceylon orig., and now in Burma, Thailand, Laos and Cambodia also. Opinions differ concerning orig. home of language. Acc. to T. W. Rhys-Davids, it was dialect of Kosala, the tribal territory in what is now Uttar Pradesh, to N.E. of the Ganges; M. Walleser suggested it was the 'Pātali-bhāsā,' lang. of Pātaliputra (Patna) capital of → Magadha. E. Windisch and W. Geiger also regarded P. as poss. a modified form of 'Magadhese,' the lang. allegedly spoken by the Buddha, and one which would have served as the *lingua franca* of elite of Magadhan empire. A more recent opinion on subject, expressed by E. Lamotte, is that P. was a lang. of C. India, a 'high middle-Indian' dialect, i.e. one of the old Prākrit languages derived from Sanskrit, but approximating more closely to Vedic form of Sanskrit than to classical. Evidence concerning characteristics of Magadhese language (or Māgadhī), has come to light in mod. times in connection with inscriptions made by Magadhan emperors, notably → Aśoka; these indic. significant differences between Magadhese and P. The most that can at present be said, therefore, is that P. is lang. of the Theravāda → Tipitaka, the separate parts of which may have come from different regions of India and thus have embodied variety of local linguistic usages; that it was transmitted orally over several cents., and that later stages of transmission, before words were committed to writing, took place in Ceylon.

For a comprehensive account of scholarly work on subject see E. Lamotte, *Histoire du Bouddhisme Indien* (1958), pp. 607–28.

Paññā (Pali); **Prajñā** (Skt.) P., or wisdom, constitutes the 3rd and highest level of the Buddh. life, the other two being *sila* (Morality) and *samādhi* (→ Meditation): (→ Eightfold Path). The wisdom ref. to in this term is that which is specifically Buddh. It consists of direct apprehension of transcendent truths, concerning nature of world and human existence, which must at first be accepted in faith, but with intention of verifying these transcendent truths for oneself, experientially (→ Faith), by living the Buddh. life. The truths thus apprehended are formally set forth as the → Four Holy Truths. P. is also direct apprehension of impermanence (→ Anicca), ill (→ Dukkha), and impersonality (→ Anatta) of all existence. A synonym of P. is → Vipassanā. Refs. to P. are frequent in the Pali → Suttas. The realisation of transcendent truth is also central concern of → Mahāyāna. P. is one of the most import. single terms in the Skt. Sutras; a body of lit. exists which is devoted entirely to Prajñā-pāramitā, i.e., transcendental Wisdom (→ Prajñā-Pāramitā Sūtras).

Nyanamoli, *The Path of Purification* (Visuddhimagga) (1964), pp. 479ff.; D. T. Suzuki, *Studies in the Lankāvatāra Sutra* (1930), pp. 283–7.

Pāramita Term used in → Mhy. Buddhism, ref. to qualities or virtues, the cultivation of which leads to enlightenment. A list of 6 P.'s is given: generosity, morality, patience, vigour, concentration (or meditation) and wisdom. Later this list was expanded to 10, by add. of skill in means necessary to help others; profound resolution to produce enlightenment; the ten powers (→ Bala); and practice of the → Jhānas. Cultivation of these virtues was regarded in Mhy. Bud-

Paritta

dhism as proper training for a → Bodhisattva. A slightly different list of 10 P.'s is given by → Buddhaghosa in his *Visuddhimagga* (section IX).

E. Conze, *Buddhist Thought in India* (1962), pp. 211–7; R. Gard, *Buddhism* (1961), pp. 145–50; D. T. Suzuki, *Studies in the Lankāvatāra Sutra* (1930), pp. 365–7; Nyanamoli, *The Path of Purification* (1964), pp. 321–53.

Paritta Protective chant, used in Buddhism from earliest period. Such a chant 'whereby both brethren and sisters of the Order, and laymen and laywomen may dwell at ease, guarded, protected and unscathed' occurs in the → Dīgha-Nikāya, in the *Ātānātiya Suttanta* (T. W. Rhys-Davids, *Dialogues of the Buddha*, part III (1921, repr. 1965), pp. 188–97). It is poss. that in this matter early Buddhism was adapting use of *raksha-mantras* (protective formulae), a practice already current among people of India; it was able to do so because the practice was made consistent with Buddh. principles by making the P. a means of converting hostile forces: 'the agencies whose power to harm is deprecated' were 'blessed with good wishes, and suffused with outgoing love' (Rhys-Davids, *op. cit.,* p. 186). A list of 6 such P.'s is given in the *Questions of Milinda,* viz.: (1) the *Ratana Sutta* (found in the → *Khuddakapatha* and → *Sutta-Nipāta* (II:1); (2) the *Khanda,* (A.N., II:72; Vinaya-Pitaka, II:109, vide *S.B.E.,* 20, p. 76); (3) the Peacock (*Jāt.,* II:159); (4) the Banner Crest (*S.N.,* vide *Kindred Sayings,* I:283); (5) *Ātānātiya* (already mentioned); (6) the *Angulimāla* (Theragatha, vide *Psalms of the Brethren,* W.874–6). The → *Visuddhimagga* of → Buddhaghosa also gives a list of 5 P.'s (ch. XII, para. 31, i.e. those mentioned above, omitting the Angulimāla), which it describes as 'efficacious.' The ceremonial chanting by monks of such P.'s at request of lay people on specific and auspicious occasions, is a feature of S. Asian Buddhism; in Ceylon the practice is quite frequent and is known as *pirit.* The use of P.'s was, and sometimes still is, employed also in connection with national ceremonies in Buddh. countries.

Path, Buddhist → Eightfold Path.

Paticca-Samuppāda A Buddh. formula, often trans. as 'Dependent Origination,' or 'Chain of Causation,' which expresses doc. that all physical and psychical phenomena are conditioned by antecedent physical or psychical factors, and that whole of existence can be shown to be an uninterrupted flux of phenomena. The doc. implies also rejection of idea of any permanently existing entity or ego, human or animal. Twelve terms are used to set forth the doc.: old age and death (*jarāmarana*) are due to antecedent rebirth (*jātī*); rebirth is due to antecedent process of becoming (*bhava*); becoming is due to clinging (to life) (*upādāna*); clinging is due to craving (*tanhā*); craving is due to feeling (*vedanā*); feeling to sense-impression (*phassa*); sense-impression to the 6 Bases of sense (*āyatana*); the 6 Bases to corporeality (*nāma-rūpa*); corporeality to consciousness (*viññāna*); consciousness to karma-formations (*sankhāra*); and karma-formations to ignorance (*avijjā*). The formula is found in canonical scriptures in the → *Samyutta-Nikāya* (II, 7), and is expounded by → Buddhaghosa in the → *Visuddhimagga,* ch. XVII (tr. pp. 592ff.). Nyanatiloka, *Guide Through the Abhidhamma-Pitaka* (2nd edn. 1957), pp. 157–73, for refs. to European writing on the subject.

Pātimokkha (Pali); **Prātimokṣa** (Skt.) Moral code of Buddh. monks, consisting of list of more than 200 offences, in descending order of seriousness, recited in assembly of whole company of monks in every monastery on → Uposattha days. A monk who is guilty of any of these offences is required to confess the matter and receive the appropriate penalty (→ Discipline).

Perfections → *Pāramitā.*

Petavatthu A minor book of Buddh. Pali canon. It is found in 5th, or *Khuddaka, Nikaya* of *Sutta-Pitaka.* It is gen. listed 7th among books of the *K.-N.* Like 6th book, the *Vimanavatthu,* the P. deals with fates of departed spirits who do not find rebirth in embodied existence; the *Vimanavatthu* describes the celestial abodes of those *devas* or spirits whose rebirth is happy, though unembodied, because of previous good → *karma.* The V. consists of 83 stories of such *devas,* arranged in 7 chapters. The P. concerns un-

Phi

happy lot of ghosts who suffer as result of some previous bad *karma;* it contains 51 stories arranged in 4 chapters. Both books are, rel. to other parts of Pali canon, late in origin, poss. 3rd cent. BC, and are clearly intended for use in popular moral instruction and exhortation (→ Dead, State of).

Phi Siamese name for spirit-beings. They are believed to be responsible for causing human sickness and misadventures of all kinds, not because of their inherent evilness but on account of some specific discourtesy or offence by person who suffers the P.'s attack. Like the → Nats of Burma, P. are thought of as inhabiting rivers, mountains, wild places, and esp. trees. They manifest themselves in variety of roles: vampires, will o' the wisps; also as house-guardians, and spirits who cause the rice to grow. The house-guardian spirit is known also as *Phra Phum* (*ex.* Skt. *bhūmi*), the earth, thus, 'the earth-spirit,' and is given a small 'house' (*sam*) outside almost every Thai home. At this *Sam-Phra-Phum,* raised from ground by short pole, are offered food, flowers, incense and candles. The manufacture of these *Sam-Phra-Phum* is a flourishing craft even in metropolis of Bangkok. Apart from these categories of P., there are spirits of dead persons; these are usually regarded as malevolent, esp. when death was result of violence or accident; it is regarded as imperative that special rites be performed to protect living from their malevolent attacks (→ Yakka).

Phongyi-Chaung Burmese name for a Buddh. monastery (*Phongyi* = monk; *chaung* = house or building) (→ Monasteries).

Pilgrimage (China) Earliest known centres of P. in anc. China were the 5 sacred mountains: T'ai-shan in Shantung; Hua-shan in Shensi; Hêng-shan in Shansi; Nan-yu-shan in Hunan; and Sung-shan in Honan. Both Taoism and Buddhism built monasteries and temples on these mountains, which grad. became enormously popular centres of P., attracting hosts of pilgrims from far and wide. In add., Buddhism succeeded in creating great new centres of P.: monasteries and temples dedicated to honour of powerful and miracle-working Buddhas and → bodhisattvas. Particularly

Pilgrimage

famous are P'u-t'o-shan, an island off the coast of Ningpo; Chiu-hua-shan in Anhwei; Wu-t'ai-shan in Shansi and O-mei-shan in Szechuan. Besides these, there are enormous number of holy places which attract thousands of P. every year. As a rule, it is special circumstances, such as sickness, poor harvests, failing business, etc., which send men on P. But grievous sins, which brought calamity to a home, may be atoned for by P. Often P. are undertaken as a result of vows being made. Occasionally they grow out of real relig. need and spiritual aspiration.

The usual season for P. is autumn. After suitable acts of worship, and choosing of a lucky day by divination, the pilgrims of a neighbourhood will set out together under a chosen leader. They wear special clothing, with red or yellow waistcoat, red being worn by those who are going to expiate sins. The pilgrims, carrying bowls with sticks of incense, move forward in groups of 10–50 in silent meditation, except when leader calls for prayer. They eat only vegetarian food, and mark their long and arduous journey by many penances. On arrival at destination, having bathed and purified themselves, they proceed to main temple hall for worship. On return the same rules, acts of worship and asceticism are observed until they arrive home.

From CE 4th cent. onwards, it became common for Chi. Buddh. monks to travel westward on pilgrimages to India and other Buddh. countries, some even reaching as far as Ceylon. The purpose was to study at fountain-head of Buddh. learning, to bring back sacred scriptures and Buddh. relics. Among most famous Chi. pilgrims are → Fa Hsien (c. 399); Sung Yün (518); I Ch'ing (634–713) and → Hsüan Tsang (629–45). The P. of these men had a profound influence on development of Buddhism in China.

K. L. Reichelt, *Truth and Tradition in Chinese Buddhism* (1927), *passim, Religion in Chinese Garment* (1951), *passim* (espec. ch. 9); H. Welch, *The Practice of Chinese Buddhism* (1967), pp. 305–10, 370–5; K. Schipper, 'Les Pèlerinages en Chine: Montagnes et Pistes,' *S.O.*, III (1960).

(Japan) The mountains of Japan are the homes of gods, and

Piśāca

over the cents. scores of mountain shrines have become centres of P. Relig. P. began with consecration of many mountain peaks as places of Buddh. worship in CE 8th cent. Besides great mountain peaks, there were several purely Buddh. or Shinto centres of pilgrimage, as e.g. the temple at Ise dedicated to the supreme Deity of Shinto. To this centre almost all Japanese aspired to go at least once in a lifetime. The habit of making P. to far distant shrines led to formation of clubs in which contributions were made monthly to a P. fund, those going each year on P. being chosen by lot, with a member acting as leader. In mod. times the mountain-P. have taken on more and more a festive and holiday nature, the relig. aspect being less emphasised than formerly.

Piśāca Anc. Indian term for a spirit-being, or demon—since the P. are usually regarded as evil, or hostile to men. As such they are mentioned in Buddh. Pali canon at various places, in connection with contemporary popular beliefs. As with → *yakkhas,* it is poss. that belief in P. has origin in idea of 'man-eating demons,' i.e. cannibals, in certain parts of India. A tribe bearing name P., among whom cannibalism was practised, is known to have existed in N.W. India; the tribe, on account of its cannibalism, may however have derived its name from that of the demons, if this was already current.

G. Grierson, 'Pisaca = Homophagoi,' *J.R.A.S.* (1905).

Polytheism (China-Far East) Popular relig. in all Far Eastern countries is incurably polytheistic. Though a supreme Deity is usually recognised, he rules over hierarchy of innumerable gods and divine beings, drawn, as case may be, from the mythologies of Taoism, Buddhism, Shinto, etc. P. seems to have developed out of the polydaemonism of a primitive nature-worship.

Prajñā-Pāramitā Sūtras Lit. 'the Wisdom-Perfection' (i.e., Perfect Wisdom), is name given to type of literature in → Mahāyāna Buddhism, the central teaching of which is the doc. of → Śūnyatā, which, says Murti, 'revolutionised Buddhism.' It is knowledge of *Śūnyatā*, which constitutes the 'Perfect Wisdom.' The *P.-P. Sutras* vary in length from the

'100,000 verses Sutra' (*Śata-sāhāsrikā Sūtra*), to the → Heart Sūtra (*Hṛdaya Sūtra*), which is only a few lines in length. Between these extremes, 9 others are known and published, of which the best known and most import. is the Diamond-cutter Sūtra (*Vajracchedikā*). The *P.-P. Sūtras* are reckoned to be among earlier productions of Mahāyāna school; in form they stand fairly close to the dialogues of Pali canon. The Buddha (here the 'Lord,' or Bhagavan) is repr. as engaging in discourse with his disciple Subhuti, whereas in other Mahāy. Sūtras he more usually discourses with another → Bodhisattva. It is thought that the *P.-P. Sūtras* had origin in S. India; thence spread to N. The great Mahāy. teachers →→ Nagarjuna, Vasubandhu, and Asanga wrote substantial commentaries on these sūtras; these commentaries were trans. into Chinese, in which form only they are now extant.

M. Winternitz, *Hist. of Indian Literature,* vol. 2 (1933), pp. 341ff.; T. R. V. Murti, *The Central Philosophy of Buddhism* (1955), pp. 83f.; E. Conze, *Buddhist Wisdom Books* (1958), *Perfect Wisdom* (1961).

Pratyeka-Yāna → *Yāna.*

Prayer From CE 8th cent. onwards, both Buddh. and Taoist priests engaged in offering masses for souls of dead. In Mahāyāna → Buddhism of China innumerable prayers are offered to Buddhas and → bodhisattvas, espec. → Amitābha and → Kuan Yin. → Tibetan Buddhism, common in N. China, makes use of prayer-wheel, whilst everywhere scrolls, flags, streamers and inscriptions carry petitions and invocations. Prayer is an integral part of the → ancestor-cult carried out in family, whilst devout Buddh. have recourse to silent meditation and petition in nearest temple at all times of special need.

E.R.E., X, p. 170; W. E. Soothill, *The Three Religions of China* (1923), pp. 133–47, 233, 243; K. L. Reichelt, *Truth & Tradition in Chinese Buddhism* (1927), *passim.*

(Japan) As in China, → Mahāyāna Buddhism brought to Japan not only techniques of spiritual meditation, but such faith in the saving efficacy of compassionate Buddhas and → bodhisattvas as to call forth in Buddh. devotees the

Predestination

most ardent prayers of adoration, penitence, petition, intercession and thanksgiving, prayers primarily directed to attainment of salvation. Buddhism has had a profound influence on mod. sectarian Shinto. P., as spiritual communion with eternal and divine source of all good, is fundamental in doc. and practice of many of most influential of mod. Shinto sects.

Predestination The B. attitude to any doc. of divine P. of human affairs, such, e.g. as is found in orthodox Islamic theology, is closely akin to the Bdm. attitude to → Determinism. The theistic P. view was known to early Buddh. as that of the Issarakārana-vādins, 'those who say that the agent in all that happens is Ishwara (i.e. God).' This view is refuted in the → *Jātaka* literature (*Jat,* V, 238), where it is argued that doc. that God is agent in human activity implies that man has, therefore, no responsibility for his actions, or that man has no freedom of moral choice. Since the premise from which Buddh. thought on this matter begins is that man has such freedom, and a theistic P. conflicts with this, P. is rejected. Another argument, put forward elsewhere in the *Jātakas,* is that the view that God is responsible for all that happens involves his being the author of injustice (*Jat,* VI, 208). This, clearly, is in itself not a disproof of the doc. of theistic P. so much as an objection to it on moral grounds.
K. N. Jayatilleke, *Early Buddhist Theory of Knowledge* (1963), pp. 410–1; Piyadassi Thera, *The Buddha's Ancient Path* (1964), pp. 63–4.

Priests → Ordination.

(China) Buddhism in China was organised monastically; till at least the ᴄᴇ 4th cent., the monks or priests were foreigners. Chi. monks were trained and ordained in monasteries, but needs of laity led to rise of a large body of priests to serve temples of popular relig. The Buddh. clergy are celibate, have shaven heads, and wear distinctive dress.

Psychic Powers → *Iddhi.*

Pudgala-Vādins Buddh. sect that appeared about 200 years after death of Buddha, i.e., at begin. of 3rd cent. ʙᴄ. A brahman named Vatsiputra, who had been converted to Bud-

212

dhism, put forward theory that while the → *anatta* doc. denied existence of an enduring individual soul, nevertheless *something* endured; this was the *pudgala,* or 'person.' He claimed that Buddha, in his discourses, had made use of notion of *pudgala,* and had thus indic. real existence of the person. The majority of Buddh.s monks demurred from this opinion; it was pointed out that use of term *pudgala* in Buddha's discourses was merely a concession to everyday usage. V., however, won a number of monks to his view, since the *pudgala*-theory appeared to satisfy demands of justice better than the *anatta* doc. For, if there is no enduring entity which transmigrates from existence to existence, there could be no proper basis for retributive justice operating through *karma;* hence incentive to responsible moral action was lost. The monks who opposed the *pudgala-vādins* did so because it seemed that notion of a *pudgala,* which transmigrated, was the reappearance, under another name, of rejected notion of the → *atta* (*ātman*). Nevertheless, the P. sect continued to grow, and as late as 7th cent. CE the Chi. pilgrim → Hsuan Tsang recorded that there were 66,000 P. monks: approx. a quarter of total no. of Buddh. monks in India at that time. The P.'s were known also as Vatsīputrīyas, after name of originator of doc. They themselves became divided on minor points into four subsects; the differences between them are now obscure, since the lit. of these sects is virtually nonexistent. A. Bareau, *Les Sectes Bouddhiques du Petit Véhicule* (1955); E. Conze, *Buddhist Thought in India* (1962), pp. 121–31.

Puñña Term used in B. trad. and usually trans. 'merit.' The task of merit-making is primary for great majority of Buddhs., whether monks or laymen; it is regarded as the production of wholesome Karma, which will secure an entail of spiritually more mature existence, or, in popular parlance 'a good rebirth.' P. has 3 aspects: (1) → Dāna or generosity, as a corrective to tendencies to egoism; (2) → Sila or keeping of the moral precepts; (3) Bhāvanā or meditational development. For monks who are spiritually more advanced (3) is their major concern; although (1) and (2)

Pure Land School

are still important; for those less spiritually advanced (1) and (2) are still their major concern. For majority of laymen emphasis is predominantly on (1) and (2), in the giving of food, robes, money or land (primarily for support of monks), and the keeping of the 5 moral precepts; when poss. also (3) (Sila). More spiritually advanced laymen, or *upāsakas,* will also acquire merit by meditating. In B. countries of S.E. Asia and Ceylon, merit-making under aspects (1) and (2) is thus basis of popular relig. and the concern of the majority.
D.N., 33; Itivuttaka, 60; *A.N.,* VIII:36; Michael M. Ames, 'Magical Animism and Buddhism: a Structural Analysis of the Sinhalese Religious System,' in *J.A.S.* (1964).

Pure Land School (Chi. Buddh.) In Chinese—Ching T'u: prob. oldest and least philosophical of sects of → Mahāyāna Buddhism in China. → Hui Yüan is considered to have founded P.L. in 402 CE, calling it the White Lotus sect; name was changed later to P.L. when a revolutionary society adopted it. Hui Yüan and successors accepted the orthodox Buddh. teaching that life is sorrow and disillusionment, governed by karma and rebirth, but directed mind to the infinite host of → Buddhas and → bodhisattvas who offered believer the assistance which only infinite grace, power and merit could give. They took as principal scripture the Greater Sukhāvatī-vyūha Sūtra (*Wu-liang-shou ching*), which proclaimed doc. of salvation by faith in Amitabha Buddha (→ Amida), and contains vivid descriptions of the P.L. or Western Paradise, ruled over by Amitabha, assisted by the two great bodhisattvas, → Kuan Yin and Ta Shih Chih.

One of greatest exponents of P.L. was Shan-tao (613–81 CE), who taught that men, steeped in ignorance and evil desire, have little power to save themselves. They must place their reliance on faith in Amitabha alone, who guarantees to all who sincerely believe in him salvation and entrance into the P.L. His saving grace, mercy and infinite merit are freely offered to all who simply call upon his name in faith. This emphasis on saving faith and devotion to all the Buddhas and bodhisattvas may be compared to the bhakti developments in Hinduism.

When, at close of T'ang Dyn., the hard divisions betw. various sects of Buddhism in China tended to be obliterated, the P.L. sects came to exert a pervasive and dominating influence in Chi. Buddhism; they remain the most effective relig. force among Chi. Buddhists in mod. times. The teachings of P.L. are condensed in the famous *Ch'i Hsin Lun* (Awakening of Faith in the Mahayana); E.T. by D. T. Suzuki (1900), and T. Richard (1910). (→ Jodo).

K. L. Reichelt, *Truth & Tradition in Chinese Buddhism* (1927), ch. 5; D. H. Smith, *Chinese Religions* (1968), pp. 125ff.

R

Rāhula Son of Gotama → the Buddha. Acc. to Pali texts, R. was born at → Kapilavatthu about time that Gotama left his home in search of enlightenment. Later, Gotama visited Kapilavatthu, when R. was still a child, and the boy was ordained a → *samenera* or novice of the Buddh. order. Thereafter he was recipient of much of Buddha's teaching, acc. to the canon; a number of → Jātaka stories and Suttas are trad. regarded as having been addressed by the Buddha to Rāhula. The collection of verses known as the → *Theragāthā,* (the Psalms of the Brethren) incl. some attr. to R. (vv. 295–8). He is said to have pre-deceased the Buddha.

Rājagaha (Pali)/**Rājagṛha** (Skt.) City in anc. India of import. in early hist. of Buddhism. It was capital of kingdom of Magadha during earlier period, until Pātaliputta (Patna) took its place. It was situated to S. of the Ganges, and a little S. of present town of Rājgir. In Buddh. hist. its chief import. is that it was scene of → Council said to have been held immediately after death of the Buddha, for purpose of agreeing on authentic version of discourses of Buddha (→ Suttas) and the monastic Discipline-code (→ Vinaya). At that time, acc. to → Buddhaghosa's commentary on the Vinaya-Pitaka, the Samantapāsādikā, there were 18 large monasteries in R. One of these was the first *ārāma,* or permanently enclosed ground, to be donated to the → Sangha, viz, the *Veluvana* or 'Bamboo-grove,' given to Buddha and his monks by King → Bimbisāra. (→ Monasteries). By time the Chi. pilgrim → Hsüan Tsang visited place in 7th cent. CE, R. was largely in ruins, with jungle closing in on the ruined buildings, and a small surviving village.

Malalasekere, *D.P.P.N.,* vol. II, pp. 721–4; S. Beal, *Buddhist*

Relics

Records of the Western World (1884), vol. 2, pp. 161–7; J. Marshall, 'Rajagriha and Its Remains,' *Archaeological Survey of India, Report* (1905–6), pp. 86–106.

Rebirth → Metempsychosis.

→→ Samsāra; Death, Buddh. view; Paticca-Samuppada.

Refuges, The Three (Buddh.) → Tri-ratna.

Relics It is claimed by Buddh. that some relics of Gotama the Buddha are still enshrined in the great pagodas; e.g. a tooth, in Temple of Sacred Tooth at Kandy, in → Ceylon; some hairs, in the Shwe Dagon Pagoda at Rangoon, in Burma. In this matter Buddhism is distinguished from the other Indian religs. of Hinduism and Jainism, which do not inculcate showing of reverence to relics of a human body. On the other hand, Islam, which, like early Buddhism, had no recognised object of worship, has developed this feature. It is poss. that it was customary in N. India at time of Buddha to build cairn over bones of a great man, and give honour to them, and that this is origin of Buddh. use of the → *stupa,* in which relics not only of Buddha, but of other Buddh. saints are said to be enshrined. Another of Buddha's relics, which it is claimed has been preserved, is his alms-bowl or *patra,* which, comments Eliot, 'plays a part somewhat similar to that of the Holy Grail in Christian romance.' Acc. to the → *Mahāvamsa,* the emperor → Ashoka sent it to Ceylon. Various legends are concerned with its subsequent travels. Acc. to Marco Polo, it was taken from Ceylon to China by order of Kublai Khan in 1284, although acc. to other legends, it is in Persia, Kandahar (→→ Buddha, the Gotama; Mahā-Parinibbāna Sutta).

Mahāvamsa; Da Cunha, *Memoir on the History of the Tooth Relic of Ceylon* (1875); C. Eliot, *Hinduism and Buddhism* (1921, repr. 1957), III, pp. 22–8.

(China–Far East) Though Japan, Korea and Siam seem to care little for R. properly so-called, when Buddhism became firmly estab. in China, one of main purposes of numerous → pilgrimages to India and the W. was to bring back holy R. of the Buddha and Buddh. saints, by possession of which great monasteries enhanced their prestige. From Han Dynasty onwards, there are well-attested discov-

Rinzai

eries of anc. seals and other regalia, amulets, inscribed stones, jade or bronze objects which were regarded as auspicious objects and tangible proofs of the ruler's virtue. Their finding was often marked by miraculous happenings, luminous emanations and other supernatural phenomena. Buddhists, wishing to prove early existence of Buddhism on Chi. soil, record at least nine discoveries of 'Aśoka-relics' (→ Aśoka) during 4th cent. CE. The numerous → pagodas were primarily memorials erected over R. of Buddh. saints. In CE 819, the emperor Hsien-tsung, a devout Buddh., proposed to bring a celebrated R., a finger-bone of Buddha, to the capital, to be lodged in imperial palace for three days and afterwards exhibited in various temples. A famous Confucian scholar, Han Yü, used occasion to write a memorial to the throne condemning Buddhism, and advising that the relic should be destroyed by fire and water, and the pernicious cult exterminated. For this he was demoted and banished.

E. Zürcher, *The Buddhist Conquest of China* (1959), *passim;* C. P. Fitzgerald, *China* (rev. edn. 1950), pp. 352–5.

Rinzai (Chinese: Lin-chi). Founded by the Chi. Buddh. Lin Chi or I-hsüan (d. CE 867), and intro. into Japan by → Eisai (1141–1215), R. became one of the two major schools of → Zen, distinguished from → Sōtō by unorthodox means employed to attain sudden enlightenment, i.e., striking and shouting, the use of nonsensical language and paradox, and the → koan exercises. It flourished in the Kamakura period; its great temples became centres of great cultural and artistic achievement. The great R. master, → Hakuin (1685–1768) laid foundation for mod. development of Zen. H. Dumoulin, *Hist. of Zen Buddhism* (1963); D. T. Suzuki, *Studies in Zen* (1955).

Rūpa Buddh. term for (1) 'corporeality' (2) a visible object. In former sense it occurs in conjunction with other terms, such as *loka* (realm or world) to denote one of three realms in Buddh. → cosmology, i.e. realm of pure form (without material substance). In this sense also it denotes first of the 5 → *khandhas,* or groups of constituent factors which make up the human 'individual'; in this case it denotes the

whole physical aspect as distinct from psychological aspects, repr. by the other 4 khandhas. In second sense, it is used espec. of representations of the Buddha used in Buddh. devotions, often ref. to in the West as 'Buddha-images' or 'Buddha-statues.' The use of *Buddha-rūpa* appears to have developed in India in 1st cent. BC or CE. Before, symbols to repr. Buddha had been used, such as the → Bodhi-tree, and → *stupa* or mound. It is uncertain whether the Buddha-R. orig. in India, from use of the *vigraha* or representation of the god in → *bhakti* devotion, or whether it was feature of Hellenistic relig., intro. into N.W. India from Hellenised → Gandhāra or Bactria. Strong claims have been made for both theories. The claim that this was an indigenous develop. on Indian soil usually takes form that it was in region of Mathurā (on Jumna River, south of mod. Delhi), a stronghold of the → Sarvāstivādins, that this occurred. There is evidence of use of the Buddha-R. in both Gandhāra and in the Mathurā area within roughly same period. The import. point of difference is that the form developed at Mathurā was distinctively more Indian in character, while the Gandharan form was obviously indebted to Greek influence; in latter case the representation of Buddha resembles the Greek god of later antiquity. Seckel, *op. cit.*, p. 163. In course of transmission through India and Buddh. lands of S.E. Asia, the style of the Buddha-R. continued to be modified acc. to local conventions, assuming different characteristic forms in Ceylon, Burma, Thailand, China and Japan.
A. K. Coomaraswamy, *Hist. of Indian and Indonesian Art* (1927); B. Rowland, *The Art and Architecture of India* (1953); Dietrick Seckel, *The Art of Buddhism* (1964), part II, ch. 3.

Ryōbu (Dual) Shintō An attempt to fuse the two great faiths of mediaeval Japan, worked out by priests of the → Shingon sect of Buddhism. R. is attr. to → Kobo Daishi (774–835), who taught the principles which formed R. in 12th cent., and which were developed vigorously in 13th cent., to become dominant form of → Shinto, highly influenced by Buddhism. Joint Shinto-Buddh. sanctuaries

Ryōbu (Dual) Shintō

were served by amalgamated priesthood (*shasō*), and Buddh. rites were conducted in Shinto shrines. Through R. the ethical content and philosophical outlook of Shinto were deepened. During course of Tokogawa shogunate, R. met with relentless attack from advocates of Pure Shinto; early in the Meiji era the forced separation of Buddhism and Shinto was effected, so that R. practically disappeared as a system of doctrine and ceremony.

D. C. Holtom, *The National Faith of Japan* (1938), pp. 36–8; W. G. Aston, *Shinto* (1905), pp. 36ff.; M. Anesaki, *Hist. of Japanese Religion* (1930), pp. 136ff.

S

Saddhā Buddh. term for → Faith.

Saddharma-Pundarīka Sūtra 'The Lotus of the True Law' Sutra, one of most import. Buddh. Skt. texts of the → Mahāyāna school, and prob. the best known. The text purports to be the teaching of the transcendent Buddha, who is here repr. as a god above the gods, a being infinitely exalted and eternal, who can say 'I am the father of the world, the self-existent (*svayambhū*).' Unlike the → Buddha of Pali scriptures, he does not go from place to place preaching message, but announces it from hill where he sits surrounded by a vast number of monks and nuns, → Bodhisattvas, gods and demi-gods. The teaching reflects a transitional stage between that of the → Hīnayāna and Mahāyāna; the former is here said to have been an accommodation of the transcendental Buddha's message to suit needs of men of lower intelligence and ability. Winternitz comments that the spirit of this *Sutra* is very like that of the Hindu *Purānas,* and espec. the Bhagavad-Gītā: the words of the Buddha here bear strong resemblance to those of the Lord Kṛṣna in the Gītā. A similar doc. of the Buddha's manifesting himself is also found: out of pity for men and their weaknesses, he appeared as a man and 'pretended' to become enlightened and enter *nirvāna*. The work is in 27 chapters, partly in Skt. prose, partly in Buddh. Skt. verse. It contains material of mixed date; the nucleus is regarded as belonging to 1st cent. CE, some of which is quoted by → Nagarjuna. It was trans. into Chinese c. CE 223, and is highly regarded by Chinese and Japanese Buddh.
M. Winternitz, *Hist. of Indian Literature,* vol. II (1933), pp. 295–305.

Saints

Saints → Bodhisatta.

Sakadāgāmin Term used in Buddhism for one who is regarded as highly advanced in spiritual progress and will return only once more (*sakadāgāmin,* once-returner) in course of cycle of rebirth, then as an → *anāgāmin;* after that he will achieve → nibbāna; i.e. in his next birth but one he (or she) will be an → arahant. The S. is said by Buddha to be one who has reduced moral imperfections of → lobha, dosa and → moha to a minimum.
D.I., I, p. 156; T. W. Rhys-Davids, *Dialogues of the Buddha,* part I, pp. 200ff.

Sakka Name used in Buddh. Pali canon for the *devānam indo,* or chief of the *devas* (i.e. heavenly beings), who in Buddh. → Cosmology rules over the lowest but one of the heavens in the *deva*-world. The → *devas* are repr. as fighting against the → *asuras,* or demons, under the leadership of S. A section of the → Saṃyutta-Nikāya, the *Sakka-Saṃyutta,* consisting of 25 short suttas, is devoted to exploits of S. He is said to be devoted to Buddha and his relig.

Sākyas The tribe in which → the Buddha Gotama was born. The tribe inhabited the Himalayan foothills in what is now Nepal. Their chief town was → Kapilavatthu, the Buddha's home in childhood and early manhood. Their form of government was that of an assembly (*sangha*) of elders, often ref. to by modern writers as republican. The affairs of government were conducted in the Mote-Hall (Santhāgāra) at Kapilavatthu. They appear to have practised endogamy to a considerable degree, although they do appear also to have intermarried with the Koliyans, a neighbouring tribe. Many of the Sākyan tribe are said to have entered the Buddh. Order when Buddha returned to Kapilavatthu after his enlightenment. One of these was the barber Upāli, who was ordained first, and was thus theoretically senior to others, who formerly had been his social superiors. (*Vin.,* II, pp. 181f.). A large number of S. were later massacred, during lifetime of Buddha, by king of Kosala in revenge for an insult.

Sākyamuni Title sometimes given to → Gotama, the Buddha, meaning the sage (*muni*) of the *Sākya* clan, a clan who in-

222

habited the foothills of the Himalaya in region of present-day Nepal.

Salvation (Chinese) Buddhism in China offered a satisfactory cosmological explanation of universe, with an ethical interpretation of world, thus providing a total solution for human frailties and social ills. It was also designed to transform suffering humanity into perfect beings in a W. Paradise (→→ Amitabha, Kuan Yin, Pure Land). Its doc. of universal S. was readily accepted by the Chinese.

The hist. of religs. in China reveals that popular imagination was, throughout the cents., profoundly stirred by the mythological constructions of Buddhism and Taoism in respect of an after-life, in which the consequences of human frailty and sin were mitigated by compassionate intervention of gods, Buddhas and → bodhisattvas. But the this-worldly and pragmatical influence of Confucian ethics has remained so strong that, even when Confucianism came to be discarded, as in modern Communist China, the ideal of national S. remains, with belief in poss. of estab. on earth of a 'perfect' society.

W. E. Soothill, *Three Religs. of China* (1923), *passim;* C. K. Yang, *Relig. in Chinese Society* (1961), pp. 229–32; D. H. Smith, *Chinese Religions* (1968), *passim.*

Samādhi, Buddh. term, meaning lit. 'concentration.' The term is used in connection with practice of → meditation, and refers to fixing of attention on a single object, thus discouraging discursive thinking. Three degrees of intensity are distinguished: (1) preparatory concentration (*parikamma-samādhi*); (2) Neighbourhood or access concentration (*upacāra-samādhi*), where the state of → *jhāna* is being approached; (3) Attainment concentration (*appana-sa-mādhi*), i.e., the degree of S. which is present when the state of *jhāna* has been attained.

Sāmanera (Pali); **Śrāmanera** (Skt.) Buddh. novice-monk (→ Ordination).

Sambhoga Kāya → Buddha-Kāya.

Saṃsāra Term used in Buddhism for transmigration; lit., moving about continuously, coming again and again (i.e., to rebirth), the term refers to notion of going through one life after another. The endlessness and inevitability of S. are described in *S.N.*, II, p. 178. It is claimed by Buddh. that to appreciate properly the Buddh. truth of the → *dukkha* or suffering entailed in all existence, it is not enough to consider one single lifetime, wherein *dukkha* may or may not be immediately apparent; one must have in view the whole frightful unending chain of rebirth and the sum of misery entailed therein. S. refers not only to round of rebirth in human forms; the whole range of sentient beings is incl., from the tiniest insect to man, and forms an unbroken continuum. Only at stage of human existence, however, can S. be transcended, and release, or → Nibbana, attained (→ Metempsychosis).

Saṃyutta-Nikāya Third of 5 → *Nikāyas* which together make up → Sutta-Pitaka of Buddh. Pali canon. The name *saṃyutta* indics. method of arrangement of Suttas used for the Nikaya, viz., that of 'yoking together' suttas dealing with same main topic. Thus first section or chapter (*vagga*) of S.-N. is made up of suttas dealing with → Devas, or heavenly beings (*Deva-Saṃyutta*), with Kosala (*Kosala-Saṃyutta*), with → Māra, the Evil One (*Mara-Saṃyutta*), with nuns, or *therī* (*Therī-Saṃyutta*), with → Brahma, Hindu deity (*Brahma-Saṃyutta*), with → Yakkas (*Yakka-Saṃyutta*), with chief of the gods → Sakka (*Sakka-Saṃyutta*) and, similarly, various other subjects. One of most famous suttas contained in S.-N. is the → *Dhamma-Cakkappavattana Sutta* (*S.N.*, V, pp. 420ff.), which sets out what is held to be first sermon of Buddha after attaining enlightenment. The S.-N. contains altogether 2,889 suttas. These are arranged in 56 Samyuttas, which in turn are arranged in five main sections or chapters (*vagga*). The S.-N. has been trans. into Eng. under title *Kindred Sayings*: the first *vagga* as vol. I (1917, repr. 1950); the 2nd as vol. II (1922, repr. 1952) by C. F. Rhys-Davids; the remaining 3 *vaggas* by F. L. Woodward as vols. III, IV and V (1955, 1956, 1956).

Sangha (or Samgha) Third of the 'three jewels' (→ Tri-Ratna) of Buddhism: the Order of *bhikkhus*, or monks. The word S. means 'assembly' and was term used in N. India at time of → Buddha for assemblies, by means of which contemporary tribal republics or confederations managed their affairs. The republican assemblies are brought into connection with the Buddh. community at beginning of → *Mahā-Parinibbāna Sutta,* where the Buddha is repr. as saying: 'As long as the Vajjians foregather thus often, and frequent the public meetings of their clan, so long may they be expected not to decline but to prosper.' Certain conditions governing way they should assemble are then mentioned in the *Sutta;* the whole saying is then repeated word for word, with same conditions, in respect of Buddh. S. It is clear from this discourse, preserved by Buddh. S. at time when the Vajjian republic had been overthrown by advancing monarchy, that the Buddh. S. was to be successor to old tribal republics, poss. even providing refuge from conditions of life under new autocratic rule.

The members of the Buddh. S. were those followers of Buddha who, having heard and received the → *Dhamma,* were prepared to leave behind life of household or family and become wandering almsmen (*bhikkhus*). The bhikkhu was also known as *pabbajaka,* one who had gone forth (from home). Their own name for community appears to have been 'the Bhikkhu-sangha'; whereas by non-Buddh. S. they were at first known as *Sākya-puttiya-samanas,* i.e., wanderers (*samanas*) of (him of) the → Sākya clan, viz. Gotama. The term *samana* was in common use in anc. India to distinguish wandering ascetic type of relig. man from the brahman; thus 'Samanas and Brahmans' was a way of ref. to the two main and contrasting types of relig. life.

The transition from the wandering life to that of settled community of almsmen appears to have been connected with practice such wanderers had of gathering together during the 3 months of monsoon rains (approx. July–September) in a common shelter, simply as a matter of convenience. Other *samanas* besides Buddh. followed this practice; but only in case of followers of Buddha did the rains-retreat develop into permanent, settled community life. The reasons for this are still not altogether clear: the characteristically Buddh. doc. of selflessness (→ *anatta*) may have had, as its reverse side, an emphasis on a wider

Sangha

community of being where notion of *anatta* could be strengthened, and where a common life could be enjoyed which reduced need for personal possessions, and hence personal identity, to a minimum. The member of the S. was allowed to possess only minimum of personal belongings: his robes and alms-bowl (in which he received food from donor-householders); these were outward sign of his dedicated relig. life, and distinguished him in eyes of ordinary householders from the mere vagabond; in add. to these he was allowed needle (to repair his robes), rosary (for use in meditation), razor for shaving head every → *Uposattha* day, and filter through which to pour drinking water, in order to save the lives of any small insects which might be contained in it. In principle these are still the only possessions allowed to monk in → Theravāda countries, although in practice he may receive gifts of various kinds from lay people; these will, however, usually be justifiable in view of some special need—e.g., a typewriter or fountain pen for monk who is a writer—and will be regarded in theory as property of S.

The code of discipline which regulated behaviour of members of the S. was embodied in the → Patimokkha. In add. there were various rulings and prescriptions concerning nature and conduct of S. life, which together formed the Vinaya, or Discipline; they were gathered and arranged in trad. form which came to be known as the → Vinaya-Pitaka. In earliest period of Buddh. hist. the way of life was summed up in the twofold 'Dhamma-Vinaya,' or Doctrine and Discipline. The earliest disagreements within S. arose over infringements of monastic discipline and were occasions of 2nd Buddh. → Council: the outcome was secession of the → *Mahāsanghikas* from orthodox Sthavira body of the S. Various other divisions within the S. have taken place from time to time; doc. differences, however, have not necessarily been a serious cause of separation; in anc. India even → Mahāyāna and → Hīnayāna monks could be found in same monastery. In Theravāda countries today the S. is divided into several sects, or *nikāyas* (→→ Burma; Ceylon; Thailand).

Sangha

The S. is, in its gen. structure, democratic. In varying degrees, however, a certain measure of authority has come to be vested in chief monk, or abbot of local monastery. In countries where the king is also Protector of the S. (Thailand, Cambodia, Laos) a hierarchical structure of the national S. has resulted, with various grades of monkhood conferred by king. In some cases these may depend also on qualifications gained in study of → Pali. The S. has a recognisable social role; it is not a body of men withdrawn from ordinary world and its affairs. It has an import. place in society of Buddh. countries, based on reciprocal relationships between monks and laymen. The former are preservers, transmitters and teachers of the Buddha's doc. (→ Dhamma) and are in many ways, spiritual and practical, counsellors of the laity; the latter, in return, provide for material needs of monks by providing them with food, robes and monastic buildings (→ Monasteries). The main purpose of life in S. is, in theory, the opportunity it provides for life of meditation, and hence of improving one's spiritual status. In practice, however, meditation is not always emphasised. Membership of S. is not necessarily life-long. A man may take → ordination for certain limited period. Such temporary monks, however, are not so highly respected by lay people as those whose intention it is to remain life-long members of Order. In some Theravada countries it is customary for boys to spend a few months as members of S. before 'coming of age'; those who do so enjoy, subsequently, a higher prestige than those who have not. Very often such short-term membership is undertaken during the 3 months of → Vassa, the rainy season, or 'Buddh. Lent.' For the various grades of monks, (novices, monks, abbots) → Ordination (→→ Patimokkha; Vinaya-Pitaka).

Bigandet, P., 'Notice on the Phongyies, or Buddhist Monks' in *Life or Legend of Gaudama the Budha of the Burmese* (*sic*) 1866; D. P. Chattopadhyaya, *Lokāyata* (1959); Sukumar Dutt, *The Buddha and Five After-Centuries* (1957), and *Buddhist Monks and Monasteries of India* (1962); R. Gard, *Buddhism* (1961), ch. V; Phra Khāntipalo, *The Patimokkha*

227

Sanskrit

(1966); E. Lamotte, *Histoire du Bouddhisme Indien* (1958), pp. 58–94.

Sanskrit, Buddhist Language and Literature Sanskrit, an Indo-European language intro. into Indian sub-continent by Aryan tribes, who began to enter from N.W. in mid. 2nd mil. BC, developed in India from the early (Vedic) form in which it was intro. (the language of Ṛg-Veda), to the 'classical' or later form. It was primarily the brāhman priests who were bearers and preservers of S.; because of this, it was language of intellectual discourse in India and enjoyed unique prestige. In gen. it was in the N.W. and W. of India that influence of S. was greatest in early Buddh. period; hence its use by Buddh. S. begins from period when there was an expansion of Buddh. community from lower Ganges valley westward, into region around → Mathura, where the S. trad. of the brahmans was stronger than in the E. A sect of the → Mahāsanghikas, the Lokottaravādins, produced a work in mixed Sanskrit, the → *Mahāvastu* which has survived to mod. times and was, acc. to text itself, part of the → *Vinaya-Pitaka* of this school. Buddh. S. works of various kinds were produced from this period onward, but no complete S. canon of Buddh. scripture has survived. Fragments of the → Sarvāstivādin canon are extant, notably the *Prātimoksa Sūtra* (→ *Pātimokkha*), and quotations from Sarvāstivādin S. canon occur in other works such as the → Divyāvadāna, and → Lalita-Vistara. These later S. works are extremely numerous; some are known only from Chinese and Tibetan trans. which were made from them and which have survived, the orig. S. texts having been lost in decay and destruction of many monasteries of N. India. The most import. of these, to which refs. are made elsewhere in this volume are: →→ *Mahāvastu* (already mentioned); *Lalita-Vistara; Buddha Carita; Avadāna; Divyāvadāna; Saddharma-Pundarika Sūtra; Prajñā-Paramitā Sūtras,* esp. the →→ Heart Sutra and Diamond Sutra; →→ *Lankāvatāra Sūtra* and the *Abhidharma-Kośa.*

E. Lamotte, *Histoire du Boudhisme Indien* (1958); M. Winternitz, *History of Indian Literature,* 25, 2 vols. (1933).

Sariputta/Sariputra Chief disciple of → Gotama, the Buddha, and a Thera (Elder Monk) of Buddh. → Sangha. S. was his 'religious' name as monk; his personal name is given as Upatissa (*M.N.*, I, p. 150). A brahman by birth, he had 3 younger brothers and 3 sisters; these also became Buddh. monks and nuns. He was highly esteemed by Buddha for his wisdom, and acc. to trad., was an accomplished preacher and expounder of Buddh. doc. There was a specially close relationship between S. and → Ānanda, Buddha's personal attendant, → Rāhula, Buddha's son, and → Moggallāna, all of whom were among his most prominent disciples. Acc. to the *Saṃyutta-Nikāya* (V, p. 161), S. died of an illness a few months before the Buddha. After cremation of his body, the relics were taken to Sāvatthi. Ānanda was profoundly disturbed at news of his death; the Buddha took the occasion to remind him of the impermanence of all things.

Sārnāth → Isipatana.

Sarvāstivādins Name of Buddh. sect in anc. India, belonging to the → Hinayana trad. They constituted one of 2 main divisions of the → Sthavira wing of the Buddh. Sangha, the other being the Vibhajyavādins, or 'Analysers.' The differences between them were over question whether present mental events (*dhammas*) only have reality, as the Vs. maintained, or whether past and future mental events could also be said to have a real existence, as the S.'s believed. Their name indicates this view: *sarva* (all—past, present, and future) *asti* (exists). They had become sufficiently numerous body by time of → Asoka (3rd cent. BC) for the dispute to necessitate calling of the Council of Pātaliputta (Patna) (→ Councils). After Council, the S.'s withdrew from lower valley of Ganges, N.W.wards to Madhura which became a stronghold of their school. They used → Sanskrit rather than (as the Theravādins did) Pali, and are regarded as constituting a transitional stage between the older, conservative schools of Buddhism and → Mahāyāna.

Sāsana The word most commonly used in Buddh. countries of S. Asia to refer to what in West. languages is called the *'religion'* of the Buddha (or Buddhism). The Pali word

Sati Patthāna Sutta

carries sense of both 'doctrine' or 'teaching,' and also 'rule of life.' Thus, the authentic way of ref. to what European languages call 'Buddhism' is 'Buddha-Sāsana.'

Sati Patthāna Sutta → Mahāsatipatthāna Sutta.

Satori Jap. term for Buddh. 'illumination' or 'enlightenment.' In → Zen, it is the state of consciousness of the Buddha-mind, pure consciousness, without mental discrimination, seeing into one's own Buddha-nature, essential wisdom (*prajnā*). If the experience can be characterised, either mentally or emotionally, it is not S. S. is an experience beyond description and altogether incommunicable. Basically, it is the integration or realisation of man in his psychic totality, the liberation of the unconscious forces of the human psyche.

H. Dumoulin, *Zen Buddhism* (1963), pp. 273ff.; E. Wood, *Zen Dictionary* (1962), pp. 114–5; C. Humphreys, *A Buddhist Students' Manual* (1956); D. T. Suzuki, *Essays in Zen Buddhism,* 2 (1933), pp. 32, 62ff.

Sautrāntika Buddh. philosophical school of → Hīnayāna trad. characterised by rejection of the → Abhidhamma, which adherents of school held to be no part of authentic doc. of Buddha. For them only the Sutras were authoritative, and were the 'end' or *anta* of the doc.: hence the name in Skt., *Sūtra-anta;* like the → Sarvāstivādin school, from which they emerged somewhere in early part of 2nd cent. BC, the S.'s used Sanskrit. Their views were not unlike those of the → *Pudgala-Vādins;* for, in rejecting notion found in Abhidhamma, of separate, instantaneous, noncontinuous *dhammas,* they posited the 'the continuous existence of a very subtle consciousness' as basis of human life; it was this, in their view, which progressed to → Nirvāṇa. They differed from Pudgala-Vādins in maintaining that it is not the whole 'person' which transmigrates, but only *one* of the 5 → skandhas which go to make up a 'person,' viz., a subtle form of *consciousness.* They placed less importance on philosophical terminology and concepts repres. by such terminology, which were, they held, but 'fruitful fictions.' Their ideas may have contributed in some measure to those of Mhy. school of → *Yogācāra.*

Self-Immolation

E. Conze, *Buddhist Thought in India* (1962), pp. 141ff.; P. S. Jaini. 'The Sautrāntika theory of bīja,' in *B.S.O.A.S.,* vol. 22 (1959), pp. 236–49.

Self-Immolation (Monks) The practice of self-immolation by Buddh. monks, notably in Vietnam in recent times, appears to have been derived from Mhy. Buddhism of China, where it is known from at least 5th cent. CE. There would seem to be some inconsistency between this practice and the Buddh. prohibition against taking life, incl. one's own. Moreover in the → Dhamma-Cakkappavattana Sutta the Buddha is repres. as saying in his first sermon that monks should avoid the two extremes of self-indulgence and self-mortification; self-immolation would appear to be a case of latter. However, justification for cult of self-sacrifice by burning, which grew up among Mhy. Buddhs., is found in approval given by Buddha to suicide of a monk named Godhika, who, after attaining state of spiritual release through meditation (*samadhika-cetovimutti*) six times in succession and then falling away from it, committed suicide the seventh time he attained it, in order not to fall away from it again (*S.N.,* I, pp. 120f.); also in practice of burning a light in honour of Buddha, which is regarded as meritorious act. The cult of self-immolation is explicitly countenanced in Skt. treatise, → *Saddharma-Pundarika Sūtra*; the story is related of a → Bodhisattva who, after eating incense and drinking oil for 12 years, bathed himself in perfumed oil and set fire to himself as act of self-offering to the Buddha. Although the Sutra goes on to say that realisation of the truth of the → Dharma is more meritorious than such acts of self-sacrifice, nevertheless the cult of self-immolation seems to have developed among Chinese Mhy. Buddhs., among whom this Sutra (trans. into Chinese in early 3rd cent. CE) was very popular.

It is this anc. practice, of which there are a number of examples in Chi. Buddh. hist. between 5th and 10th cents., which has been revived by Buddhs. of Vietnam. The motive in this revival has been devotion to Buddha, his teaching and relig., which appeared to Vietnamese Buddhs. to be threatened by those whom they regarded as persecutors of their faith. A Theravādin monk of Ceylon (the Ven. Dr. Walpola Rāhula), commenting on these recent cases, and observing that practice is alien to → Theravāda Buddhism, and 'not in keeping with the pure and original teaching of the Buddha,' nevertheless adds (no doubt with use of napalm in Vietnam in mind) 'it is better to burn oneself than to burn others' (*The Guardian*, London, 18 Oct., 1963).

Sermon, Buddha's First → *Dhamma-Cakkappavattana Sutta.*

Shingon (Jap. Buddh. sect of highly mystical and syncretistical nature, founded in CE 806 by → Kōbo Daishi. The deities and demons of various religs. are interpreted as manifestations of Mahā-Vairocana Buddha (Jap. Dainichi), whose body comprises the whole cosmos. Cosmic mysteries are repr. and symbolised in visible and tangible forms. The postures, movements and utterances of an elaborate ritual evoke mysterious powers. The cosmos is graphically repr. in diagrams called *mandala,* which symbolise two aspects of universe: its ideal or potential entity, and its vitality or dynamic manifestations. Shingon = Chinese 'Chên Yen' (True Word), itself a trans. of Skt. *mantra.*

M. Anesaki, *Hist. of Japanese Buddhism* (1930), pp. 124ff.; E. Steinilber-Oberlin, *The Buddhist Sects of Japan* (1938).

Shinran (1173–1263). A follower of → Honen, S. proclaimed → Amida as the Buddha of Infinite Light and Boundless Compassion. He founded the Jodo-Shinshu (The True Sect of the Pure Land), largest and most import. sect of Jap. Buddhism. By discarding monastic robes, marrying and living an ordinary family life, S. sought to show that secular life was no bar to Buddh. salvation. He purged → Jodo Buddhism from its assoc. with trad. mysteries and methods of spiritual exercises, and related it to common life of the people, seeking to annul distinction between relig. and secular. The Buddha's grace was a free gift, appropriated neither by virtue nor by wisdom but by faith. S. sought obscurity and shunned publicity; but his following grew, and by 15th cent. had been formed into a powerful eccles. organisation.

Sotapanna

A. Lloyd, *Shinran and his works* (1913); M. Anesaki, *Hist. of Japanese Religion* (1930), pp. 181ff.; E. Steinilber-Oberlin, *The Buddhist Sects of Japan* (1938), pp. 198ff.

Shinshū →→ Jodo, Shinran.

Sigālovāda Sutta A discourse of the Buddha found in the → *Dīgha-Nikāya* of the Pali canon. Sigāla was a young householder of Rājagaha whom the Buddha saw worshipping the 4 quarters of compass, together with the nadir and zenith. Buddha then taught him a better form of devotion—social duties towards the six directions: parents, teachers, wife and children, friends, workpeople and relig. teachers. The *Sutta* thus provides complete account of social duties of a lay Buddh. Acc. to trad., Sigāla became a follower of Buddha. The *Sutta* is also known as the *Gihivinaya* (householder's discipline). (→ Family and Social Duties).

Sīla Buddh. term for 'virtue' or 'morality' (→ Eightfold Path).

Sin → Ethics. **(Chinese)** Buddhism brought to the Chinese a vivid concept of an after-life, and a doc. of future punishment for sins committed in this life, and idea that present sufferings are result of past S. It taught that future retribution for S. could be avoided by accumulation of → Merit by such means as chanting liturgies, repentance, meritorious actions, asceticism and the like. It intro. a soteriology by its doc. of transferred merit. Buddhas and → bodhisattvas had accumulated infinite stores of merit; by appealing to them in penitence and faith, the consequences of S. could be wiped out and a blissful future life guaranteed. These Buddh. ideas exercised a profound influence on Confucians and Taoists alike, and on popular beliefs.

Skandha (Skt.) Buddh. term for a component of human personality (→ *Khandha*).

Social Duties → Family and Social Duties.

Sotapanna Buddh. term meaning lit. 'the stream-enterer'; i.e., one who has entered the stream in order to cross to the 'further shore,' viz. → Nibbana. In most gen. sense, term means a 'convert' to the way of Buddha. To have become a S. means that one is excl. from further rebirth in hell (→

Sōtō

Cosmology), or as an animal, a spirit or *peta* (→ Petavat-thu), and is guarantee of attainment of enlightenment (→ Bodhi), not necessarily in same life, but certainly in some future life (→ Samsara). The further progress of the S. is regarded as following a scheme which is set forth in a conventional form in the Buddh. scriptures as 'once-returner' (→ Sakadāgāmin), then 'non-returner' (→ Anagamin), and finally → Arahant.

Sōtō (Chinese, *Ts'ao-tung*). One of two main streams of → Zen Buddhism, founded in China by Tung-shan (807–869) and Ts'ao-shan (840–901). Its fundamental concept was that of oneness of the Absolute and the relative-phenomenal. Training, concentrating on a cross-legged sitting in meditation (→ Zazen), followed a system of five stages, called the five relationships, leading from recognition of a higher or 'real' self, overshadowing the 'seeming' self, up to realisation of complete oneness with absolute reality. Enlightenment came through silent illumination. S. was introduced into Japan by → Dogen (1200–53), and popularised by Kei-zan (1268–1325). Mod. S. tends towards quietism.

H. Dumoulin, *Hist. of Zen Buddhism* (1963); E. Wood, *Zen Dictionary* (1962); D. T. Suzuki, *Studies in Zen* (1955).

Spirits →→ Yakkha; Pisaca; Nast; Phi.

Śravaka-Yāna → *Yāna.*

Sthaviras Name given to more traditionalist wing of Buddh. monks in their disputes with the → Mahāsanghikas and others in the cents. immediately following death of the Buddha (→→ *Councils; Schools of Thought*).

Store-Consciousness Name given to Mahāyāna Buddh. doc. (*ālaya-vijñāna*) (→ Yogācāra).

Stūpa (Skt.); **Thūpa** (Pali) A 'tope,' or dome, i.e., hemispherical mound of stone and earth, or brick and earth, which, in lay Buddhism from time of → Ashoka (or poss. earlier), has served as focus for popular piety. The S., stone or brick-built, was a develop. from earlier form earth-mound, or tumulus, known in India as *cetiya* (from *ci*, to heap up). These simple mounds were a feature of folk-religion in India prior to rise of Buddhism; during early Buddh. period the folk-cult of the *cetiya* developed into Buddh. cult of the S. The latter was justified, from Buddh. point of view, on grounds that the S. was a memorial, either to Buddha, or to an early Buddh. saint. The develop. prob. took place in context of lay Buddhism rather than monastic; it has remained primarily a feature of lay Buddh. devotion. Acc. to the → Mahā-Parinibbāna Sutta, the Buddha himself commended building of S., as places for enshrinement of relics; this was, acc. to the Sutta, in answer to question raised by → Ananda, of what was to be done with Buddha's remains after death. (*D.N.*, II, pp. 141ff.; Rhys-Davids, *Dialogues of the Buddha*, part II, pp. 154ff.). Over remains of Buddha, and of other great Buddhs., S. were to be raised, to which reverence was to be paid. It is pointed out by Sukumar Dutt that this idea is not altogether easy to reconcile to other aspects of early Buddh. doc., such as the impermanence of all compounded things (→ *anicca*) and unreal nature of so-called individual (→ *anatta*). Nor does assumption that S.'s were built *in order* to house relics of Buddh. saints find corroboration in the S.'s themselves, since not all anc. S.'s, discovered in India, appear to be relic-chambers. This suggests that cult of S. is a develop. of folk-cult of tumulus or *cetiya*.

The building of S.'s was a notable feature of the Buddhism of Ashoka's time. At first, the S. appears to have been simple hemisphere of stone, surrounded by railing to emphasise its sanctity; later, the railing was elaborated and became massive balustrade, inside which a processional pavement was provided. Survivals of this type of S. are to be seen in India: (1) In C. India, at Sānchi, Bhilsā and Bārhut; (2) In S. India, on banks of the Krishna and Godavari rivers in Madras State, on sites of the ancient → Amarāvati and Nāgārjunikonda. Trad. the work of S.-building is that of kings and wealthy laymen, who are held to gain great merit thereby. Outside India a most magnificent example of a S. is the Shwe Dagon pagoda on outskirts of Rangoon, said to house some hairs of Buddha. This pagoda, which has remained in continual use down to present day, and is focus for devotion of thousands of Burmese Buddh., who

Suddhodana

visit it weekly, provides good example of what the S.'s of anc. India may have been in more expansive days of Indian Buddhism (→→ Dagaba and Pagoda).

Sukumar Dutt, *The Buddha and Five After-Centuries* (1957), chs. 12–14.

Suddhodana Father of → the Buddha, Gotama. S. was a chieftain of the N. Indian → Sākya tribe. His wife was → Māyā, who died 7 days after giving birth to Gotama. It was predicted of the child Gotama by soothsayers that he would become either a universal monarch or a Buddha. S., therefore, sought to protect the boy from any experience of unpleasant aspects of human life, such as illness, old age and death, and to surround him with pleasures. It was, in spite of this protection, that Gotama is said in trad. to have seen in one day a disease-ridden man, an old man, and a corpse, and thus to have been brought to reflection upon meaning of phenomenal human existence. When news of Gotama's having attained enlightenment reached S., the latter sent messengers inviting the Buddha to come to → Kapilavatthu. The messengers, however, hearing Buddha preach, were converted and entered the → Sangha without delivering their message. This happened repeatedly until 10th time, when message reached Buddha. On his visiting Kapilavatthu and conversing with S., the latter became a → *sotapanna*. Some years later, when S. was dying the Buddha visited him; after hearing his discourse, S. became a lay → arahant, and died soon after.

Suffering (→→ Evil, in Buddh. thought; Dukkha; Four Holy Truths). Buddh. teaching that all life is S., and can only cease by negation of Self, went counter to life affirming spirit of the Chinese. Yet to millions of Chinese, who found life an intolerable burden, the doc. that S. is result of ignorance, stupidity and greed, an inevitable concomitant of the karmic process, was attractive, esp. as Buddhism provided way of escape from S. in promise of salvation for all sentient beings.

Sumatra → *Indonesia*.

Śūnya, Śūñyatā, Śūnyavāda → *Mādhyamika*.

Śūñyatā (Skt.) 'Emptiness,' term used in Buddh. philosophy to denote the emptiness of ultimate reality and permanency which characterises all concepts (→ Madhyamika).

Sūtra (Skt.); **Sutta** (Pali) The basic unit of Buddh. scripture. From root meaning 'to sew,' *sutra* has as primary meaning a 'thread,' hence a 'thread' of discourse, a dialogue of the Buddha upon a partic. subject. Sometimes the subject of discourse is indic. by the title, e.g. *'Samaññaphala Sutta,'* the S. concerning the fruits of the relig.; sometimes the title indic. place or occasion of the S.'s being delivered, e.g., *Kosambiya* S., the discourse delivered to monks at Kosambi; sometimes the person to whom the discourse was addressed, e.g., *Kutadanta* S., a dialogue with the brahman named Kutadanta. The word S. is used also to refer to an anc. verse, or quotation, or to a rule or clause of the → Patimokkha, or code of monastic discipline. (→ Sutta-Pitaka).

Sutta-Nipāta Name of book contained in the 5th or *Khuddaka-Nikāya,* of the Sutta-Pitaka, of the Pali Buddh. canon of scripture. By gen. agreement of modern scholars this is one of most anc. sections of Buddh. canonical lit.; it provides valuable evidence of some earliest forms of Buddh. ideas and teaching. It consists of an anthology, largely of verse, arranged in five chapters: (1) The chapter of the snake; (2) The minor chapter; (3) The great chapter; (4) The chapter of 'eights'; (5) The way to the beyond. Of these (4) is sufficiently old to possess a commentary which is also a book of the canon, the *Niddesa* (in the *Khuddaka-Nikāya*). Since the *Niddesa* comments only upon the 4th chapter, this evidently existed in separate form at an early date. A commentary on the complete S.-N. was composed by → Buddhaghosa, entitled *Paramattha-jotikā.* The Pali text of S.-N. was published in Roman script in 1913 by the PTS. Trans. into Eng. have been made by Sir Muttu Coomeraswamy (of 30 sections only), entitled *Sutta-Nipāta, or Dialogues and Discourses of Gotama Buddha* (1874); by V. Fausboll, *The Sutta-Nipāta, A Collection of Discourses* (1880), as vol. X of the *S.B.E.* (rev. 1898); by Lord Chalmers, *Buddha's Teachings* (Harvard Oriental Series, vol. 37, 1932); by E. M. Hare, *Woven Cadences of Early Buddhists* (1945, 2nd edn. 1948).

Sutta-Piṭaka

Sutta-Piṭaka One of the three major divisions, or Piṭakas ('baskets'), of Buddh. canon of scripture, consisting of → Suttas, i.e., discourses or dialogues, as distinct from other two divisions of canon: the → Vinaya-Pitaka (the code of discipline governing life of Sangha), and the → Abhidhamma-Pitaka (a systematic arrangement of essential propositions and formulae). The S.-P. is made up of 5 collections or *Nikāyas:* → *Dīgha-Nikāya;* → *Majjhima-N.;* → *Anguttara-N.;* → *Khuddaka-N.* Some books contained in the S.-P. are not strictly of sutta type, e.g., the → *Jātaka,* and → *Dhammapada.* The sutta proper is characterised by a formal intro. consisting of the words 'Thus have I heard' (these being attr. to the disciple → Ananda, who, acc. to trad., recited the suttas at Council of Rajagaha immediately after Buddha's death (→ Councils), and statement of circumstances in which the sutta or discourse was delivered, viz. place, occasion, who was present, who was thus addressed, or question raised. The style of material in the S.-P. is clearly popular and intended for apologetic and teaching purposes: similes, parables, allegories and lengthy repetitions for sake of emphasis abound. The S.-P. in Pali is fullest collection extant; a Chinese collection exists which contains 4 *āgamas,* corresponding to first 4 *Nikāyas* of Pali S.-P. (→ Tipitaka).

T

T'ai Shan Most revered of the five sacred mountains of China, honoured alike by Confucians, Buddhists and Taoists. The *Li Chi* records that Chou Dynasty (*c.* 1022–221 BC) rulers made → pilgrimages to mountain to sacrifice, a custom continued throughout hist. times by Chi. emperors. It became a chief centre of pilgrimage; in early spring the Chinese in their thousands make pilgrimages to the Holy Mountain to worship at the numerous Taoist and Buddh. temples. In Taoism and popular relig. of China, the god of T.S. is greatest of terrestrial gods, belonging to a group of mountain gods known as the Gods of the Five Peaks who, since beginning of 11th cent. have been given title of Shêng Ti (Holy Emperor). The god of T.S. was entrusted by the Jade Emperor with control over human life and destiny. He appoints birth and death; in early centuries of our era he became Lord over infernal regions and judge of the dead. Souls went forth from T.S. to be born and returned thither after death. Under control of god of T.S., a whole hierarchy of spiritual beings directs all aspects of terrestrial life: birth, death, destiny, honours, fortune, posterity, etc. Pi-hsia Yüan-chün ('The Princess of the Variegated Clouds') is his daughter, known and worshipped as the Lady of T'ai Shan. Her temple on mountain is the most popular. T.S. is rich in hist. situations, recorded on innumerable rock inscriptions, and round it, through the ages, has gathered a vast store of legend, mythology and relig. lore.

E. Chavannes, *Le T'ai Chan* (1910); H. Dore, *Chinese Superstitions*, vol. 9 (1914–29); E. T. C. Werner, *Dict. of Chinese Mythology* (1932); H. Maspero, 'The Mythology of Modern

239

Tantric Buddhism

China,' in J. Hackin (ed.), *Asiatic Mythology* (1932 and 1963), pp. 279ff.

Tantric Buddhism → *Vajrayāna*.

Tathāgata Buddh. term, frequently used by the Buddha when ref. to himself; the meaning is lit. either 'he who has thus (*tathā*) come or arrived (*āgata*), or, 'he who has there (*tathā*) gone (*gata*)'; but reason for use of term is uncertain. → Buddhaghosa offers eight different explanations in his commentary on the → Dīgha-Nikāya; this indic. that there was no agreed explanation, and that he was in doubt. It is applied to → Arahants; since non-Buddhists were apparently expected to understand what it meant, it may have been a pre-Buddh. usage. It seems, however, to have been given a Buddh. meaning; it is said that the T. cannot be 'discovered,' i.e., known empirically, even during lifetime, i.e., when still associated with corporeal and mental phenomena; much less so, therefore, after death (→ *Sutta-Nipata*, XXII, 85f.).

Taxila (Taksasilā) → Gandhāra.

Temptation, in Buddh. Thought → *Mara*.

Tendai School of Jap. Buddhism (→ T'ien T'ai). Intro. into Japan by → Dengyō Daishi (b. CE 767), when he returned from China in 805 with scriptures and treatises of T'ien T'ai school of Chi. Buddhism. He emphasised universality of salvation or attainment of Buddha-hood. He estab. a great T. centre on Mt. Hiei, near Kyoto; for centuries it remained greatest centre of Buddh. learning in Japan. With → Shingon, T. was leading force of relig. faith and philosophical thought in Japan. Its teachings were based principally on the → *Lotus Sūtra* (Jap. *Hokkekyō*).

Acc. to T. the Buddha is hist. manifestation of the universal and primordial Buddha-nature, which can and will appear at any time on earth to further purpose of universal salvation. As a hist. person, Buddha attained full truth of existence; he is Tathāgata—the 'Truth-Winner.' But he is simply a manifestation of Dharmatā, the fundamental nature of universe; which, as Dharmakāya (Jap. Hosshin), the 'Truth-Body,' is the universal Buddha-soul in which all participate; as Nirmānakāya (Jap. Wo-jin), the 'Condescen-

Thailand, Buddhism in

sion-Body,' he is the concrete object of faith; and as Sam-
bhogakāya (Jap. Hō-jin), the 'Bliss-Body,' he reveals his
wisdom and power in blissful glories of celestial existence.
Since T. taught that the Buddha-nature is inherent in all existences, its ideal aim consists in full realisation in oneself
of Buddha-nature and participation in Buddha's purpose
and work. Both moral striving and contemplation are in
vain, unless founded on and aiming at faith in Buddha.
This faith means not only adoration of Buddha and dependence on his teachings, but identification with and
participation in the universal Buddha-soul; i.e. to live life
of the universal self.

M. Anesaki, *Hist. of Japanese Religion* (1930), pp. 111ff.

Thailand, Buddhism in Mod. Thailand is a predominantly
Buddh. country; approx. 94% of its population regard
themselves as Buddhists. The form of the relig. which pre-
vails (as in rest of continental S.E. Asia apart from Vietnam)
is the → Theravāda. The earliest evidence of Buddhism in
the territory now called Thailand is from *c.* 6th cent. CE. This
is of an archaeological kind, from various places in the
central plain of T., notably Nakhon Pathom (or Phra Pathom) about 30 m. W. of Bangkok, and Lopburi, about 60
m. N. of Bangkok. The oldest and largest *chedi* or → *stupa*
in T. is at Nakhon Pathom. The evidence from these places
in the central plain is from period when region was part of
a kingdom of the Mon people, whose centre was at Thaton
in lower Burma. S. T. at that time formed the Mon kingdom
of Dvāravatī; the kind of Buddhism in kingdom in early period seems to have been predominantly → Hīnayāna. From
about 8th to 13th cent. the region came under power of Sri
Vijaya kingdom of Sumatra (→ Indonesia), when the →
Mahāyāna form of Buddhism seems to have been more
prominent; evidence of this exists in Buddha- → rupas
which have been discovered, dating from this period. Between 11th and 14th cents. large parts of what is now T.
came under power of the Khmers, a people to E. (in what is
now Cambodia), and whose relig. was much more strongly
Hindu. In 14th cent. the hist. of the Thai nation proper may
be said to begin, with the setting up by the Thais (a people

related to Chinese, ethnically and linguistically, who were then moving southwards from Yunnan) of a kingdom with its capital at Sukhodhaya (about 150 m. N. of modern Bangkok). During 14th cent. the reputation of Sinhalese Buddhism (after reforms carried out by Parakamma Bahu I, the 12th cent. king of Ceylon), attracted Siamese monks to → Ceylon, who then returned to T. to spread the Sinhalese reforms. From this time onward Theravada Buddhism predominated in T. In mid. 14th cent. the capital was moved southwards from Sukhodhaya (or Sukhothai) to Ayodhaya (or Ayuthia), about 50 m. N. of the mod. Bangkok. When this was destroyed by Burmese in 1767, a new dynasty founded yet another capital, first at Dhonburi, on west bank of Chao Phya river, then on opposite east bank at what is now Bangkok. The 4th king of this dynasty, Mongkut, or Rāma IV was, at his accession in 1851 at age of 47, a Buddh. monk; his 17 years reign as king was one of most import. in the hist. of T.; it was he who laid foundations of mod. T., and initiated a reform movement within the Buddh. Order; this was seen in a reformed, more strictly disciplined sect of the → Sangha, known as the *Dhammayutika-Nikāya*; this has continued to be a powerful influence in Thai Buddhism to present day, co-existing on friendly terms with main sect, or *Mahā-Nikāya*, of Buddh. Order. Each has its large Bangkok monastic headquarters: Wat Bovornives (of the Dhammayutika-Nikāya) and Wat Mahāthat (of the Mahā-Nikāya); in each there is a large educational institution (*Mahā-Vidyālaya*) for training of monks. King Mongkut was succeeded by his son Chulalongkorn, or Rāma V (1868/1910), who also played import. role as a Buddh. ruler; during his reign an extensive modernisation of T. was carried out, largely owing to his initiative. Among other contributions which he made to vitality of Buddhism in T. was publication of the Pali → Tipitaka, or canon of scripture, in European volume-form, with text printed in Thai characters. During the six cents. since the Sinhalese Theravāda form of Buddhism was intro., it has had a deep reaching influence on whole of Thai life; in the words of G. Coedès, 'the entire population is steeped in

Buddhism'; the country has enjoyed a modest but sufficient standard of living, with remarkably little social unrest. Since second World War, however, there has been an increasing adoption of West. ways and standards, in metropolitan area of Bangkok at least; although in rural areas, where majority of population live, Theravāda Buddhism still provides the basis of belief, culture and behaviour (→→ Festivals; Holy Days).
Prince Chula Chakrabongse, Lords of Life: A History of the Kings of Thailand, 2nd edn. (1967); G. Coedès, The Making of South East Asia (1966); H. K. Kaufman, Bangkhuad (1960); A. L. Moffatt, Mongkut, the King of Siam (1961); R. S. le May, Buddhist Art in Siam (1967); J. E. de Young, Village Life in Modern Thailand (1955); K. E. Wells, Thai Buddhism: its Rites and Activities (1959).

Thera (Pali); **Sthavira** (Skt.) Term used in Buddhism for senior monk. In the → Vinaya-Pitaka distinction is made between a thera bhikkhu and a nava bhikkhu, i.e., a senior, as distinct from a junior (lit. 'new') monk. (Vin., I, 47; p. 290). In the → Dīgha-Nikāya, however, 3 grades are distinguished: thera bh., nava bh., and majjhima (or intermediate) bh. (D.N., III, p. 125). A bhikkhu was regarded as thera either by reason of number of years he had spent in → sangha or (even though junior in years) because of eminence in wisdom and learning and in spiritual attainments. Corresponding grade among nuns was idic. by Pali term theri (→ Sthaviras).

Theragāthā; Therīgāthā The Theragāthā consists of collection of verses (gāthā) attr. to 264 of senior (→ thera) monks, of early Buddhism, renowned for their spiritual attainments and virtue. Similarly the Therīgāthā is collection of verses attr. to 'senior' (therī) nuns of same period. The 2 collections form part of the → Khuddaka-Nikāya, which is part of the → Sutta-Pitaka of Buddh. Pali canon. The vv. are held by mod. scholars to contain authentic compositions of earliest Buddh. period, although some parts appear to be work of later redactors on basis of fragments of reminiscence (Geiger, Pali Literature and Language (1956), p. 21). The verses are attr. to partic. monks or nuns by name; such

Theravāda

ascriptions may not in every case be trustworthy, but in many there may be sound hist. trad. behind ascription. Like other early Buddh. lit., they are of value for reconstructing anc. Indian social hist. The Theragāthā has total of 1,279 verses; the Therīgāthā 522. These have been trans. into Eng. by C. A. F. Rhys-Davids; the former as *Psalms of the Brethren* (2nd edn. 1937, repr. 1964); the latter as *Psalms of the Sisters* (1909, repr. 1964).

Theravāda Name of one of principal schools of Buddhism, now repr. mainly in Ceylon, Burma, Thailand and Cambodia. The first major division of Buddh. → Sangha was between the → Mahāsanghikas, or Great Sangha party, and those who upheld stricter observance of monastic code of discipline, who claimed to be in true trad. of the 'elders,' and were known therefore as → Sthaviras. The controversy between the two groups was occasion for 2nd Buddh. Council (→ Councils). The Sthaviras subsequently divided into the 'Personalist' school or → *Pudgalavādins,* and the *Vibhajyavādins,* name which means poss. 'the analyzers,' or 'those who make distinctions' (sc., between reality of present events and/future events). The → Sarvāstivādins broke away from Vibhajyavādins after 3rd Buddh. Council at Patna; it was sometime after this that differentiation began to be made among Vibhajyavādins between those who became known as the Mahīsasakas, and those who assumed the name Theravādins. Acc. to Bareau, the difference between them was at first only geographical: the Theravādins being those Vibhajyavādins who were found in India south of Deccan and in Ceylon, while the Mahīsasakas were those in other parts of India. Grad. slight divergences of scriptures and doc. developed. The Theravādins claimed that theirs was the authentic and orig. form of the Buddha's teaching, as it had been contained in canon of scripture received by Sangha at 1st Buddh. Council at Rājagaha immediately after decease of Buddha; thus they applied name Theravāda, i.e., 'the Teaching of the Elders' (*Dīpavaṃsa IV,* 6, 13; *Mahāvaṃsa* iii:40). The Theravādins also divided into 3 groups in Ceylon, viz. the Mahāvihārika, the Abhayagirika, and the Jetavaniya, terms which ref. to

different great monastic centres in Ceylon. All of these schools, into which the early Sthaviras thus developed, were regarded by adherents of the → Mahāyāna, or 'great way to salvation,' as teaching and practising only a 'lesser way to salvation,' or → Hīnayāna. The latter term is sometimes used by Westerners as though it were interchangeable with Theravāda; this is not so, since the Th. was only one of the Hīnayāna schools. It is even more incorrect to ref. to Buddhism of S.E. Asia as Hīnayāna, even though it is the Theravādin form which flourishes and is predominant. Traces of Mahāyāna are still to be found in S.E. Asia, not merely in archeological remains, but also in beliefs and practices.
A. Bareau, *Les Sectes Bouddhiques du Petit Véhicule* (1955); P. V. Bapat, 'Principal Schools and Sects of Buddhism' in P. V. Bapat (ed.), *2500 years of Buddhism* (1956, repr. 1959).

Three Gems, or Jewels → Tri-Ratna.

(Marks of Existence) → *Ti-Lakhana.*

Thupavaṃsa Pali Buddh. book, attr. to writer named Vācissara of 13th cent. CE. The work is in prose, and is compilation of material drawn from older commentaries and chronicles of Pali Buddhism. As its title shows, it is a chronicle (*vaṃsa*) concerning the → stupas (*thupa*) or reliquary mounds, venerated by Buddhists, and deals partic. with one at Anuradhapura in Ceylon.

Tibetan Buddhism The hist. of T. Buddhism may be conveniently divided into two main periods, the first being from 7th to 12th cents. when the relig. was being imported as something new from India and Nepal; the second from 13th to 20th cents. when it was fully integrated with T. social life. The final eclipse of Buddhism in India at the end of 12th cent. provides the effective dividing line; for T. monks and scholars were regular visitors at the various Buddh. establishments, large and small, of medieval India right up to time of their destruction by the Moslem invaders. Thus the Tibetans became, thanks to their extraordinary zeal and determination, the chief inheritors of the later forms of Indian Buddhism, the →→ *Mahāyāna* and

Tibetan Buddhism

Vajrayāna. Indeed it is mainly from T. sources that we are able to gain some idea of the great variety, wealth and complexity of Indian Buddh. teachings and practices from the 8th to 12th cents. The Buddhism of this period is usually passed over in a few sentences in histories of Indian relig. as being so corrupt as to be scarcely worthy of mention. The evidence of the Tibetan trans. of this very period prove, however, that the great philosophic and doctrinal trads. of Mahāyāna Buddhism were still very much alive in Bihar and Bengal under the Pāla kings (8th to 12th cents.), although ritual and iconography, as well as ways of meditation and personal devotion, were strongly affected by tantric theories, of which more below. Right up to 12th cent., distinguished Indian Buddh. teachers, of which most famous were Atīśa and Śākya-śrī, visited Tibet, while the continual high standard of trans. from Sanskrit to Tibetan achieved by Indian scholars and Tibetan translators over whole range of Indian Buddh. lit. is sufficient proof of vitality of Buddh. philosophy and relig. during this period, often misleadingly referred to as the 'twilight' of Buddhism in India.

In Tibet a few small Buddh. chapels were constructed in and around Lhasa during reign of King Srong-brtsan-sgam-po (d. CE 650), who came subsequently to be regarded by T. Buddh. historians as first of Tibet's great relig. (i.e. Buddh.) kings. However this king, like most of his successors, seems to have followed the relig. practices of his ancestors and was certainly buried acc. to non-Buddh. rites (→ Bon and Tibetan pre-Buddh. relig.). During reign of his descendant, King Khri-srong-lde-brtsan, who ruled throughout second half of 8th cent., the first T. monastery was founded at bSam-yas and the first seven T. monks ordained. The prime mover was the famous Indian teacher Śāntarakshita; later accounts (unrecorded until 14th cent.) give credit to great yogin magician Padmasambhava, although there is no certainty that he was even an historical person. About 792 a great debate was held at bSam-yas in order to judge between relative merits of Indian and Chinese forms of Buddhism. The Indian party, lead by teacher Kamalaśīla, disciple of Śāntarakshita, triumphed. The new relig. was largely a court interest; but it held its own or was merely tolerated side by side with the indigenous relig. cults with which it prob. began to come to terms. During this period the Tibetans were more concerned with holding their Asian empire than with practising new forms of relig. However, two successors of Khri-srong-lde-brtsan, namely Sadna-legs and esp. Ral-pa-can, regarded as the third of the great relig. kings, sponsored the new doc. More chapels were built and methods of trans. were systematized. Also Buddh. monks began to make their appearance, still rare, however, as ministers. The murder of Ral-pa-can (836) led to fierce reaction against state-sponsored Buddhism, and in turmoil of political disruption it disappeared from Tibet until 978. In this year some Buddh. teachers returned from E. Tibet where serious Buddh. practisers seem to have been taking refuge. About same time an enthusiastic line of Buddh. kings in W. Tibet, actually descendants of old royal line at Lhasa, began to sponsor foundation of temples and monasteries, the training of scholars and trans. of texts throughout their domains, which stretched from Mt. Kailas westwards to Ladakh and southwards to Indian frontier. Their nearest sources for Buddh. teachers, texts, architectural styles and the rest, were Kulu and Kashmir, where Buddhism still flourished. The most famous Tib. scholar and translator of this period was Rin-chen-bzang-po (958–1055).

From now on T. monks and scholar-travellers from C. Tibet began to go to India in increasing numbers. Esp. noteworthy are 'Brog-mi (992–1072) and Mar-pa (1012–96), who became fountain-heads respectively of the *Sa-skya* and *bKa-rgyud-pa* orders of T. Buddhism. *'Brog-mi* studied one year in Nepal, then 8 years at Vikramashīla (Bihar), while Mar-pa spent more than 16 years at hermitage of his chosen teacher Nāropa at Phullahari (Bihar). In 1042 the great Indian teacher Atīśa, who had previously even visited Sumatra at invitation of its Buddh. rulers, arrived in Tibet at instance of rulers of W. Tibet. However, he moved on to C. Tibet, where he remained until death at Nye-thang in 1054.

Tibetan Buddhism

His personal influence was enormous; there can have been few T. relig. leaders of the day who were unaffected by his personal example. His favourite disciple was 'Brom-ston (1008–64), who founded the monastery of Rva-sgreng (1056) and the relig. order of the *bKa'-gdams-pa,* lit. 'Bound by command.' However, the strictness of its ordinances did not appeal to most Tibetans, who clearly preferred freer and more colourful forms of relig.

In 1053 the monastery Sa-skya was founded by a disciple of 'Brog-mi, and this soon became centre of a new and powerful relig. order. Chief of Mar-pa's disciples was the gentle ascetic Mi-la Ras-pa, renowned as much for his songs as his magical powers. He transmitted his teachings to sGam-po-pa (1079–1153), whose direct disciples estab. six famous schools, all based on his teachings and within the gen. relig. order of the *bKa'-rgyud-pa,* lit. 'Transmitted Word.' These six were the Phag-mo-gru, Karma-pa, mTshal, 'Bri-khung-pa, sTag-lung-pa and 'Brug-pa. Some of these schools chose their head-lamas by the reincarnation system, as subsequently adopted in the case of the Dalai Lamas.

With the estab. of these schools T. Buddhism began to come into its own, and, as by this time the bulk of Indian Buddh. lit. had been trans. into Tibetan, the Indian connection became ever less important. Also T. villagers and herdsmen were by now as ready to accept the services of Buddh. monks as of their more familiar Bon priests, and Buddhists and Bon-pos practised often quite amicably side by side. Bitter animosities sometimes developed between the various Buddh. orders, not on doctrinal but on political grounds. Many of these orders and their individual monasteries were closely connected with noble families and so became involved in their rival ambitions.

While Moslem invaders were laying waste the great relig. establishments of N. India, the → Mongols led by Genghiz Khan, who became chief in 1206, were slaughtering the inhabitants of N. China as first stage of their ruthless conquest of a huge Asian empire. Thus T. monks and lamas, now that India was lost to them as a land of religion, soon began to find scope for missionary activity amongst the Mongols, a relig. task which brought great material advantages esp. when Kublai Khan became Emperor of China. The grand lama of Sa-skya thus became a kind of vassal-ruler of Tibet and this arrangement lasted until 1354, when Byang-chub rGyal-mtshan of Phag-mo-gru overcame Sa-skya and won Mongol recognition. After 130 years of rule the Phag-mo-gru were forced out by the Rin-spungs princes, and they in turn by the rulers of gTsang. These different families all represented rival relig. interests, and throughout whole disturbed period there was a complex interplay of alliances between noble families and monastic centres. Buddhism was by now fully integrated with T. society and internal politics. Despite holiness and genuine learning of some monks and prelates, the outward worldliness of the estab. relig. orders seems to have resulted in reaction in favour of a new reformed order which had its beginnings in life and teachings of the great relig. figure Tsong-kha-pa (1357–1419). Known as the *dGe-lugs-pa,* lit. 'Model of Virtue,' this new school grew rapidly in popularity and influence under guidance of his able successors. The Mongol (Yüan) dynasty of China was succeeded by the Ming, a nationalist dynasty, but T. lamas seem to have maintained links with certain Mongol clans. The head-lamas of the dGe-lugs-pa order involved themselves with one of these, whence they received the title *Ta-le,* written as Dalai by Westerners. In 1642, thanks to the Mongol chief Gu-shri Khan, the Fifth Dalai Lama overcame his rivals, and from that time dates predominance of dGe-lugs-pa (nicknamed 'Yellow Hat') order in Tibet and the political eclipse of all older orders, although some of them have managed to keep their relig. life intact up to present day. Mongol and Chinese interference in Tibet in time of Sixth Dalai Lama resulted from 1721 onwards in a vague kind of Chinese suzerainty over Tibet, readily accepted by the great dGe-lugs-pa prelates in so far as the Manchu Emperors (until end of their dynasty in 1911) remained generous patrons of T. Buddhism.

No comprehensive canon of Mahāyāna and Vajrayāna

Tibetan Buddhism

Buddhism ever existed in India; but, by trans. into Tibetan in course of some six cents. all canonical and quasi-canonical works, as well as commentarial and independent writers of Indian Buddh. teachers that they could find, the Tibetans grad. built up their own canon, which had assumed by 13th cent. more or less its present form. Chief credit for this goes to the great scholar and encyclopaedic writer Bu-Ston (1290–1364). It was divided into two parts: the canon proper known as the *Kanjur* ('Translated Word'), containing works attrib. to the 'historical' → Buddha Śākyamuni, to various transcendent Buddhas and to tantric divinities identified as Buddhas; secondly the Commentaries known as the *Tanjur* ('Translated Treatises') containing trans. writings of Indian scholars and teachers. The *Kanjur* comprises 100 or 108 printed volumes (depending on the ed.), and the *Tanjur* comprises 225 volumes. These vast collections of Indian Buddh. lit. provide the doctrinal basis for T. relig. The most significant parts are the texts on Monastic Discipline (Skt. → *Vinaya*), the 'Perfection of Wisdom' literature (Skt. → *Prajñā-Pāramitā*), the great *Mahāyāna-Sūtras* and lastly the Tantras representing the Vajrayāna. The texts on Monastic Discipline are those of the Indian Buddh. school known as Mūlasarvāstivādin; in context they correspond closely with the *Vinaya* texts of the → Theravādin. The 'Perfection of Wisdom' texts provide philosophical basis of T. Buddhism and are prob. the most revered of all relig. books in Tibet. It would be a poor temple indeed which did not contain the 18 volumes of this partic. set. However, the works which are the chief inspiration of T. Buddh. practice are the *Tantras,* with their descriptions of the great divinities and of sets of divinities arranged as 'mystic circles' (Skt. *maṇḍala*), their collections of spells (Skt. *mantra*) by which the divinities are invoked, their refs. to consecration-rituals and to symbolic ritual of sexual union, their teachings of essential identity of microcosm of human body with macrocosm of universe, and their conviction that Buddhahood can be gained in course of a single life by those who know how. The essence of the Vajrayāna is the symbolic use of imagined divine forms, which repr. at one and same time the five components (→ *skandha*) of human personality, the five points of space (the centre and the four quarters), the five evils (stupidity, wrath, desire, malignity and envy) and the five wisdoms (pure absolute, mirror-like, discriminating, undifferentiated and active) usually repr. by the five Buddhas named Illuminator, Imperturbable, Jewel-Born, Boundless Light and Infallible Success. These five-fold sets, which stand for human personality and the infinite universe on the one hand, and the perversity of phenomenal existence and the purity of Buddhahood on the other, are the basic assumptions around which all tantric practice revolves. The main purpose of temple ceremonies is to bring a specified set of divinities face to face with the worshippers to gratify them with sacrificial offerings (e.g. lights, incense, sacrificial cakes, consecrated alcohol, etc.), to receive their empowering blessings, and to dismiss them when they came. Such a set of divinities, already well known to the participants from their earlier training in meditation upon them, act as 'integrators' of the human personality, strengthening it in its aspirations towards the perfection of Buddhahood. Watching a community of T. monks performing such a ceremony, one observes that each individual, unaware of his fellows, reverts to a form of individual meditation with his eyes fixed before him and his mind on the symbolic gestures, e.g., the miming of hand-gestures or the offering of universe in form of individual heaps of rice-grains.

T. monks and religious, perhaps numbering as many as half a million out of poss. total population of three million, repr. a large variety of relig. and social interests. From 8th cent. onwards there were always those who were scholars, usually translators and interpreters up to 12th cent.; thereafter commentators and instructors who worked entirely through medium of Tibetan, once cultural contacts with India were at an end. Despite achievement of their own vast canon and ever growing quantities of indigenous exegetical lit., oral trad. remained strong; even in 20th cent. many monk-scholars of the great dGe-lugs-pa monasteries around Lhasa might be highly skilled in philosophical and

Tibetan Buddhism

logical debate while still barely able to write their own names. In Tibet lit. scholarship has remained preserve of a minority of specially gifted individuals. Another import. minority has been concerned with methods of meditation and techniques of yoga, derived ultimately from Indian yogins and monks of 10th and 11th cents., the peak period of T. interest in mediaeval Buddh. India. The older orders of T. Buddhism trace their origins back to the more illustrious of the Eighty-Four Magicians (*mahāsiddha*), many of whose works are preserved in tantric section of T. canon. The dGe-lugs-pa (Yellow Hat) order may be seen as reform movement in that its founder and his successors insisted upon strict monastic discipline and encouraged philosophical studies, thus turning away from freer ways of thought and of living allowed to those who claim to follow tantric yoga. While the older orders never abandoned normal monastic discipline, in many of their establishments, their docs. and practices were always at the disposal of married householders, who by their professional skill and knowledge might become 'lamas' in their own right, and also of those who contracted out of the limited responsibilities of cenobitic life, living as solitary ascetics and hermits. The most famous of these two categories are prob. the translator Mar-pa, who lived as ordinary householder, and, by contrast, his foremost pupil and successor Mi-la Ras-pa, who led a life of self-inflicted hardship and solitary meditation. However, the great majority of T. monks, whether belonging to older orders or the dGe-lugs-pa, have been content with normal round of easy-going monastic life, playing a full part in temple ceremonies or performing rituals on request in laymen's homes, doing a turn of polishing or marketing, preparing their own simple meals and beloved buttered tea, or going out on excursions with friends.

The term for an ordinary monk is *grva-pa* (pronounced 'trapa'), and *dge-slong* (pronounced 'gélong'), which trans. in early lit. the Skt. word *bhikṣu,* now ref. to a monk who has taken upon himself full set of monastic vows (corresponding to Skt. *prātimokṣa*). The term 'lama' (*bla-ma*)

Tibetan Buddhism

means 'superior,' but may be used out of politeness for any venerable monk or village priest. (It corresponds to Catholic use of title 'father'). From 13th cent. onwards certain establishments, notably the Karma-pa, began to find their chief lamas when still children by making use of the regular Buddh. theory of rebirth. Thus a successor was sought in an infant showing signs indic. that he was a reincarnation of a deceased head-lama. The orig. of idea is prob. to be found in the series of Indian yogins gen. ref. to as the Eighty-Four Great Magicians; for several of these had been conceived of as reincarnations of their predecessors. This reincarnation system was adopted by the dGe-lugs-pa order at end of 15th cent. in case of their own grand-lama, and thus the succession of Dalai Lamas (Dalai represents a Mongolian title meaning 'ocean') came into existence; the 14th in this series now lives as exile in India. The idea spread to many other relig. establishments, and by 20th cent. there were more than two hundred head-lamas in Tibet who had been discovered as 'reincarnations' in their early years. Other establishments, which chose not to adopt this system, continued to elect their abbots on their personal merits. In case of the great Sa-skya order succession was hereditary, usually from uncle to nephew.

Over the cents. the Tibetans have developed an extraordinary devotion for their relig. in all its outward forms. They have depended upon their monks and lamas in times of sickness and in order to ensure prosperity. Ceremonies and relig. pageants have added colour and interest to their lives, much as was case in mediaeval Europe. The layfolk themselves often show great personal devotion, visiting temples, reciting invocations, making numerous prostrations, and going on long pilgrimages as holiday excursions. T. Buddhism has absorbed much T. pre-Buddh. relig. in form of local divinities, now accepted into Buddh. pantheon, oracles and divination, horoscopes and fortune-telling which play so large a part in life of Tibetans of all classes.

Sir Charles Bell, *Tibet Past and Present* (1924); Bu-Ston, *History of Buddhism* (E.T. 1931–2); D. L. Snellgrove, *Buddhist*

T'ien T'ai

Himālaya (1957); *The Hevajra-Tantra* (1959); *Four Lamas of Dolpo* (1967); W. Y. Evans-Wentz, *Tibet's Great Yogi Milarepa* (1928); *Tibetan Yoga and Secret Doctrines* (1935); *The Tibetan Book of the Dead,* 3rd edn. (1959); sGampopa, *Jewel Ornament of Liberation* (E.T. 1959); G. Tucci, *Tibetan Painted Scrolls* (1949); L. A. Waddell, *The Buddhism of Tibet* (1958²); R. A. Stein, *La Civilisation Tibétaine* (1662); H. E. Richardson and D. L. Snellgrove, *A Cultural History of Tibet* (1968).

T'ien T'ai (→ Tendai). The most influential Chi. sect of Buddhism during T'ang Dynasty. Founded by Chih I or Chih K'ai (538–97), in a famous monastery on the T'ien T'ai mountains of S.E. China, its basic text is the → *Lotus Sūtra,* in which is to be found the quintessence of Buddhism: → Sakyamuni Buddha is but an earthly manifestation of the Eternal Buddha. Chih I relied extensively on theories of → Nāgārjuna. He emphasised idea of totality, the whole and its parts being identical. The whole cosmos and all the Buddhas were present in a grain of sand. Absolute Mind embraces universe in its entirety. In its substance Absolute Mind is the same; in its functioning it is differentiated. In T.T. the practical expression of relig. was linked to spiritual cultivation and pursuit of wisdom by concentration (*chih*) and insight (*kuan*). A remarkable spirit of toleration pervaded T.T., for all interpretations of Buddha's teaching found place in its grand scheme. It divided teachings of Buddha into five periods, regarded not as contradictory but as progressive, leading up to the *Lotus Sūtra,* the crown, quintessence and plenitude of Buddhism. The school is not only import. for its doctrines, but for great monastic foundations which flourished during the T'ang Dynasty until great persecution of 845, from which time forward T'ien T'ai rapidly declined in China. It was also influential in → Korea, and was intro. into Japan early in 9th cent.
K. L. Reichelt, *Truth and Tradition in Chinese Buddhism* (1927), pp. 49ff.

Ti-Lakkhaṇa (Pali); **Tri-Lakṣana** (Skt.) Buddh. term for the 3 aspects or characteristics of all phenomenal existence. These characteristics are: (1) → *anicca* (Pali)/*anitya* (Skt.),

Tipiṭaka

impermanence; (2) → *dukkha* (Pali)/*dukkha* (Skt.), ill or imperfection; and (3) → *anatta* (Pali)/*anātman* (Skt.), lit. 'soullessness' or impersonality.

Tipiṭaka The canon of Buddh. scripture in Pali, regarded as authoritative by the → Theravada; it is earliest form of Buddh. teaching available and the most complete. The name Ti-Pitaka means 'three baskets.' These are (1) → Vinaya-Pitaka; (2) → Sutta-Pitaka; (3) → Abhidhamma-Pitaka. (1) consists of narratives concerning estab. of the Buddh. → Sangha, and the rules governing its life. (2) consists of the *Suttas* or 'threads (of discourse),' i.e., dialogues of the Buddha and some of his disciples with various contemporaries, and is arranged in 5 collections, or *nikāyas,* viz. →→ *Dīgha-Nikāya; Majjhima-N; Anguttara-N; Samyutta-N; Khuddaka-N.* The Abhidhamma-Pitaka consists of seven books, in which the doc. contained in popular, apologetic form in the *Suttas* is abstracted, condensed and systematised in numerical lists and under topic-headings. The Tipitaka is the form of Buddh. scripture which is regarded as authoritative in Theravada Buddh. countries of S. Asia, viz., Ceylon, Burma, Thailand, Cambodia and Laos; it is this, more than any other one single factor, which constitutes their unity as a group. Acc. to trad., compilation of this canon began immediately after death of Buddha, at Council held at Rajagaha (→ Councils). The canon was further developed at 2nd Council (at Vesāli), and was in all import. respects, incl. addition of the latest section, the Abhidhamma-Pitaka completed by time of 3rd Council, held during reign of → Ashoka (at Patna). Ashoka, who holds so honoured a place among Theravādin Buddhists, is not mentioned in the canonical lit.; he is in the post-canonical Pali chronicles. The assumption is therefore that composition of canon had been completed and settled before time of Ashoka (3rd cent. BC). Distinction must be made, however, between fixing of canon in verbal trad., and its being committed to written form; the latter took place, acc. to evidence of chronicle entitled → *Dipavaṃsa,* in reign of King Vattagamini, i.e. during latter part of 1st cent. BC (*Dipavaṃsa* 20:20–1). The text of Pali T., which until 1855 remained in ms. form, in palm-leaf collections preserved mainly in Ceylon, Burma and Thailand, began to be printed as result of interest of European scholars, notably George Turnour of Ceylon Civil Service, who in 1837 had published part of non-canonical work *Mahāvaṃsa*, and of Fausboll, Oldenberg and T. W. Rhys-Davids. Since 1855 practically the entire text of T. in Pali has been trans. into Roman script and published by Pali Text Society of London. Most of text of the 5 *Nikāyas*, which make up the T., has also been trans. into Eng. and published as: *The Book of the Discipline* (Vinaya-Pitaka) 5 vols. (1938–52) (vol. VI to follow); *Dialogues of the Buddha* (*Dīgha-Nikāya*), 3 vols. (1899–1921); *Middle Length Sayings* (*Majjhima-N.*), 3 vols. (1954–9); *The Books of the Gradual Sayings,* (*Anguttara-N.*), 5 vols. (1932–6); *The Book of Kindred Sayings* (*Samyutta-N.*), 5 vols. (1917–30); various books of the *Khuddaka-N.* separately as follows: *Khuddaka-patha and Dhammapada* (Minor Anthologies, vol. I) (1931); *Udāna and Itivuttaka* (Minor Anthols., vol. II) (1935); *Sutta-Nipāta* (*Woven Cadences*) 2nd edn. (1948); *Vimāna vatthu and Petavatthu* (Minor Anthols., vol. IV) (1942); *Theragāthā* (*Psalms of the Brethren*) (1913), (*Psalms of the Sisters*) (1909, repr. 1964); *Jataka Stories,* 6 vols. (1895–1907) (repr. as 3 vols. 1956); *Buddhavamsa and Cariva-Pitaka* (Minor Anthols., vol. III) (1938). The books of the Abhidamma-Pitaka, published in trans. by the Pali Text Society are: *Puggala-Paññantii* (*A Designation of Human Types* (1922); *Kathā-vathu* (*Points of Controversy*) (1915); *Dhātukathā* (*Discourse on Elements*) (1962).

Tri-Kāya Doctrine → Buddha-Kāya.

Tripiṭaka (Chinese) The collection of Buddh. scriptures, trans. into Chi. and known as the *San Tsang,* or Chi. T., is recognised as a most import. source for study of Buddhism; partic. the → Mahāyāna of China and Japan. From earliest days of Buddhism in China, emphasis was laid on trans. of Skt. texts. Great schools of translators worked under guidance of Buddh. scholars such as → Kumarajiva, Paramartha, and → Hsüan Tsang, and produced a voluminous Buddh. literature. Already, by time of Tao-an (CE 374), the need arose for

Tri-Ratna

catalogues of Buddh. scriptures. The most famous of early catalogues is that known as the *K'ai Yüan,* completed in 730. In CE 1883 Bunjiu Nanjio, a Jap. scholar, published a definitive catalogue of extant Buddh. scriptures in Chi. (Oxford: and repr. in 1929); an edn. of the Chi. T., compiled by J. Takakusu, was published in 85 vols., between 1924 and 1932, known as the Taisho ed. Only a small proportion of this vast collection has been trans. into Eng.

The name *San Tsang* or T. is a misnomer, as besides the → Sūtra, the → Vinaya, and the → Abhidharma, there is a 4th sect. of miscellaneous works, incl. many orig. Chi. Buddh. writings, such as the *Sūtra of Hui-nêng,* the *Huang-Po Doctrine of Universal Mind,* and many other → Ch'an (Zen) writings.

In the *Sūtra-Pitaka,* though most of works are Mahāyānist, incl. the great works of the → *Prajñā-Paramitā,* there are also → *Nikayas* by the → Theravadins and → *Agamas* by the → Sarvastivadins. In the same way the *Vinaya-Pitaka,* and the *Abhidharma-Pitaka* contain both Hinayānist and Mahāyānist works.

In all, the Chi. T. is estimated to be about 70 times the length of the Chr. Bible. Many of the works, preserved by various schools of Chi. Buddhism, are highly repetitive and differ very little from each other in essentials. But the Chi. reverence for the written word has allowed little to be discarded throughout the cents. (→ Tipitaka, Buddh.).

S. Beal, *Catena of Buddhist Scriptures from the Chinese* (1871); E. Conze *et al., Buddhist Texts* (1954), pp. 271ff.; C. Humphreys (ed.), *A Buddhist Students' Manual* (1965), pp. 159, 178, 249ff.

Tri-Ratna The 'Three gems' or *Tri-ratna* are the 3 principal features of Buddh. relig., viz., the → *Buddha,* → *Dhamma* (Skt. *Dharma*) and → *Sangha.* Throughout S.E. Asia, Buddh. devotions, incl. those of lay people, always begin after ascription of honour to Buddha, with chant in which the devotee affirms his dependence on these three: *'Buddham saraṇam gacchāmi; Dhammam saranam gacchāmi; Sangham saraṇam gacchāmi,'* i.e., 'I go for refuge to the Buddha; . . . to the Dhamma; . . . to the Sangha.' They are

Tri-Yāna

therefore known also as the '3 refuges.' Ref. to devotional practice of taking refuge in these 3 is found in Pali canon, in the → *Saṃyutta-Nikāya* (E.T., *Kindred Sayings,* vol. I, p. 283). In the → *Mahā-Parinibbāna Sutta* the Buddha is repres. as saying that he who steadfastly trusts in virtues of the 3 gems has already 'entered the stream,' i.e. a → *sotappana,* one who has set out on way to enlightenment.

The three are regarded as interrelated and interdependent, and from early refs. to three as a conventional formula, it is clear that affirmation of all three constitutes the bare minimum of Buddh. relig.; thus a system which affirmed the Buddha and his doc. only, without affirming also necessity of the relig. Order, the Sangha, would not properly be called Buddh. (→ Devotions).

Tri-Yāna → *Yāna.*

Tun Huang For over 1000 years, one of most import. Buddh. centres in China. From Han Dynasty (206 BC–CE 220), an import. stage-post at the E. end of the 'silk-road' to C. Asia, it became a great Buddh. centre and place of → pilgrimage. In 366 the first of the Buddh. cave-temples was begun; the construction of temples and grottoes continued throughout the next mil., until close of Yüan Dynasty (1368). At height of its fame, it boasted 1000 grottoes, of which only 480 remain, in which have been preserved thousands of sculptures and murals, recording the triumphs of Buddh. art in China. The earliest murals (386–581), revealing considerable foreign influence, present adaptations of anc. Chi. mythology and legends, together with stories from Buddh. scriptures. With the Sui Dynasty (581–618), the sculptures and paintings became more realistic and distinctively Chi., opening the way to the highly developed art of T'ang Dynasty (618–907), in which what is ostensibly relig. art depicting the ideal Buddh. paradises becomes excuse for a fascinating social commentary on the times. During Sung Dynasty (960–1279), when flames of war spread to T.H., the monks of the cave temples, before taking flight, sealed up their scriptures, scrolls and documents in one of the caves. These were accidentally discovered by a Taoist priest in 1900; in 1907 Sir Aurel Stein, and later Paul

Tun Huang

Pelliot, brought thousands of these scriptures, pictures and scrolls to the W., where their study has immeasurably enriched our understanding of Chi. relig. and culture.

P. Pelliot, *Les Grottes de Touen-Houang,* 6 vols. (1920); A. Waley, *A Catalogue of Paintings from Tun Huang* (1931).

U

Uccheda-vāda Buddh. term for the doc., repudiated as false, of *uccheda,* or annihilation, i.e., that no life of any sort continues after death of the body. In the *Brahma-jala Sutta,* the Buddha distinguished 7 diff. sorts of such annihilation doc. over against which he set the higher truth (*D.N.,* i, 34). The doc. of the Annihilationists is sometimes referred to as *uccheda-ditthi,* or the 'annihilation-illusion,' which, together with *atta-ditthi,* or the 'soul-illusion,' constitute the 2 illusions, or false views, regarding personality.
T. W. Rhys-Davids (tr.), *Dialogues of the Buddha,* Part I (1956), pp. 46–9.

Udāna Book of Buddh. Pali canonical scriptures, the 3rd book of the → *Khuddaka-Nikāya.* It consists of collection of 80 solemn utterances (*udāna*) of the Buddha, each of which is preceded by a prose or prose and verse narrative indicating occasion for the solemn utterance. Under title *Verses of Uplight,* the U. was trans. by F. L. Woodward and pub. as *Minor Anthologies,* vol. 2 (1935), of the *Sacred Books of the Buddhists.*

Upagupta → Divyāvadāna.

Upali A barber, of the → Sākya tribe, who was ordained into Buddh. → Sangha in time of the Buddha.

Upāsaka Term used in Buddhism for devout layman (or laywoman—*upāsikā*). U. indic. one who 'follows,' 'serves,' 'attends,' or 'accords honour.' The Pali texts ref. to existence of large numbers of these U. (e.g., *D.N.,* III, 148; Rhys-Davids, *Dialogues of the Buddha,* III, p. 142). The term is in current use in S. Asian Buddh. countries to describe laymen of pious disposition who on → holy days keep the 8 moral precepts, fasting from midday, and poss. engaging in meditation. These are usually more elderly members of laity, though not exclusively so.

Uposatha (Buddh. sabbath) → Holy Days.

V

Vajji Name of tribal republic of N. India at time of Buddha, mentioned several times in early Buddh. lit. The name V. indic. both a geographical region and its people, consisting of confederate tribes. During life-time of Buddha, the V. were a peaceful and prosperous community; soon after his death they were conquered by King Ajātasattu, and absorbed into kingdom of → Magadha. Ref. is made to the V. in the → Mahā-Parinibbāna Sutta, where Buddha draws parallel between the V., with their republican form of government, and the Buddh. → Sangha. The implication of this for the monks may have been that, after destruction of old republican form of society by new expanding monarchies, the Sangha was only preserver of old democratic order.

T. W. Rhys-Davids, *Buddhist India* (1903), *Dialogues of the Buddha,* Part II (1966), pp. 78–85.

Vajrayāna Name given in Indian Buddhism to last phase of develop. of the → Mahāyāna, of which V. is the continuation, although by its name it is designated as a separate *'yāna'* or means to salvation. An alternative name, used more esp. of earlier stage of develop., is → *Mantra-yāna.* The → Yogācāra school, which arose in 4th cent. CE, had emphasised practical importance of meditational methods and disciplines; the Mantrayāna developed this still further, and gave prominent place to use of *mantras,* or sacred chants, the use of which, in combination with mystical symbols and gestures of various kinds, was held to be most potent method of achieving more advanced spiritual states. Much material for such practices was taken over from popular, indigenous Indian relig., e.g., magical spells similar to those contained in the Hindu *Atharva-Veda.* Sys-

262

Vasubandhu

tematisation of use of this material is the stage of develop. known as V. The aim of system was infinitely enhanced psychic experience here and now, rather than distant goal of → *nirvaṇa* after countless rebirths; hence V. entailed much greater concern with the occult, with magical transformations and miracles, than earlier forms of Buddhism. One region of its greater strength was E. India (i.e., modern Bihar, Orissa and Bengal); the great Buddh. monastic centre or university of Vikramaśīla was stronghold of V., from whence it was carried to Tibet, notably by Padmasambhava, where too it became dominant form of Buddhism, and where it was preserved to mod. times (→ Tibetan Buddhism).

D. Snellgrove, *Buddhist Himalaya* (1957).

Vassa (Buddh. Lent) → Holy Days.

Vasubandhu Buddh. writer of fourth cent. CE. Born at Purusapura (Peshawar) in → Gandhara, capital of Kanishka's kingdom, he entered Buddh. monkhood. At first a → Hīnayānist of school of the → Sarvāstivadā, V. composed compendium of the Abh. teaching of this school, his → *Abhidharma-Kosá*. This came to be considered most authoritative treatise of Sarvāstivadā. His conversion from the Sarvāstivāda school to the → Mahāyāna is trad. attr. to efforts of his brother, → Asanga. His life story is related by 6th cent. writer Paramartha. This was trans. into Eng. in 1904 by Takakusu (in *T'oung Pao,* Serie II, vol. V, pp. 269–96). This translator raised question whether the biographer Paramartha had confused material appertaining to separate V.'s, thus merging two figures into one. The view that there were 2 V.'s was argued by E. Frauwallner in 1951. In his view there was a Sarvāstivādin writer of name in 4th cent. ('the elder V.') and brother of Asanga, who was converted to Mhy., and wrote an import. Vijnānavāda (Mhy.) work. There was another Sarvāstivādin in 5th cent. ('the younger V.'), who was the author of the *Abhidharma-Kośa.* Doubt was thrown on Frauwallner's theory in 1958 by P. S. Jaini, who presented new evidence to uphold trad. view that writer of the *Kosā* was converted by his brother Asanga to the Mhy., and subsequently composed at least one

Vatsīputrīyas

import. work of the Vijñānavāda sch. S. Dutt, in 1960, inclined to theory of 2 V.'s, and maintained that author of the *Kosá*, 'in spite of his intellectual leanings to Mahāyānism, was not a Mahāyānist, but a Vaibhāsika of the Kashmirian school.' It is to the second, younger V. that Dutt attr. the three treatises on logic, *Vāda-hṛdaya, Vāda-vidhi,* and *Vāda-vidhāna* ('Heart of Dispute,' 'Method of Dispute,' and 'Rule of Dispute') trad. attr. to writer of the Kosa. This younger V., in Dutt's view, was author of the Mhy. *śāstras,* a learned monk who lived at imperial capital, Ayodhya and had the Gupta King Skandagupta as his patron.

J. Takakusu (tr.), 'Paramartha's Life of Vasubandhu,' in *T'oung Pao,* Serie II, vol. V (1904), pp. 269–96, 'The Date of Vasubandhu,' in *Indian Studies in Honour of Charles Rockwell Lanman* (1929); E. Frauwallner, *On date of Buddhist master of the law Vasubandhu,* Serie Orientale, Roma III (1951); P. S. Jaini, 'On the theory of two Vasubandhus,' in *B.S.O.A.S.,* vol. XXI (1958); S. Dutt, *Buddhist Monks and Monasteries of India* (1962), pp. 280–5.

Vatsīputrīyas A school of Buddh. thought, founded by Vatsiputra (3rd cent. BC), which, unlike the orthodox, affirmed the reality of a human 'person,' which transmigrated from one existence to another (→ Pudgala-Vādins).

Vesak (Vesākha, Pali/**Vaiśākha,** Skt.**)** →→ Holy Days; Festivals.

Vesāli (Pali); **Vaiśālī** (Skt.) In early Buddh. period an import. city of N. India, to N. of Patiliputta (Patna) between the Ganges and Himalaya. Between V. and the Himalaya there extended uninterruptedly a natural forest. The city was visited by Buddha on several occasions and various discourses (→ *Suttas*) are reputed to have been first uttered there. It was also stronghold of the Nigantha sect (known as Jains); they regarded Buddhists as their rivals, and on occasions of Buddha's visits to V. are alleged to have made considerable efforts to prevent their own followers from coming under his influence. It was a place said to have been greatly admired by Buddha, who, on his last visit, 3 months before death, took a long deliberate final look at the familiar scene. About a cent. later it was at V. that the

2nd Buddh. → Council was held, to decide points at issue between → the Sthaviras and their critic Vajjiputtaka. By time the Chi. pilgrim → Hsüan Tsang visited place in 7th cent. CE, V. had suffered great decline and was a small insignificant place, apart from its hallowed assoc. for Buddhists. It is identified with village of Basrah in Muzafferpur district.

Vietnam Composed of two great deltas of the Red River in the N. (formerly Tongking), and the Mekong River in the S. (formerly Cochin-China), and the narrow coastal plain between (Annam). Little is known hist. before 111 BC, when the Chi. Han Dynasty annexed Red River delta and coastal plain, which became a province of the Chi. empire known as Nan-Yüeh (Nam-Viet). It remained an integral part of China for 1,000 years, during which the V. people adopted Chi. religs., philosophy, writing, social and administrative patterns, etc. In CE 939, V. gained independence under native rulers, and, except for short period (1413–27) under Ming Dynasty, remained independent, though acknowledging Chi. suzerainty, till French conquest in latter half of 19th cent. The Japanese took over control during World War II. In 1954 the country was divided into two zones, Communist in N., and Nationalist in S., since when the country has been bitterly divided by civil war. The combined population of N. and S. V. is about 33 m. The religs. are Buddhism, Taoism and Animism, with about 1 million Christians in the S.
Guy Wint (ed.), *Asia: a Handbook* (1965); B. R. Pearn, *Hist. of S.E. Asia* (1963).

Vihāra Lit. 'an abode,' 'a dwelling place'; in Buddh. usage, a large building where *bhikkhus* (monks) resided, hence, a monastery. In → Ceylon and → Thailand word is now used to ref. to large hall or sanctuary which contains the → *Buddha-rupa*. The name of mod. Indian state, Bihar (where Buddhism originated), is another form of word.

Vijñāna-Vāda Alternative name for Buddh. school of → Yogācāra, meaning 'those who affirm' (*vāda*) 'consciousness' (*vijñāna*), i.e., as the ultimate reality.

Vimānavatthu → *Petavatthu*.

Vinaya-Piṭaka

Vinaya-Piṭaka First of the 3 *piṭakas* or 'baskets' of Buddh. scriptures, i.e., the → Tipiṭaka (Skt. Tripiṭaka). The V.-P. is the 'discipline' *piṭaka,* i.e., its contents are concerned principally with rules governing life of the Buddh. → Sangha or Order of monks. A number of different versions of V.-P. are known: that of the → Theravādins, in Pali; of the → Mahāsanghikas, the Mahīśāsakas, the Dharmaguptakas, and the → Sarvāstivādins, preserved in various Chinese versions, in Tibetan, and in Buddh. hybrid Skt. The gen. scheme of contents is same in each case: (1) Section dealing with the Patimokkha rules for monks, or bhikkhus; this is called the bhikkhu-division (*bhikkhu-vibhanga,* Pali; *bhikśu-vibhanga,* Skt.); (2) Similar section for nuns, or bhikkhunīs; (3) A section called 'the groups' (*khandhakas*), each 'group' dealing with a special aspect of life of Sangha, such as ordination, the → Uposattha, meeting-rules concerning dress, robes, medicine, food, dwellings, furniture, etc. In the Pali V.-P. of the Theravādins, these groups are arranged in two series: the first is called the Great Chapter (*Mahāvagga*); the second, the Lesser Chapter (*Cullavagga*). The rulings in the *Vibhanga* and *Khandhaka* sections are given a narrative setting; the occasion on which an offence occurred or practice began to be followed is described, together with the Buddha's decision on subject given on that occasion. The rules regarding ordination, in the *Mahāvagga* of the *Khandhaka,* are given in context of founding of the Order, after Buddha's enlightenment. In case of the V.-P. of the Sarvāstivādins and Mahāsanghikas, the *Khandhakas* section is intercalated between the *Bhikkhu-vibhanga* and *Bhikkhunī-vibhanga.* In all extant V.-P.'s, except those of the Mahīśāsakas and the Mahāsanghikas, various additional items have been appended, at a time after compilation of main work; some of these appendages are as late as 1st cent. BC. Prob. the oldest material which now comprises the V.-P. is the → *Patimokkha,* list of offences which is recited on *Uposattha* days by the monks in assembly and confession made by a monk of any offence of which he is guilty (→ Discipline, Buddh. Monas-

Visuddhimagga

tic). In the *Bhikkhu-vibhanga* this *Patimokkha* list of offences is amplified by addition of a commentary on basic text.

The *Bhikkhu-vibhanga,* or *Sutta-vibhanga* has been trans. into Eng. by I. B. Horner in 3 vols. as *The Book of the Discipline,* vols. I, II and III (1938, 1940, 1942); the *Mahāvagga* of the *Khandhaka* as vol. IV (1951); the *Cullavagga* of the *Khandhaka* as vol. V (1952).

Viññāna (Pali); **Vijñāna** (Skt.) Term used in Buddh. analysis of human existence; usually translated 'consciousness,' the most import. of the 5 constituent groups (→ Khandhas), that make up human individual. It is V. which is regarded as the regenerative force, that which passes on, at termination of one human individual existence, to form another. V. is incl. in the 'chain of causation' (→ Paticca-Samuppada) as the 3rd link.

Vipassanā (Pali)/**Vipaśyanā** (Skt.) Buddh. term, usually trans. 'inward vision,' 'insight.' V. is one of the 2 principal factors in attainment of enlightenment; the other is *samatha,* or quietening of the mind. V., in sense of transcendental insight into, or analysis of, the nature of things, is regarded as the second and more import. It is by V. that the Buddh. truths concerning the suffering (→ Dukkha), impermanence (→ Anicca), and impersonality (→ Anatta) of all existence are seen and acknowledged. The pair of terms *samatha-vipassanā,* are regarded as synonymous with *samādhi-pannā* (meditation) and wisdom (→→ Samadhi; Panna). The develop. of this pair of factors, mental quiescence and transcendental insight, is connected very closely with cultivation of the absorptions (→ Jhāna). → Meditation.

Visuddhimagga Title of one of most import. books of post-canonical Pali lit. of the → Theravāda. Its author → Buddhaghosa was instrumental in restoring some of prestige which Pali as a language for Buddh. writing had lost to Sanskrit by 5th cent. CE. The title of work is usually trans. as 'Path of Purification'; it indic. primary concern of book, viz., a thorough description and exposition of the Buddh.

life. This is reflected in the 3 main divisions of book: morality (*sīla*), meditation (*samādhi*), and wisdom (*paññā*), i.e., the threefold description of the Buddh. life (→ Eightfold Path). The first section, on morality, consists of 2 chs.; the section on meditation, or concentration, contains nine chapters (III–XI), setting out various methods, in partic., the 40 poss. objects which may be used to aid develop. of concentration; some of these are physical objects, some mental. Still on subject of meditation, chs. XII and XIII describe its rewards. The third section, concerned with wisdom or understanding (*paññā*), contains 10 chs. (XIV–XXIII). Of these, XIV–XVII provide theoretical analysis of experience, after manner of the → Abhidhamma lit. The 4 following chs.; XVIII–XXI, are entirely practical, and show how the meditator's own experience may be analysed in terms of theory set out in XIV to XVII. Ch. XXII sets out nature of truths which are directly perceived as climax of the Buddh. life, and ch. XXIII, as a parallel to XII and XIII in the previous section, sets out benefits of transcendental wisdom. A new transl. from Pali into Eng. has been made by Bhikkhu Nyānamoli, *The Path of Purification* (1964).

Void, Doc. of → *Mādhyamika*.

Vows Relig. V. are common in Buddhism and Taoism, and are taken by both monks and laymen, those of former being stricter and more comprehensive. In Chi. Mahāyāna Buddhism, the 48 'bodhisattva V.' are detailed in the *Wu-liang-shou Sūtra,* and may be summed up in the V. never to rest until salvation of all sentient beings is achieved. Buddh. monks, on reception into the order, take numerous V.; the four great V.: (1) To seek salvation of world; (2) To root out from self all evil and passion; (3) To study law of Buddha; (4) To attain to perfection of Buddhahood, are taken by monks and devout laymen alike. In gen., Taoism copied Buddhism in practice of taking V.

A common practice in China, in cases of severe sickness, etc., is to make a V. (*hsü yüan*) to offer gift to a god or temple, to do some act of merit, to fast, or to go on → pilgrimage.

J. Legge, *The Chinese Classics* (1861–72), vol. 5, *passim*; H. Welch, *The Practice of Chinese Buddhism* (1967), pp. 285ff., 361ff. For a full discussion and numerous refs. see *E.R.E.*, XII, pp. 646ff.

W

Wat Siamese name for Buddh. monastery (→ *āvāsa*); → Monasteries.

Wên Shu Chi. name for the bodhisattva → Manjusri, who is personification of thought and knowledge. He is repr. as riding on lion, and holding in his hands a sword and book. The Chinese regard the holy mountain, Wu-t'ai-shan, as his chief resting place.

S. Couling, *Encycl. Sinica* (1917, 1965), p. 326.

Wisdom → *Paññā*.

(Books) → *Prajnā-Pāramitā Sūtras*.

Worship →→ *Devotions; Holy Days; Pagoda; Stupa.*

Y

Yakkha Class of supernatural beings mentioned in Buddh. Pali canon; in some cases the Y.'s appear to be semi-divine spirit-beings possessing supernatural powers but morally neutral; in other cases Y.'s are repr. as wicked beings, hostile esp. towards human beings who seek to live a holy life. Buddh. etymology explained the term Y. as being derived from root *yaj*, to sacrifice. Even though etymology may be incorrect, it indic. that in early Buddh. times Y.'s were beings to whom sacrifices were sometimes offered. They are certainly ref. to in Pali texts as 'flesh devourers'; in many cases the ref. appears to be to the Y.'s eating human flesh. This has led to suggestion that idea of wild demonic beings inhabiting lonely places (characteristic of Y.'s in Pali canon) may have been orig. from existence of cannibal tribes in certain parts of anc. India. On other hand, Y.'s are also assoc. with disease, and idea may have its roots in the 'flesh devouring' aspect of certain diseases, held to be work of Y.'s. The horrific character of the Y.'s finds expression in Buddh. texts mainly in refs. to loud noises made by Y.'s at night or in lonely places, to disturb or frighten monk or nun engaged in meditation.

J. Masson, *La Religion Populaire dans le Canon Bouddhique Pali* (1942), ch. 9; T. O. Ling, *Buddhism and the Mythology of Evil* (1962), pp. 15–19.

Yama Lord of death, in Buddh. trad., Y. repr. element of anc. popular Indian belief which Buddhism has preserved and given its own features. Old age, illness, punishment and approaching death are his messengers, sent as warnings to men not to live careless and immoral lives. At death men are examined as to whether they have heeded these mes-

Yāna

sengers; if they have not, they are despatched to various appropriate hells. (*M.N.*, III, pp. 179f.). Y. thus repr. in popular, mythological terms, Buddh. idea that a man's moral actions inevitably bring their appropriate rewards or penalties. In the *Mahāsamaya Sutta* of the → Digha-Nikaya, 'twin Yamas' are mentioned, which Rhys-Davids takes to be conception similar to that of Castor and Pollux. (*D.N.*, II, p. 259; cf. Rhys-Davids, *Dialogues of the Buddha*, II, p. 290). (→ Yen Wang).
J. Masson, *La Religion Populaire dans le Canon Bouddhique Pali* (1942), ch. 5.

Yāna Term occurring in Buddhism (Pali, Skt, and Buddh. Hybrid Skt.), signifying a means of attaining Enlightenment. In course of Buddh. history various Y.'s came to be distinguished, each characterised by different methods and scope from others. The use of these terms began with rise of the self-styled 'Great' means to salvation, the → Mahāyāna. Adherents of this form distinguished the way of those known as Śrāvakas, who heard the teachings of the Buddha and followed his way, but were unconcerned about Enlightenment of others, as the Śrāvakayāna. Those rare individuals who discover the way to Enlightenment without hearing the teaching of Buddha, and without being concerned for Enlightenment of others were described as 'private' or 'pratyeka'—buddhas, and their way to Salvation was known as the Pratyeka-yāna. The way of those who are destined to become enlightened, but who postpone their final full Enlightenemnt for sake of assisting others on the way were known as → Bodhisattvas, and their way was the Bodhisattva-yāna. It was this which was called also the Mahā-yāna, while the Śrāvaka-yāna and the Pratyeka-yāna were together regarded as the two-fold way, Dvi-yāna, which was also → Hīna-yāna or a 'Lesser' means to Enlightenment—'lesser' that is, in sense that it was less widely embracing, less inclusive than Māha-yāna; not that it was necessarily an inferior method. Since Hīna-yāna was characterised as two-fold (Dvi-yāna), the Mahāyāna was also characterised as Eka-yāna (single). Occasionally the Hīnayāna and Mahāyāna (i.e., the Dvi-yāna and Eka-yāna) are together spoken of as the Three-fold means, the Tri-yāna, in some Mhy. texts (see D. T. Suzuki, *Studies in the Lankavatara Sutra*, 1930, pp. 358–61). A further yāna was that which developed in India during period CE 500–1000, which made great use of symbolism and sacred chants, and was known as → Vajra-yāna or Mantra-yāna. This is some-times referred to as Tantric Buddhism.

Yen Wang (or Yen-lo Wang). Chi. name for → Yama, who was orig. the chief of the ten kings of hell; he was de-graded to become ruler of the fifth hell, because he was considered to be too compassionate towards criminals who came before him for judgement. Buddhism borrowed this god and his functions from Brahmanism; he is adopted also by Taoism. He alone of kings of hell is depicted with a dark face.

Yogācāras Name of those Mhy. Buddhists who professed doc. of → Asanga and his brother → Vasubandhu. The doc. was known also as Vijñānavāda, and the adherents as Vijñānavādins. The name of doc. ref. to its central idea: that *vijñāna* (consciousness) alone is real, whereas objects of consciousness are not. The doc. was a reaction to, and to some extent directed against, views of the → Mādhya-mika, acc. to which both subject and object in conscious-ness are unreal (in characteristic Mādhyamika form, reality is → *śūñyatā*). Acc. to the Y., occurrence of *illusion* demon-strates that consciousness can have 'content,' 'without there being a corresponding object outside.' This shows 'the self-contained nature of consciousness' (Murti); for the so-called object or 'content' of consciousness is result of an inner modification of consciousness. On other hand, the doc. was a reaction to, and was directed against, the extreme rigour of →Theravādin Abhidhamma school, with its assertion that there is a certain fixed number of ulti-mately real → *dhammas,* or psychic 'atoms,' of which all existence is made up. This, acc. to the Y., is to attr. reality to ultimate nonentities; consciousness alone is real, and it is the *yogācāra,* the man deep in meditation, who alone re-alises the truth: 'The yogācāra sees what is as it really is.' It was emphasis upon the practical clearing and purifying of

Yogācāras

consciousness by means of *yoga* which led to alternative name Y., by which school of the Vijñāna-vādins was known. Thus, the title V. refers to the *speculative,* and the name Y. to the *practical* aspect of this school. Since *vijñāna* alone exists, it alone receives false impressions and makes false constructions, and has to be cleansed of its false dualisms and illusions. As Conze points out, adherents of this school have no special or superior right to the title Yogācāra, 'practitioners of Yoga'; the name is given them largely because it occurs in title of one of Asanga's chief writings, the *Yogācāra-bhūmi Śāstra.*

To some extent the Y. were developing ideas found in earlier Buddhism, incl. poss. those of the → Sautrantikas, who taught that of the 5 → skandhas it is vijñāna alone which transmigrates from rebirth to rebirth. The Y. developed the doc. of → ālaya-vijñāna, or 'store-consciousness,' by which was meant pure consciousness, before it particularises itself as substratum of a human mind or consciousness. This is a concept somewhat similar to that of Hindu idea of the universal Brahman; there was, however, another closer affinity within Buddhism itself, viz, with the → *Lankāvatāra Sūtra.* This 'store-consciousness' thus performs role of a permanent 'self,' although the Y., in accordance with their Buddh. tenets, denied existence of a self. In this respect they have been accused of attempting to reconcile the irreconcilable. (Conze, *Buddhist Thought in India,* pp. 133f.)

However, the Y. had also a practical, indeed, relig. concern. Against the excessively intellectualist, extremist and negative analysis taught by the → *Mādhyamika,* they sought to recover importance of meditational practice and restore this to its proper place in Buddh. system. The Mādhyamika was a critique of phenomenal existence based on logic, whereas the Vijñānavāda was critique based on psychology, i.e., Buddh. psychology, and in this respect it constituted return to attitude and methods of early Buddhism.

Vijñānavāda is sometimes given credit for formulation of doc. of the three Bodies of Buddha (→ *Tri-Kāya*); but in this also → Asanga and his followers were but giving systematic shape to ideas found in earlier Buddhism. The Tri-Kāya doc. worked out by Asanga corresponded with Y. view of the three kinds of truth. The first is 'conventional truth' (*parikalpita*), i.e., concepts based on sense-perception, which are not really inherent in what is perceived, but are due to the perceived. The second is examined truth, concepts as they are examined concerning their cause, that out of which they have originated, and the conditions of their decay. This second kind of truth (*paratantra*) thus goes deeper than conventional truth. The third is final or highest truth (*parinispanna*), which is without origin or decay, changeless, and devoid of distinction of subject and object. The 3 'Bodies of the Buddha' were understood in similar fashion. The *nirmāna-kāya* was like conventional truth, purely imaginary; it was held that the Buddha-nature made an appearance of ordinary human existence. The *sambhoga-kāya* was akin to second kind of truth, while the *dharma-kāya* was the eternally true nature of Buddh. Different Buddhas may have differing *nirmāna* bodies or even *sambhoga* bodies, but all constitute the one eternal *dharma-kāya*, which like highest kind of truth, is unknowable, except in so far as it can be realised by the Buddha within himself.

While the Y. made explicit ideas which they had derived from earlier stages in development of Buddh. thought, they also provided basis for further develops., notably that of the → *Vajrayāna*, or tantra. With its combination of ritual, worship and yoga in context of absolutist ideas, its double aspect as both relig. and metaphysics, and its aim of transmuting human personality by mystic institution with the Absolute, Vajrayāna would appear to owe not a little to system of Y. school. There is a great deal of Y. lit. (→→ *Asanga, Vasubandhu*); but most is in Tibetan or Chinese trans. (i.e., from Sanskrit).

T. R. V. Murti, *The Central Philosophy of Buddhism* (1955), ch. 13; E. Conze, *Buddhist Thought in India* (1962), Part III, chs. 1 and 3.

Z

Zazen → Zen meditation while sitting in an approved posture, hallowed by Buddh. trad. The body is maintained upright, the legs crossed, the breathing regulated, whilst the mind is freed from all attachments, desires, concepts and judgements. The aim of Z. is → Satori, to enter the 'dharma gate of great rest and joy.'
H. Dumoulin, *Hist. of Zen Buddhism* (1963), pp. 159ff.; E. Wood, *Zen Dictionary* (1962), p. 157.

Zen (→→ Rinzai, Obaku, Sōtō). A form of Buddhism developed in China as → Ch'an, which, transplanted to Japan, became one of most import. and influential of Buddh. schools, and unique in hist. of relig. It upholds the direct, mystical experience of Reality through maturing of an inner experience. It claims to transmit the essence and spirit of Buddhism directly, without reliance on scriptures, words and concepts, and the reasoning based on them. It seeks inner spiritual enlightenment, and encourages practice of meditation or contemplation, teaching that man's orig. nature is the Buddha-nature, unrealised through ignorance.

Z. has had profound influence on Jap. culture, inspiring finest works of art and literature. Its principles were applied to military arts of Judo and Kendo (fencing), and in the tea ceremony, flower arrangement, landscape gardening, etc. Z. monasteries are usually places of great aesthetic appeal, marked by quiet, order, cleanliness and strict relig. discipline. In life of the monks, meditation, worship and energetic manual labour alternate. There is no great stress on ascetic practices. Self-realisation and one's Buddha-nature are equally found in practical affairs and in meditation.

The intro. of Z. to the W., notably by D. T. Suzuki, has led to keen interest, resulting in many import. studies; but also to Z. cults which are often a caricature rather than a true expression of Z. Buddhism.

Of many important works in Eng., the reader will find those of D. T. Suzuki, A. Watts, C. Humphreys and Chang Chên-chi interesting. See espec. H. Dumoulin, *Hist. of Zen Buddhism* (1963), which contains an adequate bibliography.